£6.95

the
snows
of
yesteryear

the
snows
of
yesteryear

portraits for
an autobiography

◆

GREGOR VON REZZORI

Translated from the German by
H.F. Broch de Rothermann

Chatto & Windus
LONDON

Published in 1990 by
Chatto & Windus Ltd
20 Vauxhall Bridge Road
London SW1V 2SA

A CIP catalogue record for this book is available from the
British Library.

ISBN 0 7011 3666 9

Originally published in the Federal Republic of Germany as
Blumen im Schnee
Copyright © 1989 by C. Bertelsmann Verlag, GmbH, Munich.

This edition published by arrangement with
Alfred A. Knopf, Inc.

Printed in Great Britain by
Mackays of Chatham PLC, Chatham, Kent.

For Beatrice

with love and in unending gratitude

Mais où sont les neiges d'antan?

—François Villon

Contents

The SNOWS of YESTERYEAR

Cassandra

Swarms of waxwings have settled in the ripe clusters of rowanberries. It is said that they come only every seven years from high up north, from Lapland or Siberia, and only when the winter threatens to turn exceptionally severe. They're also called plague birds, even though they appear rather pretty: plump and colorful, with a saucy crest, velvety black heads and throats, white-banded wings on scarlet pinions and tails edged in lemon yellow. Their fluffy breasts, of a rosy mother-of-pearl hue, crowd against the spiky gridwork of the cluster stems as they busily pick the red berries. A sudden detonation: someone is shooting with birdshot into the swarm, which rises like smoke above the crowns of the rowan trees. But a good dozen of the birds tumble from the fruit

clusters down into the snow amidst fallen
berries and drops of blood. Who can tell
whether the survivors will ever return? The
clusters are torn to shreds and the denuded
twigs show as a rigid pattern against the pale
winter sky.

When she joined the household, it was said, she was hardly more than a beast. They had peeled her out of her peasant garb and had instantly consigned the shirt, the wrap skirt, the sleeveless sheepskin jacket and the leather buskins to the flames. But clad in city clothes, she looked so utterly absurd as to be frightening. People would say in rude jesting that if a pregnant woman encountered her, she might well miscarry. Forthwith they dressed her once more in her traditional costume, though a somewhat stylized version, devoid of the many-colored embroideries on shirt and skirt, without the vermilion sash and the saffron-colored kerchief: a nunnish garb in subdued black, white and gray shades. "They turned a goldfinch into a sparrow," she would say of herself. It had not been anticipated that she would be even more conspicuous in this contrived costume than in her traditional clothes, notwithstanding which she wore it with great and dignified pride, as if it were a monastic vestment.

No one ever found out how she had come by the name of Cassandra. Under no circumstances could she have been baptized under that name. The godforsaken hamlet in the Carpathian

Mountains whence she had come—she still knew its name but no longer where it was located, in any case, "way back in the woods"—consisted of a handful of clapboard hovels whose inhabitants slept with their sheep in winter, while in summer the plangent sound of their shepherd pipes mingled with the wind rushing through the pine trees of their mountain fastness. To what name she answered there she stubbornly refused to reveal, nor did she divulge who first had called her Cassandra. Probably it was someone at the monastery where my father had found her, but even that seemed doubtful: no one but the abbot himself would have been likely to bestow on her, out of the bevy of maidservants—perhaps by reason of some evil-boding prophecy?—the name of the seeress from *The Iliad*. The monks in their black frocks, the stovepipes of their rimless hats on their shaggy-haired heads, shy, wildly ecstatic or half mad in self-absorption, were no less ignorant than their village brethren. Anyway, she came to us as Cassandra and took care of me from the day of my birth—as my nanny, my mother said; as my wet nurse, Cassandra claimed.

It is typical of my mother's misguided pride that no photographs of Cassandra have come down to me. When the northern part of the Bukovina where we used to live—formerly a crown land of the Austro-Hungarian monarchy and after 1919 a province of Romania—was ceded to Russia in 1940 as a result of the pact concluded between Stalin and Hitler, or more accurately between their lackeys Molotov and Ribbentrop, the authorities in charge of Interests of Germans Abroad "repatriated" us and all other former Austrians "of German blood" to the German Reich. Each person was allowed to take fifty kilograms of belongings. My mother had a Russian colonel quartered in her town house in Czernowitz who gallantly permitted her to take with her twice as much, of which at least a third consisted of memorabilia of the family. Among the hundreds of photographs, all those showing Cassandra were eliminated. Not because of her ugliness, although she must have looked, with me in her arms, like a female gorilla costumed as a nanny kidnapping a white infant. That Cassandra had been in our service, first as nanny and later, when

I was growing up and my parents had separated, as my father's housekeeper, my mother could not help admitting. But that the "savage one," as Cassandra openly was called in the household, had also been my wet nurse—this my mother resolutely denied. To have nursed me with her own milk was a distinction she claimed for herself alone.

I know better. Not only because I felt all my life that, nursed by Cassandra, I had suckled the milk of that soil, with all its light and dark powers, from which she, Cassandra, but not my mother, had sprung; but because the myth of my mother's boundless maternality was inconsistent with the hardly more credible but steadfastly maintained other myth of her delicate health. Until proof incontrovertible emerged, toward the end of her life, of the remarkable toughness with which she endured the vicissitudes of existence, she managed to convince almost everyone that, as someone in constant poor health, even the simplest life tasks were beyond her. Before I was born she had spent most of her time in health spas, allegedly to recuperate from the birth of my sister, which had occurred four years earlier.

Her supposed delicacy was aggravated by historical events, which drove us for the first time, though then only temporarily, from the Bukovina. I was born in 1914; the First World War broke out in August of that year. The Bukovina borders directly to the north on Galicia, where, right from the start, bloody fighting took place and the Russians advanced almost unopposed. Because someone claimed to have seen their flat caps—in truth, he had mistaken the visorless field-gray caps of our German comrades-in-arms—panic broke out among the population. My mother, left alone, as my father had gone to war, allowed herself to become infected by the general hysteria, and so we too fled more or less helter-skelter. Our objective was a summer house near Trieste belonging to my paternal grandfather, who had died shortly before.

Obviously I remember nothing of this flight, which occurred soon after my birth. My sister, who was almost five, spoke of it as a darkly shadowed experience; sometimes it recurred for her in anxiety-ridden dreams. My mother avoided talking about it. My father maintained that she was ashamed of the rashness of our flight, which he dismissed with a shrug as "headless." But ultimately events confirmed that she had been right: Czernowitz (now Chernovtsy in the Soviet Union), the capital of the Bukovina, repeatedly fell into Russian hands during the ever changing outcome of the ensuing battles. At best, we might have chosen a more favorable moment and a more comfortable means for our flight.

As to the route we took in our flight, I also know about it only vaguely and through hearsay. I was told that we had to cross the Carpathian Mountains in horse-drawn carriages and over a rather arduous pass, by night and in a blizzard, so as to reach Bistrice (now Bistriţa), in the district of Marmorosh, then still belonging to Hungary, whence the railway was to carry us to Trieste by way of Budapest and Vienna. This mountain pass can have been only the Bargău, where, according to legend and Bram Stoker's novel, the castle of Dracula once stood. To reach it and Bistrice must have taken us several days by carriage, all during which Cassandra acted as our protective genius.

Our mother neither spoke nor understood any of the local languages. Although German had been the official idiom in the Bukovina during the Austrian era, that language became increasingly mangled and incomprehensible, both to us and to the variegated nationals, the deeper one penetrated into the Bukovina. Cassandra, on the other hand, who spoke no language correctly, expressed herself in snatches of Romanian, Ruthenian, Polish and Hungarian, as well as Turkish and Yiddish, assisted by a grotesque, grimacing mimicry and a primitive, graphic body language that made everyone laugh and that everyone understood.

What this kind of flight is like, we now know well, at the latest from the days at the end of the Second World War when the tide was turning in 1944–1945, if not sooner from the time of the defeat of France, when populations of entire regions were in headlong flight. Among the hand-drawn carts and open rack-wagons on which children in rags are starving and freezing, the closed barouches with their fur-clad passengers and yapping terriers, their attendant vans loaded with mountains of luggage, are an object of scandal and inspire hatred rather than respect. Resentment against us could not be mitigated by the finishing-school French and nursery English to which my mother resorted when she couldn't make do with German. The decrepit old coachmen, my sister's frightened, indignant and frozen governess, the Bohemian cook and two peasant girls barely trained as maids were of no help. But Cassandra was at home in the Carpathians and to her the sharp air was as balsam. Had she heard the howling of wolves, it would have sounded to her as a familiar melody. She spoke to the people as her own kind and in their own idiom. Her strange garb invested her with authority. When it was a question of finding quarters for the night or a place close to a warm oven, a pitcher of milk or merely some water for tea, it was she who negotiated and sought understanding, it was she who called for mercy and sympathy, and she did so with the impish, weirdly droll vivacity that was her very own and that no one could withstand. Much later my mother, still resentful, and unaware of how this contradicted her description of Cassandra, used to recriminate over the remembrance of how Cassandra, a barely born infant at her shamelessly bared breast, exploited me as a means of sentimental blackmail when expatiating on our wretchedness as refugees.

Of the house near Trieste where we finally found refuge I have no memories either, unless it be subconsciously in my feeling of intimacy with Mediterranean landscapes, the homelike ambience which for me pervades those stony shores, scanned by the black obelisks of cypress trees, that ocher-colored coastland over which the Adriatic blue fades into the barely more translucent azure of the skies. No telling whether this familiarity is not derived rather from some early impressions of postcards. We stayed in the little villa near Trieste for less than a year, until the entry of Italy into the war against us Austrians required that we flee once more, this time much less dramatically and in greater comfort—specifically, to Vienna and in three sleeping-car compartments.

Whether for Cassandra this stay in the Karst region around Trieste, a region totally different from Bukovina's wealth of fields and forests, was like an exile, she never told. Among Italian-speaking people she became mute, although she might have achieved at least some measure of understanding in Ukrainian with Slovenes or in German with some of the German-speaking Triestines. Not only must she have seemed, in that motley mixture of Slovenes, Friulians, Greeks and Jews, like some exotic specimen from the sideshow of a traveling circus, but the opportunities for such encounters would have been rare. We lived a very secluded and cloistered existence; even my mother, mindful of her role as refugee and of her perennially fragile health, hardly ever drove into Trieste. Later, my sister told me that *she* almost died of boredom. Apart from endless hours of instruction with her governess, her sole distraction consisted in the game of diabolo, in which a rotating hourglass-shaped spool is balanced and spun on a string stretched between two sticks, then thrust into the air and caught again on the string—a game Proust had already described as obsolete at the turn of the century. Thanks to untiring practice, she managed to acquire a mastery of diabolo with which she often used to humiliate me later on. Photographs from that period show her, flowerlike, among gigantic agaves in a rock garden, clad in a white summer frock and a large linen hat to protect her against the Mediterranean sun. The strange plants, appearing to have originated in some other geological era, look like a stage backdrop, and this invests the figure of my sister with an air of artificiality and precociousness. At home—our home in the Bukovina, which she was to come to hate—her blossomlike appearance was natural. There is another picture of her in the garden of our true home that shows her at eye level with her stubby-haired setter, Troll, the dog my father had laid as a puppy in her cradle shortly after her birth—much to the dismay of the still ailing mother, the nurse and all the other females in the household. The dog and the little girl are as organically harmonious in the cheerfully overgrown garden as its trees and shrubs and lawns turning into meadows rank with wild flowers. The picture, taken no more than a year and a half before the one in the garden near Trieste, epitomizes an irrevocably lost period in my sister's life. That childlike innocence, the existential oneness with all living creatures, the deep embeddedness in the ever astounding richness of all nature became a thing of the past and ceded its place to the realization of the complexity of being.

More especially for Cassandra, the encounter with an alien world was not an enriching experience: she—who relished the anecdotal and raised any occurrence, however banal, to the level of an event and knew how to embroider and enrich it with fantasy, so as to incorporate it into the never ending garland of cameos that gave our life story (and thereby her own) glamour and drama—was incapable of telling us anything about the time near Trieste. Whether her memory was blurred by the homesickness she may have suffered there, or whether the sullen patience, legacy of an old line of slaves, with which she bore any dispensation of fate (a condition of psychic torpor similar to the physical rigor that certain bugs or birds assume at the approach of danger) prevented anything memorable from even dawning on her—this remains a moot question. That she had no eyes for the beauty of the landscape was but natural: as my father used to say, primitive people have no grasp of the abstract concept of beauty in nature, since for them, sensory perception of nature flows together with love of the ancestral soil; anything else is merely alien. Whenever I asked Cassandra whether she hadn't liked the sea, she remained glum and taciturn. I had the impression that her sullen reticence had to do with some unpleasant occurrence she didn't care to think about. Through some kind of spiritual osmosis there rose in me an image, somewhat in the Art Nouveau style of that period: a young woman in silhouette, like a figurehead on a galleon, stands on a foam-sprayed cliff by the sea, and in her I seem to recognize my mother; sitting before her, in a half-adoring, half-masterful attitude, is the dark-clad figure of a man combining all the traditional attributes of the southerner, the artist and the lover in a single epitome—dark hair, a flowing black lavalliere, a black slouch hat carelessly held in his hand. I have an inkling that the fierce antagonism between my mother and my sister, which arose originally between an obstreperous child and an authority who asserted herself too late and never self-assuredly, at some time had assumed the form of an archfemale enmity, the true motive of which resided in jealousy over a man. That something of this sort also might have colored the relationship between Cassandra and my mother seemed to me too abstruse a fancy to be worth thinking about, and yet in the end I came to believe it. Both my sister and Cassandra idolized my father. To them, the stay in Trieste dimmed his image as husband and sole master of the household—and thus as the safeguard of that family unity which alone bonds a home in togetherness.

For me all this experience dwells in the golden haze of the mythical. Conscious recall sets in only after we left Trieste and found refuge in the house of friends in Lower Austria. Here it is a different landscape: a valley rich in meadows, embedded between the wooded slopes of hills. This is more enticing and gives much more evidence of the human imprint than the Carpathian land that remains my true home; nevertheless, this Austrian landscape is an intimately familiar part of myself. For my mother, the church and the tiny village nearby were merely admonitory markers of our bitter existence as refugees, but for me they signal my awakening to the world. I can see myself on a meadow, its grass not yet mown and so high that I cannot see above it. I raise my arms to Cassandra so that she may pick me up. To me she represents the mediator of the reality all around, she is the embodiment of all security, of the safe assurance with which I experience the world. The miracle of my discovery of the world occurs under her protection and with her encouragement. For anyone else, she is but a barely tamed savage. My mother could never get along with her and would have sent her packing, had she not understood intuitively that without her I could not exist.

I loved Cassandra dearly, and it was due only to constant hearsay, both within and outside the house, that ultimately I too came to believe that she was inhumanly ugly and primitive. Her large simian face, heartwarming and protective, grotesque and impishly comical, presides over everything that the memory of my childhood days transforms from that inexhaustible pool from which I draw my confidence in life. Cassandra was the standard-bearer of the mood that made those days fair and bright and full, somehow, of desperate merriment—a merriment boldly militating against the prevailing tension and exploding any impending drama into absurd humor, shattering it in laughs. As I realized later, Cassandra, in all this, was the distorted funhouse-mirror image of each of us. She imitated, paraphrased, parodied and derided not only the flickering yet imperturbable jolliness of my father, whom she adored with doglike devotion, but also the often hysterical boisterousness of us children. We followed her in her comical exaggerations: she led the procession of clowns, harlequins and Punch-and-Judy characters that we mustered each day to counter the tensions within the household, to resist and balance my father's eccentricities and my mother's ever more uninhibited nervous susceptibilities, her irritability, her panic anxieties, her inflexibility and her artful enticements.

Thanks to my father's happy disposition, the ever shorter spans of time he spent at home always felt like vacations, only occasionally torn by the storms of his choleric outbursts. When he was gone again on one of his so-called assignments, which usually and in fact were hunting trips, my mother's migraines and changeable moods hung over the house like a curse. Yet nothing could equal the effervescent charm of her smile and cajoling voice when she thought to persuade us, in a sudden spurt of maternal dutifulness, to wear a warmer jacket or eat another spoonful of spinach, just as nothing could better rupture the fine mood of a carefree hour than the cold haughtiness with which she might reprimand Cassandra or my sister's mademoiselle if either of them dared to contradict her and assert that, after all, the day was too warm for heavy clothes or that we had already eaten enough spinach. Then we had to bear not only her own ill humor but also that of those she had rebuked.

It was probably between 1916 and 1918 in Lower Austria, during the last years of the war, that Mother's exaggerated solicitude for me and my sister turned pathological. The times were somber and threatening. The rural environment heightened the sense of remoteness into claustrophobia. The distrust of the peasant neighbors toward foreign strangers who had come from the city to escape the urban scarcity of food, the unheated apartments, the riots and possible epidemics were bound to suggest to a young mother that she adopt a circumspect domesticity, irrespective of how little she was cut out for it. Mother's highly susceptible pride generated in her a totally abstract sense of duty, an a priori bad conscience that dictated certain rules of conduct to be followed with iron rigidity—often in patent disregard of contradictory evidence. Thus motivated by notions of some obsolete and outlandish behavior pattern, she was prone to interfere in securely established traditional relations and to disrupt them.

Our old Bohemian cook, who had accompanied us faithfully wherever we went, turned rebellious and threatened to give notice because Mother suddenly thought of determining not only the already skimpy menus but also, on the strength of some "thrift" recipes picked up in the newspaper, how the dishes were to be prepared. Her relationship with my sister, who during her first years had grown up unhampered under the care of her nannies, had been a neutral one that in the course of time could have developed readily into mutually acknowledged independence, but it now became openly antagonistic under the impact of this newly asserted Victorian maternal authority. Cassandra, with her simian ugliness and nunlike vestments, speaking her higgledy-piggledy garble of incomprehensible foreign idioms, was bound to appear as an open challenge to the village peasants with their age-old customs. If they tolerated her at all and had not driven her out with scythes and flails, it was only because they admitted her as the not fully human guardian and mascot of me, a three-year-old lad; she was like the sow on whose cringle-tail the youngest of a farmer's sons clung when he let her guide him to the pasture each morning and back home at night. When my mother started to insist that she henceforth would accompany us on our walks and supervise our games, she trespassed a subtle, irrational borderline within which the master's privileges were either acknowledged or denied. For the peasant women in the village she was confirmed now more than ever as an idler. And from then on, Cassandra's clowning seemed even more sharply parodistic. It began to undermine my mother's authority even with other members of the household.

Was it because of excessive perspiration due to overly heavy clothing or because of cooling off too abruptly at the onset of a rainstorm, or perhaps on account of psychosomatic reasons? In any case I contracted pneumonia in August 1917 — for the second time, at so tender an age! To measure my fever, my mother put a thermometer in my mouth which I promptly crushed between my teeth. Fearful lest I swallow a splinter of glass, she scrabbled on her knees around my bed until she had recovered all the glass slivers from the cracks in the flooring of the old house. This strenuous effort — it was alleged — together with the exertion in carrying me home at the unexpected outbreak of the storm, added to her previous chronic kidney and nervous disorders, as well as her heart defect. It compelled us in later years to tiptoe through the house during many anxious hours, and it was used against us as a terrifying means of blackmail whenever our own idea of what to wear or whether to go on a sledding party in winter or a bathing excursion in summer (both in Mother's eyes detrimental or even injurious to our health) clashed with the maternal view.

The vegetative calm with which Cassandra bore these household turbulences (to which were added, after our return to the Bukovina, marital conflicts between our parents) she managed to camouflage behind crazy parodies by which she distorted into farce any imminent tragedy. By magnifying everything grotesquely, she reduced the trifles at the bottom of most of these commotions to their true size; as my father used to say, she "pricked the soap bubbles of our family squabbles" and burst them, thereby opening our eyes to the absurdities of an unreflected life, hidebound in rigid patterns. More than anyone else, she taught us the healing power of laughter.

Today I appreciate the strength that she needed to withstand the vicissitudes of fate and that she communicated to us for the rest of our lives — a feat all the more remarkable when one remembers that war overshadowed each hour of our everyday life. The smell of blood and steel pervaded everything, even places where these had not yet had a direct impact. No one could believe any longer in the possibility of a victory by the Central Powers. Its defeats threw the discouraged into gloomy despair. It was not just an empire that broke apart: a whole world went under. And it was as if, with the end of the Austro-Hungarian monarchy, a light was extinguished that until then had bathed the days in a golden sheen. This struck not us alone: a new era had begun.

We grew up with the myth of a lost bygone world, golden and miraculous. By 1915 we were already what later hundreds of thousands of Europeans were to become: refugees, exiles, leaves tossed by the storms of history. Toward the end of the war we were forced to leave the village in Lower Austria that had been our refuge; it became even more inhospitable than it had been from the beginning. Vienna, with the dimming of its glory, had become a gray and squalid slum. My mother's relatives who lived there recommended that we return to the Bukovina. My father, whom I saw for the first time when he returned from the war, agreed. Although the future of this former crown land was still entirely unsettled, it seemed a more promising place to live in than any of the other splinter states of the dismembered monarchy. We went home.

This too was not accomplished in unmarred serenity. In Galicia, the stretch between Lemberg (now Lvov) and the Prut River, marking the border with the Bukovina, was bordered by the simple wooden crosses crowned with the helmets of fallen soldiers. Swarms of crows dotted the gray skies. The closer we came to the Prut, the more frequently we could look through burnt-out window frames into houses through whose torn roof timbers one perceived storm-swept clouds and from the floorings of which nettles were growing. Czernowitz, on the other side of the Prut, had become restive and shabby, peopled by a wretched species of individuals, hitherto encountered only alone or, at worst, in shady twosomes or threesomes but never before in such compact exclusiveness.

We had fled the Bukovina from a house in the country my mother had never liked. It had been my sister's birthplace. That I, too, had not been born there I owed to her panic-prone disposition. My sister's birth had been a difficult one, and my mother did not want to face once more the risk of perhaps bleeding to death in the hands of some rural midwife, far from medical assistance. When she went into labor, she had herself driven to the city· by horse carriage—a distance of some fifty miles. I was born before she reached the clinic. The experience may well have contributed to her hatred of that country house. Now, after four years of rural seclusion and with the disconcerting uncertainty of the times, it was decided to stay in Czernowitz.

But uncertainty also yawned all around our new house: it was located at the outermost edge of the city, where, beyond the villa gardens and small farm holdings, the views broadened to open country. The East was threateningly close. The great trees of the public park, adjacent to our own, were denuded. Impacts of howitzers had opened craters at the bottom of which rainwater formed murky pools. The monstrously swollen corpse of a horse lay by the roadside a hundred meters away. And yet this was to become the house of a merry, happy childhood, though all too short and filled with tensions that were alien to what is commonly understood as cozy and homelike.

Visitors may have thought it comfortable and even elegant. The furnishings that had been destroyed or plundered were soon replaced by new acquisitions. For this my mother had a deft hand. Jubilantly, my sister and I moved into the large and airy children's rooms. But before the beginning of that span of my life, which I recall as my true childhood, threatening storms once more overshadowed our life.

Those were the days shortly before the Romanians, in 1919, occupied the Bukovina. The sinister species in rags that had begun to fill the streets of Czernowitz was a constant reminder that a few hundred kilometers to the east, just beyond the Dniester River, Russia lay waiting, where, for the past two years, the Bolsheviks made short shrift of our kind of people. The revolutionary spirit of 1917 had degenerated into bloody madness and might easily spread over to us. Gangs of plunderers drifting about had already targeted the ration warehouses of the departed Austrian army as their first objective. Besmirched with lard and plum jam, totally inebriated and with their bellies full, the howling gangs of rabble staggered past our house; they were more or less held in check during the day but became menacing at night. My romantic father provided everyone in the house with firearms. Even Cassandra was handed a pistol, which she hid comfortably between her voluminous breasts—with the safety catch off. The precautionary measures with which this pistol then had to be retrieved enriched the anecdotal treasure trove that accumulated around my remarkable nanny over the years. But for the time being there was no cause for laughter. These are clearly remembered images: we, the children, are fetched from our beds and hastily dressed; all lights are extinguished; I see Mother's hands in the moonlight as she frantically hides her jewelry; the glitter of pistol barrels. But the danger passed us by. Within the next few days, Romanian soldiers occupied Czernowitz. Occasionally some shots were heard, and then it was announced that order had been restored.

But it was an eerily nervous order. We had no idea how the Romanians would deal with us. Our father stayed in the city all day long to find out how the situation was evolving. We children were strictly forbidden to exchange so much as a single word with any stranger. Of course, we were not to go beyond the garden under any circumstance. (Nor were we allowed to do so later on without accompaniment, and when once I did so, my punishment was draconian.) But this seclusion was difficult to maintain. Like all children of a nation at war, we were enthusiastically patriotic but at the same time ardently attracted to anything military, even in the form of an enemy. When Romanian troops marched by, I could not be restrained; I had to get to the garden fence to see it all. In so doing one day, I had failed to consider that I was holding in my hands a doll called "The German Brother": a childlike soldier in a field-gray uniform and with a black-white-and-red cockade decorating the German recruit's visorless cap covering his blond locks (the very same headgear the sight of which, five years earlier, because it had been mistaken for Russian, had caused our first flight). A sergeant of the Romanian battalion filing past saw this toy and in a rage ran over to me, reached through the fence, tore the offending object from my hands and flung it, cursing, into the gutter. But he hadn't noticed Cassandra, who, driven by the same curiosity as my own, had joined me at the fence. A wild sow whose piglet has been threatened could not have broken from the underbrush with fiercer speed: she threw herself with such uninhibited vehemence against the iron fenceposts that the sergeant, frightened, jumped back. A torrent of bawdy Romanian curses was loosed on him which, together with the weird appearance of the scolding fury, triggered a wave of derisive laughter in the troop. Had there not been this outburst of rude amusement, Cassandra's impetuosity could have cost her dearly: without a moment's hesitation, she grabbed a handful of earth and flung it after the retreating figure. She could have been shot on the spot.

All memory of early childhood is episodic, embedded in the moods of separate periods which later we interpret as stages of our development. It is a year later, a summer day of almost unbearable heat. The foliage of the trees around the house hangs listless. Our mother exacerbates her growing fear of just such threats even though the times are by now more peaceful: we are citizens of the Kingdom of Romania. My father's monarchism has proven to be more enduring than his Austrian patriotism: he prefers the monarchy with a foreign language to the now ex-clusively German-speaking republic of the shrunken Austrian rump state, contrary to my mother, who feels like an exile cast out in an inferior culture, a world full of menacing forces, includ-ing climatic ones. A hot day such as this hatches unforeseeable perils. It is only natural, therefore, that on a sudden impulse it is decided to drive to the nearest lookout point in the gently rolling landscape. Even though the difference in elevation is minimal, it might be expected that the air would be cooler there, where large tracts of forest abounded.

In those days, such excursions were not made easily. One drove in horse carriages that took hours; to protect oneself against the sun, parasols were taken along, together with dusters, as well as blankets and overcoats for the return in the evening. Since there was no inn along the way, cold drinks were brought in thermos bottles and sandwiches were packed in baskets. And toys: thin loops of reed that were thrown in the air with small sticks and then caught again with swordlike thrusts; balls; and of course, my sister's diabolo game, that hourglass cone rotating on a string stretched between two sticks, which was thrown up whirring high above and caught once more to run back and forth along the length of the string with micelike fleetness. Mother liked to watch us playing these tame games harking back to her own youth. They soon bored us to tears.

Usually, when Cassandra came along, I was excused from these choreographic, rather than sportive, exercises. On the pretext that under all circumstances I had to avoid congesting my affected lungs, we withdrew to the shade of some tall trees in a grove. This is the key image of that period and bearer of its mood (I would have been just over five years old at the time): in the wide-open expanse of the landscape stands one of those clumps of splendid trees in the mighty crowns of which golden orioles are whistling and warblers are flying hither and thither. A light breeze sweeps over the fields, where one can hear the rustling of the dry corn sheaves; big pumpkins with yellow-white and black-green tiger stripes lie heavily on the rich black earth, attached to their hairy vines. Far away the call of a cuckoo is heard and the warble of bobwhites; closer by, frogs croak in the reeds of a swampy water hole; a stork stalks with careful deliberation under the willows of a brook, then slowly rises over their crowns with a heavy flapping of its wings and flies off. Cassandra cradles me in her arms and tells me a fairy tale.

But this time Cassandra hadn't come along. Mother didn't quite trust yet the newly established peace and even less the good-natured disposition of the rural population, which had run wild during the war and was in any case degenerating as a result of the city's proximity. Therefore as many people as possible had to come along for protection and proper supervision: everybody went with the exception of Cassandra and the maids, who were given one of their rare days off. Cassandra stayed home because someone had to take care of the house, and much to our chagrin the dogs stayed with her—to defend the house and her and, chiefly, because it was feared that they would go hunting on their own if let loose in the fields.

Dogs played an important part in our childhood. There was at least one dog for each member of the family and all of them were instinctively drawn to Cassandra. They acknowledged her as an authority in the hierarchy of the household on the strength of her being, so to say, their own companion in fate and dependent on their common masters. But strangely enough, and notwithstanding their passionate love for my father and for us, it was Mother whom the dogs considered the supreme authority. They had— and I cannot express it more clearly—an order of rank ascending from secular precedence to spiritual supremacy. With the exception of the dogs, all of us trembled under my mother's febrile humors as under a metaphysical power that could not be explained rationally and even less could be denied. She embodied the eternally threatening and fragile nature of all existence. The drama of life confronted her at every moment with the potential to turn suddenly into tragedy. She saw it as her duty to prevent the worst by constantly alerting everyone around her to watch out. (Had she realized that the name of Cassandra fitted her better than it did my nurse, she would have been deeply offended.) In any case, the dogs seemed to sense her innate and tragic comprehension of the ever threatening evil in all existence, and whenever a storm gathered they all sought refuge at her feet.

At the opposite end stood Cassandra's full-blooded animal vitality. Her almost frightening merriment—like my father's hardly ever dampened good spirits—was perhaps nothing more than a robust physical disposition's natural consonance with the surrounding world. While my mother and sister were both incomparably more frail, Cassandra and my father both enjoyed the rudest health, the best of appetites, the most perfect digestions and therefore also the sunniest of temperaments, ready at all times for jokes and laughter. That this readiness to make light of life resulted from insights into its inscrutability at least as profound as Mother's can be only surmised and hardly proven. To recognize what is absurd and to accept it need not dim the eye for the tragic side of existence; quite on the contrary, in the end it may perhaps help in gaining a more tolerant view of the world.

Our excursion to the refreshing breezes on the hill was probably as chaotic as most undertakings that had their roots in Mother's rather touching intention to rearrange the world for us as it had been in her own childhood at the turn of the century. We drank cold tea with the metallic taste of thermos bottles, ate sandwiches that had fallen into the sand, played with our hoops and balls, jumped rope and did charades until we became cranky and bawled and scuffled with each other. Soon a storm came up. Our excursion had to be curtailed and we returned to the city sooner than anticipated. The house seemed deserted. The door stood open. The first rooms we entered were in a terrifying state of devastation. Our immediate thought was of robbery. Then Cassandra appeared, naked as the day she was born, out of breath, her chimpanzee face congested to a scarlet hue, her hair loose and barely covering her nudity: a Lady Godiva with a pitch-black mane. She had taken advantage of our absence to have her fill at romping with the dogs all afternoon—bare-assed, a beast among beasts. The wild chase had gone through the garden and the house, and our premature return had left no time for the riotous bacchante to tidy up. She was not in any way embarrassed, but merely declared that the dogs occasionally needed such an untrammeled spree. My mother was on the point of dismissing her right then and there, but my father, who as usual was away hunting at the time, on his return took Cassandra's side. With that the "scandal," as my mother saw it, took its place in the long list of humiliations which it was her lot to endure. To her, Cassandra once more had been declared the winner in a decisive either-or situation. We, on the other hand— Father, my sister and I—saw in the bizarre happening not merely proof of the untamable nature of our strange housemate but also something mystical, almost mythological: the primeval essence of our country embodied in one of its own chosen daughters. For us she was imbued, henceforth, with the power of an arcane native priesthood. When I think back to the house of my childhood, which my memory places in a bright, wide-open land-scape, surrounded by birches, beeches and rowan trees (in style somehow akin to the pagan neoclassicism of paintings like those of Franz von Stuck), there is always present in it the image of Cassandra, running wild and naked, and behind her the pack of dogs snapping at the black banner of her mane.

Cassandra's hair, the beauteous counterpart of her homeliness, was one of the delights of my childhood. She usually wore it tied in two braids, thick as arms, coiled on top of her enormous head and crowning it like a flattened Kurdish turban, a style—she told us—favored by all the women in her village so as to serve as a kind of pillow on which better to carry heavy baskets and pitchers. When she loosened her hair, it would fall down over her shoulders and back in a silkily crackling, glistening wealth, reaching down almost to the hollow of her knees. To grab it and dip my little hands in its dry flows was for me an inexhaustible pleasure. Evenings, when she undressed me to put me to bed, I would stand on the nursery dresser in front of her and take the pins out of her hair, unwind the braids and cover her face with them. Laughing and joking, she let me have my way. At times I would wrap myself entirely in its folds, hiding myself as behind a curtain, and call to my sister—already in bed and usually reading a book—to come and find me. Blissfully I inhaled its pungent smell of almonds and frankincense. Such flowing hair has re-mained for me the epitome of the sweetly voluptuous darkness in all that is feminine—once more in perfect harmony with the late Art Nouveau style of the era I was born in, but in antithesis to that other, more problematic and refractory feminine element, so different as to be almost inimical to the first, which found its purest incarnation in my mother's and sister's ethereal skin and all but translucent eyelids.

This puzzled me later on, since it seemed inconceivable to me that I ever could have perceived in Cassandra anything that could be defined as sexual, let alone the quintessence of "woman." For me she belonged to those objects and beings of my own, most intimate childhood sphere, among which some—my dog, my magpie, my rabbit or a favorite toy (my teddy bear, an elephant made of some rubbery substance from which I hardly ever was separated)—were especially "soul endowed" through the strength of my love for them. To all these objects I was tenderly attached and I would mourn their loss bitterly, but they had nothing to do with the factual, real world I was growing into: the world of adults, who guarded the secrets of sexuality and death. Cassandra was of my own world, and if I discovered that my domino set was the object of erotic fantasy, this would not have seemed more absurd to me than if this were claimed to be the case with regard to Cassandra.

Naturally, I was not without libidinous stirrings. Thoughts of the feminine rose in me early. Even as a six- or seven-year-old, I was perennially infatuated: with a youthful aunt; an elegant lady who had come to visit; a pretty girl I had seen in passing; or merely a picture in some illustrated journal; the daughter of our physician, more or less of my own age; and many more. My imagination was replete with images of blissful embraces, tender kisses exchanged in fondly silent togetherness, even temporary misunderstandings between myself and the loved one, and the ensuing all the more delightful reconciliations, when all would be cleared up once more—to my own satisfaction, of course. But such emotions were purely "platonic," in the parlance of that period—"chaste," as my mother would have said. They had no connection with the signs of budding sexuality that my infantile body exhibited upon chance arousals—much to the delight of Cassandra, I need admit, who on such occasions, with loud praises, half derisive and half in earnest, accompanied by much laughter, was wont to show me off in my proud condition to the cook, the chambermaids and whosoever else happened by or readily could be called to witness the spectacle. This too I saw as nothing but a boisterous prank, all the more so since the chambermaids, almost all of them—like Cassandra herself—barely domesticated daughters of Carpathian shepherds, fled screaming with laughter from this exhibition. Nevertheless, adherents of Professor Freud may find some satisfaction in knowing that then my direst nightmare consisted in my sitting on the potty in an open passageway, exposed to all eyes and unable to flee since, on rising, my naked behind would be fully revealed. The feeling of self-inflicted distress in this dream was every bit as terrifying as the recurring nightmare of a treacherous murder I had supposedly committed, which frequently haunted me as an adult.

At that time, matters scatological played a paramount role in this world I shared with Cassandra. For Cassandra carefully watched over my digestion, expertly commented on its variable functioning, on the consistency and color of the excretions, further elaborating her diagnoses with many a homespun anecdote and earthy rustic proverb, regularly interweaving the matter of defecation into most of her stories. In almost all the fairy tales chronicling the adventures of two lovers—as, for instance, in my favorite story of the miraculous steed that always catches up with the princess repeatedly abducted by the Storm King, until the abductor finally manages to escape on the equally fast twin of the miracle stallion—the conclusion of such symbolically engaging yarns was signaled thus: "And then the two squatted down and together they crapped on the ground." Cassandra always concluded her tale with this bald simplicity, nor was there any doubt that this function signified a ritual sensory expression of a happy ending, the consecration of a connubial union more pure, solemn, on a higher moral and even aesthetic level—because performed in the full possession of one's own individuality instead of in mutual abandon—than the rude couplings we knew all too well from our dogs and the other animal life around the house, couplings that we also called, in equally unabashed innocence, "marrying." It would never have entered my head that animal copulation might have anything to do, or even be equated, with the blissful conclusion of the love romances in my dreams. The ritual of joint crapping—a shared and mutual catharsis—came closer to the idea of my fantasized epiphany.

All this might never have become known, for it occurred only in the intimacy of a like-minded world view, the exclusive twosomeness of Cassandra and me, sealed, so to say, in the piecemeal piebald gibberish I had learned from her, which we developed into a kind of secret idiom understood by no one else. Ever more frequently I had to translate word by word some utterance of Cassandra's for the other inmates of our household. The linguistic crudity and drollness that emerged in such endeavors amused my father and those others in the house who relished the humorous as much as it repelled and, at times, even horrified my mother. I was careful, of course, not to divulge any of the most intimate bond between Cassandra and myself—her fairy tales and the almost trancelike attention with which I listened to them. So the strange act of consecration that always concluded the conjoining of two lovers (comparable though not similar to two lovers in Indian folktales partaking a meal from the same cup) would have remained Cassandra's and my own secret if childhood's pressing urge to comprehend the incomprehensible had not driven me to unintentional treason.

It happened one night in my sister's and my bedroom, when Cassandra no longer slept with me. The lights were out, but my sister went on babbling as if to herself—something that always annoyed, excited or frightened me. This time she was embarked on a description of my clumsiness as a toddler still learning to walk, breaking whatever fell into my hands, putting anything within reach into my mouth, bawling, dirtying my pants and so on. She harked back to our exile near Trieste. Spitefully my sister embroidered on my helplessness at a time when she already knew how to behave like a young lady and was chattering in Italian— all of which was even more tormenting since I had no memory of that phase of my life and no remembered image with which to test the truth or falsity of her allegations. I had to accept whatever she said, as if my impotence of those days was extended to the present and into all future time still to come: I would always remain the latter-born, the less developed, the underdog, and she would always have an advantage over me in a world of exquisite experiences and superior knowledge and abilities. The only thing that remained for me from that time near Trieste—and even this merely as a blurred image, picked up I could not say where—was that female figure standing on the cliff by the sea in whom I seemed to recognize my mother, and the man I did not know.

Naively, I told my sister about this image in an anxious murmur and asked her—my heart throbbing in hope that the old puzzle would now finally be explained to me—whether she thought that then these two had squatted down together to crap on the ground.

Many experiences with my sister, who was bound to regard me as an unwelcome interloper, should have told me she would not pass up this opportunity to use such a compromising utterance against me. I was eventually subjected to a third-degree inquisition which, while it made clear from whom I had gotten this unspeakably vulgar and obscene metaphor, did not convince the inquisitors that I had no inkling of its true meaning. I was suspected of knowing only too well the real facts masked behind the offending allegory. That alone was shame enough. Even worse, I had credited my own pure mother with being capable of this debased act, not to speak of the ignominy of the denunciation itself, which, were it ever to be brought to my father's attention (and my sister saw to it that it was), would direct his wrath not on the putative wrongdoers but on me, the slanderer.

Cassandra too was hauled over the coals. But the effort to obtain additional damning evidence from her or to wring from her a confession of further pernicious influences failed by reason of her total incomprehension. This was not merely for linguistic reasons: she didn't even grasp what was being talked about. Yet I began to understand, intuitively, though by no means fully, something of the underlying implications. Henceforth I suspected complex hidden meanings in the most innocent figures of speech, the intent of which was not immediately obvious to me. I would have kept my innocence much longer had I not been suspected so early of having lost it.

It never entered my mind to interpret my sister's spiteful and malicious acts as expressions of a spiteful and malicious character. She simply followed her impulse to pay back in kind whatever bothered and annoyed her; and what bothered and annoyed her was purely and simply my existence as her brother. Understandably so: a talented and imaginative ten-year-old girl, happily busy on her own, is bound to view a willful and irascible six-year-old who constantly invades her world of games and dreams as a hateful troublemaker. I have often wondered that she didn't take advantage of some chance to wring my neck. For my part, I considered her a natural given of life, to be likened to the variable and sometimes hard weather of our country, its white-hot summers and bone-freezing icy winters, also its heartrendingly beautiful springs, as well as its autumns ripening in blue-golden splendor; also to the enticing yet cannibalistic love of my mother, with her lures and bribes and increasingly monotonous reminders, warnings, proscriptions, prohibitions, threats, condemnations and punishments; and generally, to other predicaments of childhood—the helplessness, the impotence, the groping, urgently stressing and distressed existence in unenlightened ignorance.

But primarily my sister was unable to put up with me because I lacked everything that fell under the concept—broadly inclusive in her understanding—of being domesticated. For the crude familiarity with bodily functions and the lack of physical taboos which I owed to Cassandra contributed to widening the distance between my sister and me, a distance set by our difference in age, until it became an unbridgeable one of principle, indeed of culture: we belonged to two different civilizations. She had been born before the general proletarization of the postwar era, in a world that still believed itself to be whole, while I was the true son of an era of universal disintegration. The foundation of her good breeding lay in the self-assurance, however deceptive, of an imperium basking in glory and resting on a punctilious system of rules of comportment and behavior. In contrast, I grew up in the dubious shakiness of one of those successor states described, rather derogatorily, as the Balkans. That this would give me the advantage of a more robust psychic makeup, which greatly facilitated my adaptation to our changed circumstances, in due time received dramatic proof. But in the days of our childhood together—later we saw each other only sporadically, when home for vacations from our separate schools—we expressed our differences in our own ways: she in the sovereign consciousness of her superiority, with her books and her precocious knowledge; I with a feeling of marked inferiority, in suppressed and impotent outbursts of rage, my fists raised against her, more brutish in every respect but, on the other hand, more natural, less inhibited, more free of illusion and closer to the raw realities of nature, less in jeopardy of fancies and abstractions. Only Cassandra knew how to effect temporary conciliations between us. With diabolical slyness she managed to bring out what was still genuinely childlike in my sister, a regression to a more primitive and infantile phase which she then magnified into the comically ridiculous, thus reducing her precocious pretensions to their proper proportions. I know of no better example of this than what we termed our "potty war."

In accordance with Mother's instruction (who once had heard something or other about a "kidney shock"), whenever some small mishap or alarum occurred — which was often enough — we were first of all set on our potties. What we called "peepee" thus became a kind of purification rite to be performed devoutly, posthaste after some fall or injury while still swallowing the last tears, or routinely at night before going to bed and entering the dark world of sleep, and then again in the morning on awakening from the weirdness of dreams. The vessel receiving these offerings became a symbol of well-being. Each of us had our own and guarded it jealously as an emphatically personalized property; if one of us, in haste or by mistake or in mischief, happened to lay hands on the other's potty, wild screams were heard. Cassandra was in the habit of stirring up these feuds by exchanging, seemingly by chance, the hardly to be confused receptacles: my sister's classic, spherically rounded and handle-equipped one and my own more masculine, beaked and cylindrical one, or she promoted our own confusions, so that all too frequently the nursery was rent by outraged scream: "He" — or she — "is peeing in my potty!" Fueled by demonic Cassandra, the emotions then rose to the level of murderous intentions, and often things got so noisy and boisterous as to reach the rest of the house, until the governess of the moment would profit from the opportunity to intervene and put "the savage one," Cassandra, in her place. (This relation, in any case, was never a good one. It was conflict not between personalities but between different classes and different worlds.) Finally the hubbub reached the earthly proximate Olympus, so that either Mother would come rushing into the nursery like an angered swan and, instead of soothing our boiling emotions, would conduct fidgety interrogations, meting out punishments that diverted our wrath from each other and directed it instead against the despotism of adults and our own impotence; or my father himself—rarely enough, when he happened not to be away hunting—stepped in and staged some humorous "divine ordeal," a race for the potties or a "noble contest," challenging us as to which of our toys we would be ready to sacrifice to buy back the usurped right to use the contested vessel. What until then had been a deadly serious conflict, fought with a ferocity all the more embittered as it centered, in truth, merely on the agonizing "as if" of childhood, then resolved into a game, became irrelevant and lost its sharp-edged reality. In return, I gladly accepted any outcome, even though I said to myself that my father patently favored my sister because she was closer to his heart than I.

I could always be sure of one consolation: behind the black silken curtain of Cassandra's hair, in the baking-oven warmth of her strong peasant corporeality, I found refuge at all times from whatever pained me. I was so obviously her favorite that she was often denounced to my parents and then chided for her undisguised preference for me. The more my sister outgrew the nursery and came under the thumb of a succession of more or less neurotic, pretentious governesses—neurotic because they lacked a man and were unattractive and poor, pretentious because, with their semieducated Occidentalism, they presumed they had been relegated to a Balkanic backwater and degraded to the level of domestics—the more Cassandra made me exclusively her own. I was the apple of her eye.

I granted her all maternal privileges more willingly than to my own mother, without regard to its being disputed whether she had been my wet nurse. Cassandra affirmed it as steadfastly as my mother denied it—out of shame that she hadn't been *able* to nurse me, declared Cassandra behind a hand secretively raised in front of her mouth. This, in some perfidious way, was convincing as only such believable fabrications can be. Add to this that Cassandra mourned the loss of a son of her own, whom she allegedly had to desert because of me.

Time upon time she told me—and told me alone, in our private jargon and in a singsong as plaintive as an old folk tune—of the unimaginable poverty she grew up in, the oldest of twelve children. At the birth of the youngest her mother had died, while the father had been crippled by a felled tree; she had raised her brothers and sisters, always on the verge of starvation, and whenever they had a slice of cornbread or an onion, they would thank God "on bent knees"—all her life, in pious gratitude, she drew a cross with the knife over each loaf of bread before making the first cut. Then came a night "as full of stars as a dog's pelt is full of fleas," and a village inn where gypsies fiddled and "the light cast from the windows shone like golden dust," while crickets chirped in the meadows "like water boiling in the kettle." Someone passing by plucked her from the fence on which she was perched so as to see and hear the better—"it was our picture show," she told me (having meanwhile been enriched by urban experience), "and we sat next to each other like swallows in autumn on a telegraph wire, young and old, Granny asleep with the baby in her lap, and only woke when some of the men came out of the inn to fight or throw up." But then someone had picked her from the fence and taken her into the golden roar of the gypsy fiddles, the clouds of tobacco smoke and men's voices, given her a drink and then another, and when the dazzling images began to go round and round in her head like the merry-go-round at the kermess, he took her outside and down to the side of the creek where the honeysuckle grows so thick between the tree trunks that "you can crawl and hide in it completely, like you in my hair." "And then you both squatted down together and crapped on the ground, yes?" I asked eagerly.

Graphically, she described to me the shame of having a belly "as big as a pumpkin." The girls in the village spat at her when she passed, and her father beat her with a fencepost, so that she hoped she would lose the child. She tried to drown herself in the creek under the tangle of honeysuckle which by then was leafless and gray like cobwebs. But the water was so shallow that she could plunge only her head into it, facedown, and since it was winter, the frost was bitter and she couldn't hold out long enough to die. Thin ice formed over her face and when she lifted her head out of the water, the glaze of ice broke like glass—and that's what made her so ugly, she said.

Then the pope came and took her to the monastery, a day's journey away, and that is where my father found her. "But I had to leave the child behind," she mourned, "your little brother"—and once more she laughed impishly. There were times when she sobbed bitterly over the loss of my little brother, usually when some incident made her sad, but she reverted soon enough to her usual spunky jollity. "Nothing but fancy notions," it was said in the household, "not a word of truth in the whole story. She's not quite right in the head, anyway." Nevertheless, I longed one day to meet my milk-brother and be reunited with him forever after in brotherly love. He was stronger, more noble and more courageous than I, and he was unconditionally devoted to me. He would accompany me through all the perils of life like one of those otherworldly helpers in times of distress who are the rightful companions of fairy-tale heroes.

Since we were not sent to school like other children when we got to be six or seven years old but were taught at home, and because those entrusted with our education devoted so much of their time and attention to my sister, who showed not only much greater intelligence but also pronounced talent and a sharper thirst for knowledge, I stayed much longer than usual in the world of childhood in which Cassandra was the most constant and direct influence. Cassandra herself was of course illiterate, and if, ultimately, she was able laboriously to form the letters of her own name, she owed this to my own and our shared efforts to penetrate the secrets of the alphabet. At first, neither of us got very far in this endeavor, and when finally I outdistanced her, she gave it up altogether and without regret. Meanwhile I owed her a much more valuable piece of knowledge than I ever owed later to my despairing teachers. It came to me out of Cassandra's attitude toward the written word.

Cassandra was not one of those semiprimitives who are haunted by hundreds of superstitions but take for real only what they can see with their eyes and grasp with their hands, and for whom any writing belongs to a phony world created by pettifogging lawyers, in which every word is twisted and turned around topsy-turvy as if by sleight of hand. That may be how the dimwitted people of her home village thought. But Cassandra's superstitious awe of the reality of letters, and her ultimate and voluntary rejection of their decipherment, originated in a much more archaic insight. The serried rows of books on the shelves of my father's library were truly demonic for her. That certain things had been recorded between the covers of these books which could be grasped mentally and transformed into speech and knowledge by initiates in the shamanic craft of coding and decoding those runic symbols—this could be understood only as a supernatural phenomenon. It irritated her to see that we had lost the sense of its terrifying uncanniness and that reading was an everyday custom, publicly performed, nay, that it could even become a vice, as exemplified by my sister. With the instinctive certainty of the creature being, she felt that such casual handling of the irrational was bound in turn to generate irrationality.

She realized that for those who had acquired it, the ability to read conferred power over those to whom the written or printed word remained a sealed mystery. But she also knew that this was a power pertaining to black magic—that it turns against its own practitioners and transforms them into slaves of the abstract. She saw in it a truly devilish power, since its manipulators, who also were its most immediate victims, were not even aware of its nefarious effects. To be sure, she was unable to say what was meant by the abstract and, even less, in what consisted its peril. Yet she carried within her innermost self—not only since she had left the monastery, where, on the walls of the church, the angels, devils and saints, as well as the tormented or redeemed bodies of the mortals, together with the beatitudes of heaven and the torments of hell were most wondrously and graphically depicted in ocher, red, blue and gold — she carried from her very beginning the clear and unshakable conviction that anything supernatural that does not lead directly to God and His heavenly kingdom must bring about a downfall into damnation. Books were either sacred or devilish, and since almost all books could be interpreted either way, they also could have both holy and diabolic effects. It seemed to her that with the opening of the covers of a book both the gates of heaven and the jaws of hell were being unlocked, and the angel or devil who then emerged from its pages separated the questing spirits according to either their longing for the one and only truth or their susceptibility to devilish, pernicious lies. To expose oneself to such a momentous decision in trite everyday circumstances seemed to her downright sacrilegious. And from that she protected me.

My father's infatuation with my sister, his loving understanding of her fancies and moods, the constant interest he devoted to all her doings bestowed upon her an exaggerated importance throughout the household, which she also displayed impudently in the nursery in her dealings with Cassandra and me. Everybody thought the world of her cleverness, and all too often my ignorant nurse and I had to acknowledge her unquestionable superiority. She was able to read long before I had learned to speak properly, and she read almost all the time. But when I was five years old and she was nine, she claimed to understand Latin — which she hadn't yet been taught.

Cassandra and I knew this well enough. But how could we call her bluff? She strutted in front of us, an open book in her hand, and moved her lips as if speaking the words she was allegedly reading, but when we challenged her to read aloud, she only replied disdainfully: "You can't understand that; it's Latin!" I was about to jump on her and wrest the book from her hand when Cassandra restrained me, wrapped me in her hair and murmured in my ear: "Don't you believe her, she is only pretending to read. She's probably holding the book upside down and lisping nonsense to annoy you." But against the visible evidence of the purported reading, which we could not contest, this was a mere supposition, further weakened by my father, who, laughing maliciously, made himself my sister's accomplice by confirming: Yes, what was written in the book was indeed Latin.

The looks I shot at my sister from the haven of Cassandra's sheltering hair and under the fire protection of her flashing black monkey eyes were white-hot with impotent rage. Nevertheless I exulted in the certainty of a later, all the more powerful vindication—a steadfast faith in the revelatory power of truth which stayed with me and reassured me all my life whenever I saw through some mental sham that, for the time being accepted as valid, could not be exposed because of some vested interest or simply because of general stupidity.

Among the experiences from which we learn nothing that we didn't know already, there is to be counted the insight that the reality we consider as all-dominating in truth consists mostly of fictions. My family's fictions were only too transparent: we lived the years 1919–1939 in the illusion of having a pseudo-feudal position in the world; this was based neither on prestige enjoyed in an existing society nor on wealth, but merely on the position my parents and particularly my grandparents had held before the First World War.

This strange make-believe, challenged by no one, was promoted by the leftovers of colonial gentry in which we were left, powerless relics, at the end of the Dual Monarchy. We considered ourselves as former Austrians in a province with a predominantly Austrian coloring, like those British colonials who remained in India after the end of the Raj. Neither my father nor my mother had been born in the Bukovina. My father had arrived there before the turn of the century as a government official of the Empire. My mother's parents had lived there temporarily, connected with the country by an originally Greek bloodline that over the centuries had become Romanian. (None of this was in any way singular in the great spaces of the former Habsburg Empire. In many ways—but mainly through the constant migration to far-off provinces by individuals of the most variegated backgrounds, military men or civil servants, pioneers or traders or fortune-seeking entrepreneurs—the situation was not unlike that one finds in the United States. Indeed, the fad for all things American which soon was to conquer all Europe fell on especially fertile ground in our neck of the woods.) So as long as we lived there, albeit as citizens of the Kingdom of Romania yet in the presumptuous feeling of belonging to another, superior civilization, the country in which my sister and I were born held only a provisional and specious character for our parents. Even we, constantly reminded that we were born there only by chance and were not real natives, could not free ourselves of a certain skepticism about our homeland, whose "Balkan" character now sharpened noticeably under our new sovereigns.

My sister in particular, who was eight years old when the old Austria fell apart in 1918 and who thus spent the formative part of her childhood in the ambience of a bygone era, never managed to feel at home among the sheepskin- and caftan-wearers, the spur-jingling operetta officers and garlic-scented provincial dandies. I, for my part, had no difficulty in that respect. I loved the land and its beauty, its spaciousness and its rawness, and I loved the people who lived there: that multifarious population of not one but half a dozen nationalities, with not one but half a dozen religions, and with not one but half a dozen different tongues— yet a people showing a common and very distinctive stamp. I could not have been connected to it more intimately than through Cassandra.

Our house stood at the edge of Czernowitz in a garden which on one side bordered the spacious and attractive public park and on the other, the botanical garden, also under the city's administration. This embeddedness in park greenery, and the nearby opening out into agricultural countryside, conveyed an illusion of living in something like a manor—a fair deception, strengthened by the severe isolation in which we children were kept, without any contact with our coevals. A large arterial road bordered by poplars and leading out into the country separated us from the extended grounds of a cavalry barracks where, in Austrian times, lancers and, after 1919, Romanian Roşiori were quartered. Notwithstanding the barely concealed scorn of my father for those "victors" who, as he was wont to say, "pounced on the dying old monarchy at the very last minute," I myself was passionately attracted by their uniforms, their weapons, and their manly and self-assured demeanor, in short, by everything that demonstrated the lethal seriousness of their profession.

Cassandra shared this passion with me, though not for the same reasons. I was never alone when I rushed to the garden gate to see if the sound of hoofbeats announced merely the passage of a hackney or the spectacle of a lieutenant riding by with his orderly, or perhaps a sergeant major with the fierce mien of a bronco tamer. In her eagerness, Cassandra was almost quicker than I. The officers were in the habit of visiting in the neighborhood and liked to show off their horses to the ladies living in the nearby villas. Cassandra, of course, was out for lower ranks. When the weather was bad, I did not have to beg to be let into the front drawing room or onto the balcony, so I could see better whenever a squadron, rain-soaked or dust-covered, returned from its exercises: Cassandra, alerted by some sixth sense, would already be at my side and take me by the hand or lift me up in her arms, and together from the best vantage point we watched the oncoming ranks in rapt silence, following them with our eyes long after they had filed past, our emotional harmony as perfect as that shared by art lovers before a masterwork.

Soon we harbored a common secret: during one of our walks (my sister was at home doing lessons), a noncommissioned officer accosted Cassandra. We already knew him by sight: in his squadron he rode a white horse that I especially admired. For several weeks we met him regularly. He wasn't much taller than Cassandra and at least equally unprepossessing, bowlegged, with arms hanging almost to his knees, a diminutive pitch-black moustache of exactly the same width as the nostrils under which it was glued, framed by two sharp wrinkles like two parentheses. Whenever he opened his broad mouth in a friendly grin, his big teeth shone white like an ape's. He could have been Cassandra's brother. But his tunic glittered with gold braids, spurs jingled on his boots, the spit-polished shafts of which were decorated with brass rosettes on heart-shaped cutouts below the knees, and it was with the unmatched verve of the experienced Lothario that he raised his arm to his shako in salute. I resolved to imitate all this in due time: this was supersharp and had true class; this was the right way to deal with women. I kept secret even from Cassandra that I exercised these gestures at home in front of a mirror.

The encounters were not limited to strolls along the so-called Nut Lane in the public garden—the name derived from the thick hazelnut bushes bordering the path, bearing to everyone's delight a profusion of fruit, almost always stripped bare before they could ripen to their full doe-brown, glossy hardness. Fairly soon our chaste perambulations ended with the three of us in our garden, into which a narrow door in the wall gave access and where a small pavilion, hardly more than a toolshed, invited strollers to rest. There the cavalryman, to my joyful delight—so overpowering as to make my temples throb—took off his saber and handed it to me to play with. I quickly withdrew to the remotest corner of the garden, where I could relish to the full the agonizing thrill of drawing the naked blade from its heavy, dull-metal scabbard, letting it glitter in the sun and then using it for nothing more martial, to my sorrow, than the beheading of nettles. My fantasy was excited even more passionately by the gold filigree of the saber knot, which in a most tactile way manifested the reality of the military world, making me realize all the more acutely the mere "as if" of the world of my games.

It was, alas, only a borrowed reality and it mocked me: I could not include it in the world of my games without feeling that I was deceiving myself—especially since I knew full well that I had been bribed by Cassandra and her corporal to get lost. I also knew that by letting myself be seduced so willingly, I was giving them time for their own games—games of factual reality, not make-believe ones. I did not have the slightest doubt that I had become their accomplice in something prohibited, though what this was I could imagine only vaguely. According to the degree of my enlightenment at that time, it could hardly be anything else than that these two were now squatting together to crap on the ground. After I had been called back and had returned the bribe and both of them had gone on their way, I felt impelled to return secretly to the pavilion, where I searched for the traces of their encounter. But when I failed to find any, my conscience was not appeased. The secret that separated the world of adults from my own make-believe one remained impenetrable, even though it seemed to be present, shimmering provocatively, everywhere and in everything.

The idyll was not to last long. One evening we strolled in vain along Nut Lane: our cavalryman did not appear, nor did he come the following day or the day after that, and so on for a stretch of one or two weeks. Then, quite unexpectedly, we met him once more. The verve of his salute was restrained. No, he could not accompany us to our garden but allegedly had urgent business in the opposite direction. A violent argument ensued between him and Cassandra, the words flying out so fast and vehemently that I did not understand any of them. Suddenly he hit her brutally across the face. I screamed. The impulse to throw myself at him lapsed in futility, for as he hit her he turned and walked away quickly, almost at a run. Cassandra loosened her hair and wrapped me in it. The jingling of his spurs was lost in the distance. She took me by the hand as I sobbed uncontrollably, and silently she walked me home.

Cassandra had no tears. She brought me to her little room in the attic, rummaged in one of her drawers and produced from under a pile of laundry a photograph of the cavalryman: it showed him in the traditional lady-killer pose, leaning on a rudimentary birch-lattice fence (the standard background of the while-you-wait photographer at the entrance to the public park), one arm bent akimbo, the sleeve embroidered with a filigree of gold braids and his hand nonchalantly holding a pair of white cuff-gloves, the saber hanging low in the belt. Cassandra placed the picture on a table, lit a candle in front of it, knelt down, crossed herself and started to pray . . . at first in a murmur, then ever louder, first in deep seriousness and apparent piety, then ever more satanically, her rising rage driving her into demonic merriment, praying ever more wildly and interjecting into her prayers

increasingly terrifying invectives and the most shocking gestures
. . . until she finally grabbed the picture, drew a pin from her hair
and with it pricked out his eyes, drove it through his heart and
time and time again at the juncture of his legs; then she tore the
picture into small scraps with which, after lifting her skirts, she
wiped her behind, finally burning each scrap separately in the
flame of the candle.

At first, I was deeply frightened. Cassandra, the piously strict,
for whom God the Father, Jesus Christ and all the saints were part
of the world as real as the mountains, the rivers and the trees in
the forest where she had been born, all of them as firmly
grounded in her life as the walls of the monastery in which she, a
sinner, had found refuge, she who never failed to make the sign of
the cross before speaking the name of something holy, she who
had led me into every church that happened to be on our way —
she now celebrated right here before my very eyes a black mass,
she sinned in the most blasphemous manner imaginable, she
indulged in shamanic magic and invoked satanic powers for the
lowest of purposes: to take revenge on one whom she had loved. It
was so monstrous, so unexpected and so baffling that, irresistibly,
it reverted to the comical. I ended up raked by laughter. I could
not wait to tell my sister about it and I rejoiced in anticipation of
that moment, even though I knew this would constitute a betrayal
of Cassandra and our twin togetherness. Our family storehouse
of anecdotes had gained another pungent Cassandra story — and I
had lost one more part of my innocence.

Retrospective perception of the milestones of life, which tends
to make you see existence as divided into distinct phases, leads me
to see this episode as marking the end of my true childhood. After
it I could no longer identify myself with Cassandra naturally and
spontaneously. For the first time I "saw" her consciously and
perceived her through the eyes of the others to whom I betrayed
her. I had left the safe haven of her hair, in which I had been
sheltered from those others, and I had switched over to their
camp. We still lived in a time in which an almost unbridgeable
gulf gaped between the so-called educated classes and the so-
called common people. My family's situation, based on the ab-

stract image of a once privileged position—mainly the myth of former wealth, which encouraged us to live beyond our true means and to indulge in expensive habits we could no longer afford—placed us absurdly far above the "common people," who, for the most part, lived in abject poverty, a poverty borne humbly and with eyes raised in admiration to their "masters." For the first time I thought of Cassandra as belonging not to my own lineage but to that other race of the poor, the know-nothing and the lowly. At the same time, there awoke in me a sense of the social pecking order. The longings for my putative milk-brother began to fade. Had I met him then, I would have felt separated from him by the same gap that set me apart from the neighborhood children with whom we were forbidden to play.

It may be that this event was preceded by another less spectacular one that had an even greater impact, an initiation of a different sort, the dark terror of which, though belonging wholly to childhood, at the same time presaged its end. My magpie died. One afternoon she lay dead in her cage. That very morning she had been hopping around as gaily as ever. I could not believe that this cold and rigid piece of rubbish that lay in the sandy gravel at the bottom of her cage was she. I trembled with sorrow. My sister was all eagerness to arrange a solemn funeral, but Cassandra with bewildering roughness forbade any such un-Christian nonsense and saw to it that the little corpse was discarded with the garbage. In so doing she was seconded by my mother, who thought the magpie had died of tuberculosis and might possibly infect us; this only increased my grief. For the first time, Cassandra was not my ally. My lamentations went for naught. Cassandra remained coarsely peremptory, as if, faced by the unavoidable fact of life and death, her unbroken peasant sense of reality revolted against citified fussing. "Dead is dead," she said gruffly. "One day you too will be dead."

Had she said what surely I had heard before—"You too will have to die one day"—it would have remained in the abstract. When hearing such sentences, comprehension glanced off from the purely verbal, but "being dead" meant what was clearly manifest by the bird's corpse on the garbage heap. I understood.

Terror struck at me like a dead weight. I saw myself stretched out on my bed, rigid and cold, rubbishy in my cerements, rotting underneath, something to be discarded as quickly as possible, like the dead magpie. Around me stood my sobbing family. I saw the hearse carrying me away and, behind, my sister in black veils, triumph in her eyes dutifully red from crying. I saw my grave and my dog refusing to leave it. All that was unavoidable, inescapable. It could happen tomorrow or many years on—but it had to happen, and against that no revocation or merciful exemption was possible. I was overcome by great fear. Clouds like black cinders stood over cooling embers in the scarlet evening firmament. I felt like fleeing—but where? Wherever I might go, this fear would go with me. This death fear would henceforth be with me, inextinguishably and forever, and it would hollow out my whole being: even if fleetingly I might forget it, it would rise in me at some moment and gnaw at my happiness or joy, or be ready to sink down to the bottom of my soul like a heavy stone; henceforth I would always know what it meant when someone told me that I too was mortal. In utter despair I asked Cassandra whether this was truly so, whether it had to be irrevocably so. Cassandra was incorruptible: "Everything has to die!" she said. "Your father too, and your mother and your sister, and I too, we all have to die one day!" And I knew she was telling the truth: Cassandra, the seeress.

I cannot dissociate the memory of Cassandra from that of the landscape that produced and nurtured her, the land whence she had come to us: the melancholy spaces of a landscape peopled with peasants and shepherds through which the silver band of a river meanders lazily, edged by hills and mountains shaded by forests. The view from the windows of our nursery carried the eye over the green humps of the treetops in our garden, out to the two rows of poplars bordering the big arterial road which led straight as an arrow to the pallid blue remoteness where the great forests stood. It may well be that the apelike sorrow in Cassandra's jet-black eyes originated in her longing for the stillness of those forests, filled with the drumming of woodpeckers and the scent of waving grasses in the meadowed clearings, and that her impish merriment was meant only to shield this incurable homesickness. Whenever her glance happened in that direction, it clung there, stretched out to the vague faraway somewhere, which, like an incontrovertible fate, exerted a steady undertow on our own souls as well. Cassandra could not turn away from that perspective without a deep sorrowful sigh, as if she saw herself as a wanderer on the wide dusty road between the poplars, forever drawn by her own inescapable destiny. And each time she would clasp me in her long simian arms only to thrust me away abruptly, as if pushing me out of her life. Even I—that God-sent gift replacing her own child, the sweetly restored core of her life— even I she saw merely as a short-term wayfaring companion on her road through life, the road that ultimately she had to travel alone. And because I sensed this in my innermost self, I also took up life as if it were but a succession of leave-takings in the course of a long journey.

In the image I hold of her in my mind, she is part of the prospect from the window of our nursery. She moves in front of it in all her scurrilous and farcical animation, haunting and weird even when sad, angry or moody, reminding me of a figure in one of those Turkish stick-puppet shows: the female counterpart of Karagjös, the jester. We never were able to determine her nationality with any degree of certainty. Most probably she was a Huzule—that is, a daughter of that Ruthenian-speaking tribe of mountain Gorals, who, it is said, are the purest-bred descendants of the Dacians who fled before the Roman invaders into the impenetrable fastness of their forests. Yet Cassandra just as well could have been a Romanian—that is, a product of all those innumerable populations who coursed through my country during the dark centuries of the decaying Roman dominion. She spoke both Romanian and Ruthenian, both equally badly—which is not at all unusual in the Bukovina—intermixing the two languages and larding both with bits from a dozen other idioms. The result was that absurd lingua franca, understood only by myself and scantily by those who, like her, had to express themselves in a similarly motley verbal hodge-podge. Even though it may be questioned whether I was actually fed at Cassandra's breast, there can be no doubt that linguistically

I was nourished by her speech. The main component was a German, never learned correctly or completely, the gaps in which were filled with words and phrases from all the other tongues spoken in the Bukovina—so that each second or third word was either Ruthenian, Romanian, Polish, Russian, Armenian or Yiddish, not to forget Hungarian and Turkish. From my birth, I heard mainly this idiom, and it was as natural to me as the air I breathed. Just as naturally, I repeated guilelessly everything I heard from her, at least at first, and only when I was constantly corrected, when some of my expressions brought on irrepressible laughter while others were greeted by an uncomprehending shake of the head and yet others severely prohibited, did I begin to realize that Cassandra's and my way of expressing ourselves was something out of the ordinary, a secret idiom within the general means of communication, albeit one with so many known patches that confidentiality itself was somehow full of holes without, for all that, being readily decodable.

Cassandra certainly could have limited herself to her ancestral Ruthenian or Romanian, both of which she spoke in a highly colorful manner with a strong dialect and rurally coarse inflection. That instead she chose to speak her laborious linguistic farrago, newly minted with every sentence and ultimately corrupting even her native tongues, was probably due to her innate humility. Submissively she tried to adapt herself to the languages spoken by her masters; and where German failed her, she filled it up with words from all the other idioms she knew. She made do with linguistic tidbits, like a beggar who collects the crumbs fallen from a rich man's table. If this, like her sterilized folkloristic garb, led to the grotesque opposite of unobtrusive assimilation, the blame should be put once again on the furtive ambition for betterment. German had been the language of the masters in the Bukovina during Austrian times and remained that of the educated classes. That Cassandra was allowed to live and work in and be part of a German-speaking household, that she was permitted to use German herself, even though corrupted with foreign borrowings to the point of incomprehensibility, constituted for her an admittance to a more exalted world and to a higher life form. She thought of herself as raised above her own kind on the strength of her speaking German, as much as on account of her fictitious nurse's uniform. In contrast to the black, white and gray abstraction of the uniform (in her own inimitable way, she is supposed to have said: "I go about like photograph of myself!"), her linguistic garb was composed of thousands of many-hued patches; whoever did not happen to know their multifarious origins could hardly understand what she was trying to say. Maybe I was the only one to understand her completely; the others, who couldn't plumb the etymology of her neologisms, found in them a source of unending merriment. In our household, she played the role of linguistic court jester. Through her speech patterns, and prodded and guided by my father, we developed a rare awareness of language, an almost maliciously acute way to listen to the spoken word and an interpretative feeling for written expression, to a degree that otherwise I have encountered only in students of Karl Kraus, whose linguistic education certainly was less fun than ours, even though it too stemmed mainly from the satirical pointing up of the ridiculous and the corrupted.

It goes without saying that my growing linguistic conscious-ness distanced me from Cassandra. At the same time, the distance from my sister, rather than decrease, also widened in those years. While I emerged from childhood and began my adolescence, my sister's teenage years were almost over and her full ripening was just around the corner. While I approached the difficult years of puberty with grim determination, she had left this phase effortlessly behind her, scarcely encumbered by the usual awk-wardness or silliness, and was about to change over gracefully to the side of the grown-ups, whom I now faced alone in avowed enmity. Cassandra no longer was always on my side.

Before long, anyway, our family life disintegrated completely. Our parents separated. My sister and I were sent to separate schools, she to Vienna and I first to Transylvania and later Austria. We saw each other only during vacations, which we spent partly with our father in the country and partly with our mother in town or at various Austrian lakeside resorts. What bound us together despite this separation was our growing sense of the comical and absurd, which often enough marked our family situation. The resulting tensions would explode in such convulsions of laughter that we were left in tears and stitches, as if after some physical excess. In all this we had had sufficient practice before the final breakup of what, all our lives, we were to mourn—not without a strange trace of guilt—as our lost home.

Shortly before my parents' separation, there occurred a momentous incident between Cassandra and me which, incongruously, once again centered on those mythically significant chamber pots. I was eight years old and for some time already thought of myself as much too grown-up to let myself be cared for by my nurse as I had been in the days of my childhood. But Cassandra would not be deprived, at the very least, of seeing to it that I scrubbed myself each evening in cold water with a bristle brush, that I brushed my teeth and my hair—all this as conscientiously as she had done so hitherto on the instructions of our governesses. It did not help that I told her repeatedly in no uncertain terms that this was no longer any of her business. One evening, as I was climbing into bed, she held out for me, with an admonitory remonstration, what she called (in a corruption of the French phrase *pot de chambre*) a "potshamba," and I angrily jumped down her throat. Cassandra bared her monkey teeth and looked at me with such fierce malevolence that I would have been frightened had my own fury not made me insensitive to her threats. Without a word she slammed the receptacle back to its habitual place under the bed, turned and wordlessly left the room. The door banged shut behind her.

The next day she failed to wake me up. The luckless person to whom my mother had assigned the role of governess to my sister had to take care of this task in her place, and she did it with the tips of her fingers, as it were, as if she had been expected to clean out the rabbit hutches. Cassandra had gone into town first thing in the morning, she explained. We gave it no further thought. Toward noon, when I was in the garden, my sister staggered toward me, tears in her eyes, hardly able to speak. Finally she managed to gasp: "Come, come right away! Cassandra . . ." She had to take a deep breath before continuing: "Cassandra—

bobbed her hair!" A new paroxysm of laughter cut her short. She
had to hold on to me, bent double by laughing.

I ran to the house, followed by my sister. At the sight of
Cassandra, we both succumbed. She looked like one of those
dwarfs whom Spanish court painters place as pages at the side of
princes. Her glorious hair had been cut off in a straight line over
her brow and at her neck. What remained stuck out at a slant on
either side of her wrinkled simian cheeks, jet-black and oily, like
the blubber-stiffened pigtails of an Eskimo woman, and its effect
was all the more comical as she, in expectation of our appraisal,
had raised her arms at the same angle, so that she stood there, legs
spread wide, like a Samoyed in her furs. She looked like nothing
so much as an Eskimo in a soccer gate ready to ward off a penalty
kick. Our irrepressible merriment infected her forthwith, and she
too began to laugh until tears ran down her face. She raised the
corner of her apron to wipe her cheeks, slapped her thighs and
boomed her raucous peasant laugh: "Hohohoho! Have become
modern lady now!" That it was meant as a symbolic act of
vengeance, we all forgot.

It was in those days that my mother had put an end to the
constant succession of misses and mademoiselles by calling to the
rescue a Miss Lina Strauss. *Strauss* in German means "bunch of
flowers," and therefore it was but natural that soon she was
nicknamed and lovingly called by everyone in the household *das
Strausserl,* "the little bunch," or Bunchy for short. Bunchy had
been Mother's tutoress and she combined in her person all the
talents and qualities that, singly, had been hoped for in her
innumerable predecessors. Unlike those "English" and "French"
governesses, perennially dismissed in short order, she did not
originate in Gibraltar, Tunis or Smyrna, but in Stettin, in
Pomerania, which, however, did not prevent her from teaching
good French, English and Italian, as well as the history of art, and
from soon establishing herself, thanks to her clear-eyed intelligence, poise and experience, and, last but by no means least, her
sense of humor, as an undisputed figure of authority in the
household. That this household held together at all was due
largely to her conciliatory presence. Nevertheless, distinct en-

campments began to take shape, even though much crossing over occurred between them. My father and sister stood together as ever before; and although Bunchy was in a certain sense an heirloom of my mother's, she had to be counted willy-nilly with this alliance because of her unconcealed affection for my sister and her respect for my father. On the other hand, my mother felt somehow betrayed by Bunchy and thought to compensate for this by trying ever more jealously to get a firm hold over my own person, lining up in a close though competitive collusion with Cassandra, who, in actual fact, "belonged" to my father—the way each of our dogs belonged to one of us and thereby became "mine," "yours," "his" or "hers." Thus, the pecking order in our family was constantly shifting and from now on was fought over openly, as in a kind of class struggle.

Heretofore my mother—together with her follow-ing—had had the upper hand. Strangely enough, her windblown irrationality counted for more than my father's overbearing jolli-ness, malicious wit, and vitality, his knowledge and his skills. Her physical frailty and delicate nervosity, though it concealed a steely toughness, made her seem superior to my father in all his booming robustness; her sensitivity endowed her with greater depth than my father's naive huntsman's sentimentality. But as a group, the opposing party now gained a tremendous advantage as a result of Bunchy's towering cultural superiority over Cas-sandra, "the savage one." While Bunchy was reading with my twelve-year-old sister the poems Michelangelo addressed to Vit-toria Colonna, Cassandra was feeding me, the eight-year-old, her inexhaustible fairy tales—telling them in her very own patched-up patois, gathering words from all over to form her linguistic collages, randomly found vocables, scurrilous verbal creations, word-changelings, semantic homunculi—I never again encoun-tered language in such colorful immediacy. The fairy tales them-selves I met again, it is true: in conscientiously compiled collections of folklorica, in prize-winning anthologies, one of them even by Dostoevsky; Cassandra knew them all and a few more to boot that have nowhere been recorded—and what's more, she knew how to tell them as if they were happening right in front of your eyes.

I need hardly expand on the enormous legacy she thereby bequeathed to me. But at that time, the "culture of the Occident" conveyed by Bunchy was regarded as more valuable. In this respect our parents were of one mind: we did not belong to Romania, which had surrendered to its Balkanization and was therefore part of the East. It was the year 1922; Europe was not yet divided, as it was to be after 1945, yet even then we felt definitely and consciously that we were "Occidentals." That this would make us doubly homeless we were to experience later on, when we moved to the West and in many respects felt like Easterners there, felt this even more acutely at a later date, when our homeland irrevocably became part of an East that was fundamentally and ideologically separated from our own world. The disintegration of our parental home preceded by two decades the disintegration of Europe.

For Cassandra this meant what in the ugly legal parlance of today is termed "deprivation of existential legitimacy." It started for her with the appearance of Bunchy. Cassandra came to realize that she had become superfluous, for I too was leaving the world of the nursery forever. In truth, there was no longer any use for her. She helped out here and there and temporarily, in whatever it was, but pretty soon she mainly took care only of the dogs. And the dogs themselves felt that something was amiss—as they always sensed whenever a trip was planned on which they were not to be taken along or when one of us was banished to his or her room as punishment or was about to be taken sick—and reacted with dazed distress; some forgot that they were supposed to be housebroken and all of them were disobedient and irritable, at times even biting each other. Troll, the old stubby-haired setter who had been placed as a puppy in the cradle of my newborn sister, was almost throttled to death by my Airedale, who had been my first birthday present and was thus younger by four years. This prompted my sister to conduct a fierce vendetta against me that lasted for months and also was directed at Cassandra, who still loyally stood by my side.

My memories of that period are clouded. I was rebellious and must have been greatly trying to my father. I usually committed some infraction during his absences when he was off hunting or at what he called "business assignments," with which he legitimized his week-long disappearances, and these infractions were deemed too grievous to be judged and punished fittingly by the household's female judicial system. Because he was annoyed by the very fact of being made to play the family bugaboo, his punishments generally turned out even more severe than his hotheaded temper in any case would have dictated. Such things sank too deeply in me to be amenable to Cassandra's consolations. Though she managed to come up with comforting pleasures, such as a choice tidbit secreted for me in the kitchen, or puppies from a new litter: Mira, my father's favorite pointer bitch, was as fertile as a queen bee, and Cassandra was as merry and efficient a nursemaid in the kennel as she had been of old in our nursery.

Cassandra became more easygoing and, if not engaged in one of her clownish pranks, exhibited a somewhat comical but undeniable dignity. She held herself stiffly erect—as much as she could with her short neck and huge, lopsided head—erect "with the pride of a Stone Age female who has discovered that she can stand on her hind legs," as my father used to say. Sometimes the family thought of marrying her off—"to a blind man, perhaps," it was suggested maliciously. Bunchy even thought of the possibility of further cultural improvement, although she knew of the failed attempt to rid Cassandra of her obstinate illiteracy. "How about an educational trip to Florence?" wondered my father in ironic allusion to Bunchy's own past. "If only she were a little smaller, we could get her hired in a circus sideshow," quipped my saucy sister, who always maintained that Cassandra was in reality a giant dwarf.

Cassandra herself would have acknowledged this collective racking of brains with incomprehending surprise. What, after all, was wanted of her? Surely we could not think of depriving her of her claim to residence in our house! She lacked nothing. She had a roof over her head—even a room to herself, with a bed, a cupboard, a table and a chair; she had plenty of good food and as much fun with the dogs as she could wish for. She was alive. She'd had enough of men, once and for all. Of her children, one was lost and the other was about to go his own way, as was but natural: such was life. In passing, I began to notice ever more numerous silver strands in her bobbed hair.

When my parents separated and my sister and I were sent to schools abroad, so that two separate households were established, Cassandra at first stayed with Father. There she exhibited hitherto unknown talents which enabled her soon to transcend her duties in the kennel and assume brilliantly her new and rightful place as housekeeper. She became expert at just about every household art: she knew how to cook, how to clean rooms, how to sew and iron, how to set a table and how to serve; she knew how to manage the linen closets and the pantry, how to tend flowers, harvest the fruit of the orchards and train servants. When in doubt, she visited with my mother to get advice. Because my father was even more frequently absent, the house remained almost exclusively under her sole management. When my sister and I came for a few weeks' vacation, we found almost everything as it had been—though somewhat airlessly inanimate, as in a museum, and pervaded by that peculiar boiled-cabbage fustiness which creeps into houses deserted by their masters. "There's a smell of servants' quarters," said my sister. Cassandra herself was much too keen-witted not to notice this herself. One day she declared that the time had come for her to leave. "Is come my tshyass," she said: her hour had struck. She repeated it for weeks and months, but then one day the hour really came. A widower with three small children needed her more urgently than we.

I could never have imagined a day when she no longer would be in our house, and it is not to my credit that when the day came I accepted it as a matter of fact. She spared me seeing her leave. She was there when I left for school, and she was gone when I returned. But by then so much had changed in my world that I considered this disappearance of Cassandra as a kind of logical sequel. I was thirteen years old, an age when one doesn't look back. Although I suffered homesickness when I was away at school, I also found myself being homesick when at home. I guess this was probably due to that persistent undertow emanating from the wide poplar-lined wayfarers' roads that crisscrossed our countryside, leading to a dove-blue never-never land that filled my soul with nostalgia for something forever lost, something I had already lost the moment I was born. When I asked about Cassandra, I was told that she had found a noble task in life with the widower's children and had every reason to be happy. Czernowitz being so small, I did not have the impression that Cassandra had disappeared from my world. She occasionally visited us when her responsibilities toward her new foster children allowed.

She raised those children. When their father died, she stayed on alone and worked her fingers to the bone for them: flourishing children, two pretty girls and a dark-eyed boy who may have reminded her more than I of her own lost son. I saw her for the last time shortly before the Second World War, in the winter of 1936–1937. She still had her sterilized nurse's costume, threadbare by then, a bit slovenly, and not so scrupulously clean as when she was with us, yet worn with great self-assurance. Her ugliness may have been frightening for someone who had not known her, particularly when she stuck out her gigantic dwarf's head and laughed so that her white teeth—set in pink gums and by now showing some gaps—seemed to jump out of her dark simian countenance. Her hair was as straggly and Eskimo-like as ever, but by now it had turned iron gray: "Like tail of white horse my accursed corporal rode—does Panitshyu remember him?" She called me Panitshyu, or "young master," and when I reproved her, she replied in her own patchwork language: "How else shall I call such a tall young gentleman? Nowadays I would no longer be allowed to hold the potty for you—would I?" She laughed her full-throated peasant's laugh: "Hohohoho!"

A friend who was with me at the time and who knew nothing of the role she had played in my life, asked in surprise: "Who is this Cro-Magnon female?" "My second mother," I replied.

Two years later the Russians were in the Bukovina, this time for good, and I never learned what had become of her.

As I recall her now, there is one scene that stands foremost in my mind: a day in winter; it must have been immediately after the end of the First World War and upon our return to the Bukovina after four years of nomadic refugee existence. Cassandra and I are on our way to fetch fresh milk from a neighborhood farmstead. It is surprising that my mother has allowed me to accompany Cassandra, for it is bitterly cold. But fresh milk is a prized rarity and Cassandra has probably taken me along so as to exact compassion—as she had done earlier, during our first flight from the Russians in 1914. The open country into which the large gardens at the edge of town imperceptibly merge lies under heavy snow below which one senses earth in the icy grip of winter. The frost bites so sharply that we are more running than walking. To distract my attention from the cruel cold, Cassandra cuts all kinds of capers, turning us both around, so that we walk a few steps backward, our new tracks now seeming to run parallel to our old ones. Or she makes me hop alongside her, holding me by the hand, first on one foot for a stretch and then on the other, and pointing back she says: "Look, someone with three legs has been walking here!" And then, when I tire, she does something that intuitively I feel is not a spontaneous inspiration but rather the handing down of an age-old lore, a game with which numberless mothers before her in Romania have transformed for their children the agony of the wintry cold into a momentary joy. She places the bottom of the milk can in the snow so that its base rim forms a perfect circle in the smooth white surface; then she sets four similar circles crosswise on both sides and at the top and bottom of the first circle, intersecting it with four thin crescents—lo and behold! a flower miraculously blossoms forth in the snow, an image reduced to its essentials, the glyph of a blossom, such as are seen embroidered on peasant blouses, where these fertility symbols are repeated in endless reiteration to form broad ornamental bands. I too insist on an ornamental reiteration and, struck by this magical appearance, I quite forget the strangling cold. I do not tire of urging Cassandra to embellish our entire path with a border of flowering marks, an adornment of our tracks which I wish all the more to be continuous and without gaps, since I know full well that these tracks will soon be blown away by the wind and covered by the next snow, ultimately to be dissolved entirely in spring with the melting of the snow and thus fated to disappear forever.

The Mother

A piece of brocade woven in silver and burgundy lozenges. It may have been part of a harlequin costume that once fitted a female body so tightly as to make it look androgynous, even while accentuating its femininity. I visualize only the body: it has no face. It lies in a treasure chest, the body of a mermaid ensnared in ropes of pearls as if in a net, together with fishes, shells, crabs, starfishes and corals. The mermaid is blind; her world has turned to rubbish. The chest contains the tinsel of a forgotten carnival of long ago. And the mermaid herself is rotting.

A man who admired her when she was a young bride and then as mother—incidentally, a most artistic, scintillatingly witty man who later was to become my friend and teacher, though unfortunately only for too short a time—this man told me once that it was hard to imagine what subtle fascination had emanated from her when she was relaxed and serene or, even more, when she thought herself unobserved and was lost in thought, enraptured in a transfixed expectancy, an inner-directed listening, awaiting some ineffable occurrence. Only in her last days, when she hoped soon to be rid of the burden of her eighty-six years and longed to be released by death, she recovered some of that shy grace, wafted on her tremulous smile, a dream-bemused question, an expression of bewildered but no longer expectant hearkening. What lay in between was a life of continuous disappointments: an increasingly warped and ever more dreary existence in which anxieties both foolish and legitimate, neuroses both real and imaginary, afflictions, terrors and true obsessions were accompanied by uncontrolled outbreaks of impotent rage that twitched her eyebrows skyward and dimmed her glance as if in frozen

panic, senses blunted and mind benumbed, head cowering between hunched-up shoulders, motions jittery and her whole
being—now brittle and clumsy and always distraught—shackled
in fated abasement. Only the fine facial bone structure and the
still full hair which never turned entirely white gave some hint
that once she had been beautiful.

Her flowering as a woman was short. The early images of her
that I hold in my mind are of great comeliness. It is 1919, the First
World War is over and we are back in the Bukovina, where there
had been hard-fought battles. Here and there rubble is still rotting in ruined buildings; naked walls and yawning gables rise up
to the skies, outlined against indifferently speeding clouds. But
some things have remained untarnished. After four years of
refugee existence in other people's houses, my mother is finally
mistress of her own home once again. I see her in the light of a
summer afternoon ceremoniously putting the last touches to the
table set for afternoon tea, arranging cups and flowers. Her face is
happy; she dreams of an idealized present, not as it is but as it
should and could be. Shortly thereafter she is joined by my father
and immediately the atmosphere becomes strained and frosty.
The tea is drunk in hostile silence, which torments me because I
sense that she is suffering. My sister is unaffected and soon
scampers away, luring my father after her into the garden. I too
should like to escape to the safety of Cassandra's hair, but my
mother embraces me vehemently, and I love her passionately, love
her in a way different from my love of Cassandra. She belongs to
that promised land beyond my child's world; I see in her the
embodiment of what one day will be entrusted to me when I too
will be a grown man and part of her world: the very essence of
frail, vulnerable femininity in need of protection. No doubt my
later realization of what toughness and occasional callousness
hid behind her apparent delicacy did not favorably influence my
subsequent attitude toward women.

Her love for me was stormy. I do not care to call it passionate,
for that would presuppose impulses and initiatives, and one failed
to find anything in her being that emanated directly from her. She
lived not according to any immanent motive but by preconcep-

tions. She loved me as "the mother" should, according to a fixed concept of what mother and child were supposed to be, a fickle love that depended on the submission with which I conformed to my role as child. No other torments of childhood were so painful as the intensity of that love, which constantly required me to give something I was unable to grant. She required more than my goodwill to be a well-mannered child, to grow and to thrive under her care. I felt I was expected not merely to fulfill the stereotype of the perfectly educated, well-bred son, unconditionally loving his mother, but in addition to provide something lacking in herself. In her hands, I was both tool and weapon with which to overcome her emptiness — and perhaps also some anticipatory foreboding of her own destiny, whose fated finality she refused to accept.

My mother's restlessness and nervous insatiability were discharged against my sister even more virulently than against myself. She could not stand this darling of my father's, even though she claimed maternal rights and also exacted the demands flowing from a mother's responsibilities in regard to my sister. She could not cope with the rapidly maturing girl whom she had left alone during the first four years of her infancy. It was said that after the birth of my sister she was stricken with a kidney disease which she tried to mitigate but never could hope to cure entirely by protracted sojourns in health resorts. Until the outbreak of the First World War (and my own appearance in this world) she spent the greater part of the summers in Swiss spas and the winter months in Egypt — and it is in the latter country that, for a time, I matured in embryonic safeness. Meanwhile my sister was in the care of well-tried nurses under the supervision of our maternal grandparents in the country house in which she had been born, the so-called Odaya which had been allotted to my mother as a kind of conditional dowry. The girl hung on her father with passionate love and in ever more intense closeness.

Our mother's frail health and almost yearlong absences from her house (the furnishing of which was only scarcely completed to suit family occupancy), a house she hated, did not benefit her young married life. Nor did the four years of war that followed bring our parents any closer. We had left the house when the Russians arrived, and I believe that their appearance came as rather a relief to her. It was a ramshackle old building, in appearance half monastic and half a Turkish konak located in a most remote region and of a rusticality that only my huntsman father did not mind. My mother much preferred our house in town. In 1918, upon our return to the Bukovina, we resumed our family life in Czernowitz; the family was split into contending parties and, in view of our father's absences, owed its cohesion only to the permanent old-time domestics—Cassandra; Olga Hofmann, the Bohemian cook; Adam, the coachman; and finally Bunchy, those firm pillars amidst the coming and going of all the others. My parents were already so alienated from each other that for my own part I could not have found any pretext for the formation of an Oedipus complex. Jealousy I felt only toward my sister and her close bond with my father, a relationship from which I was totally excluded.

During my childhood days, my father was more a mythical than tangible figure for me. I saw him as rarely as my sister had seen her mother during *her* first years. Now he was away from home most of the time on hunting expeditions: Nimrod, the great hunter, whom from afar I marveled at, admired and envied and whom at close range I feared. I grew up among women, and it is through them that I experienced "the female" in three archetypal embodiments: through Cassandra, a brood-warm, protectively enveloping motherliness; through my sister, forever outdistancing me by four years and by nature's favor or disfavor the superior, the more airy, spiritual, always nimbly evasive figure of the nymph; and through my mother, an iridescent interplay of all archfemale characteristics—sensual excitement paired with the fitful capriciousness of the potential mistress, forever vacillating between stormy tenderness and pretended indifference, between lovingly passionate empathy and cruelly punishing iciness.

A potential mistress, yes, but one in the sentimental guise of a turn-of-the-century painting. The essential of my mother's femininity I perceive in her clothing. She was very attractive in those years, with her still girlish though gently rounded slimness. I never imagine her body but always as she appeared, formally clad, in society. To my mind she is the prototype of the lady. I love her movements, her posture, as well as certain graceful details: her smooth arms, the nape of her neck with the line of her chestnut-colored hair artfully teased into an airy, fluffy fullness — not like Cassandra's tightly wound pillow for baskets and pitchers. But I find even more appealing the elegant line of her clothes: the long narrow skirt, slightly gathered at the hips, the tightly laced waistline and the accented high bust of the period. Her favorite color is a light pearl-gray that invests the fabric with a discreet, self-assured neutrality which brings out the bloom of her delicate skin. For jewels, she prefers pearls. Her thin pointed shoes and soft kidskin gloves that cover her arms to her elbows are endowed for me with an erotic fascination. I develop a sharp eye for the quality of hats, handbags, umbrellas and other accessories. In winter, her furs flatter her with a voluptuous sheen that speaks eloquently to me. And all this is suffused with the scent of a fastidiously cared-for womanliness.

As if she meant to transpose this ethereal physicality to a spiritual and psychological sphere, she has an unworldliness, a remoteness from life that removes her as a possible object of my sensuality and places her in a category of sublimated eroticism. What is feminine in her awakens merely a mediated desire so that it remains platonic, as one used to put it. One might say the desire was directed at the brassiere rather than at the breasts. What I perceived as "womanly" in my mother were her female accoutrements: a totality of culturally distinguishing characteristics. The inevitable attraction of the totally different, forever unattainable and eternally incomprehensible female being, though belonging to the same zoological human species, was summed up for me in the onion skins of feminine clothing.

Whether that remoteness from the world and from reality also sublimated the desire of the men in my mother's life remains a moot question. As far as my father was concerned, this would seem paradoxical, but it can't be ruled out. He loved her very much, even though he never took her entirely seriously and cheated on her left and right. She accused him of unbridled sensuality, thereby probably expressing her inhibitions regarding any overt assertiveness. She feared reality; her life seemed to her a spell that had cast her into irreality. She always felt guilty about not fitting, as she saw it, into a world where everyone else was at home. Nothing around her or in herself corresponded to the conceptions she had formed about her life, and this nourished a culpability that she then angrily rejected. She felt constantly reminded of her subservience to the call of duty, as if she were forever failing at some task. This unfulfilled, unfulfillable sense of duty magnified ultimately into a nervously obsessive need for self-imposed duties. She assigned herself duties like self-inflicted punishments.

My remembrance of that early time is murky. The sunny days of childhood came later for me. I was still frightened by the stormy skies and the blood-red sunsets over the deeply melancholy spaciousness of the landscape, of which we had an unobstructed view on three sides of our house and garden. Clear-lit images, such as that of my mother at the tea table on a summer afternoon before her elfin dreaminess iced over, are rare. If there hadn't been the brood-warm love of Cassandra and her comical buffooneries, I would now be visited in an even worse way by the anxieties that in those days permeated our problematic family life. None of them are forgotten. My allergies to all kinds of tensions, exaltations and neurotic resistances have their throat-tightening origin in those days, when, presumably, the hardness I displayed to my mother at the end of her life also originated. Her endearments were of a tempestuousness that frightened more than delighted me, and in addition prompted venomous remarks from my sister. Even though I surmised, with the uncanny ability of children to plumb the reality behind the surface, that the bluntness with which my mother interfered in our harmony stemmed from her need to find some firm ground in a life that was slipping away from her, I never forgave her for it. Nor did I forgive her her absentmindedness, which she tried to correct with unyielding opinions and rigid prejudices. The hostility to anyone not sharing her opinions and intentions resulted directly from existential panic. When she was alone or thought herself so, her glance would drift away and she would lose herself in a remote nowhere, initially filled by dreams, perhaps, but later peopled by phantoms from her misspent life—in any case the true scenery of her mind.

I see her at table, our meals a silent ceremonial. She holds herself stiffly erect and eats automatically, without visible enjoyment, the eyes either downcast to the plate or directed unseeingly straight ahead, apparently indifferent to what happens around her. She herself—or her soul, her fantasy or whatever; in any case, her true life—is miles away, beyond the dining room walls. All the more persistently she insists on the ceremony of the meals, on our table manners, on a letter-perfect service; she devises sophisticated menus, watches over our nutrition by serving us foods that promote our health, appetite and digestion, and punishes us excessively if, overfed and sated, we reject it. She requires sound corporeality to convince her of our physical reality. We have to prove that we actually exist, by means of thriving health, growth, appetite, regular bowel movements, red cheeks and bubbling exuberance as much as by unconditional submission to her unending instructions, prescriptions and proscriptions. What she understands to be maternal love clutches at the visible and the tangible. Intellectual development is by tradition left to professionals, hired employees: governesses, tutors, teachers. But the supervision of our weal and woe devolves upon her alone and it turns into a rankling obsession. She holds on to it desperately, as if it were her only support in the whirlwind of the times.

And it is true that that whirlwind was exceptionally violent. One no longer realizes today the extent of the changes that the 1914–1918 war wrought in the world in general and Europe in particular, though it did not bring so much destruction as its continuation in the even fiercer 1939–1945 war. Only the regions of the embattled fronts lay in ruins; the hinterland was largely spared. There was not the terror of aerial bombardments night after night, nor the horror of flattened cities across the continent, nor the misery of their ruins and the wretchedness of swarms and mobs of bombed-out populations and refugees. On the surface, the world seemed unchanged, but it was all the more spooky for that. In the first installment of the worldwide war which had come only to a temporary halt in 1918 and broke out all the more fiercely two decades later, an order had been destroyed in which, up to then, everybody had put faith. Critical voices had not been lacking: the world before 1914 no longer considered itself the best of all possible ones. But it was a world in which culture still rated high. The meat grinders of Ypres and Tannenberg, the hellish barrages of Verdun and the Isonzo shattered all illusions. A species of men arose from that ghostly landscape of bomb craters and trenches whose bestiality was unconstrained. A free field was given to the Hitlers and Stalins to come.

For the class to which my parents belonged, this meant a fall into chaos, into impotence and deprivation, hopelessness and squalor. What today is designated by the collective noun *bourgeoisie* lived with an imperturbable faith in what Robert Musil's Count Leinsdorff called "property and learning." All the trust in life that these two pillars had supported collapsed together with them. The resulting changes in reality were so sudden, unpredicted and incomprehensible that at first they seemed more like a monstrous nightmare. The desire to wake from the bad dream gave rise to the utopia of the 1920s, one of the worst by-products of which was to be the Third Reich. But most people remained stunned and paralyzed: sleepwalkers in an alienated present.

My mother, born in 1890, was almost thirty years old when the First World War ended and had—as she used to say—"hardly lived at all, in fact." She had been raised in a golden mist of expectations about the future, which in the imagination of a young girl of her generation were nourished by ambiences and impulses, lights, colors and sounds, an intoxicating vision of an enchanted, permanently celebratory existence: the "grand life" in the style of Madame Bovary. Seen in this light, her first married years, in a hated house which she had fled for the daffodil meadows of Montreux and the palm shades of Luxor, were indeed a time devoid of meaning. Those years of refugee subsistence in the remoteness of a small villa near Trieste and in a cowherd hamlet in Lower Austria must have seemed even more estranged from what she thought of as the "true" life. She had borne two children and had assumed the role of a conscientious mother, but the dream of her life had remained unrealized. For this she blamed mainly my father, but also in part the country we lived in.

After the collapse of the Austro-Hungarian monarchy, the Bukovina became part of Romania. While in Austrian times its linguistically and sartorially kaleidoscopic mixture of people had given an attractive touch of color to the placid and mannered everyday life of a flourishing crown land, the opposite now occurred: a thin foil of civilization appeared to have been superimposed on an untidily assorted ethnic conglomerate from which it could be peeled off all too readily. Neither my father nor my mother belonged to the indigenous population. Each in his or her own way lived in a kind of exile: they had both ended up in a colony deserted by its colonial masters. Hardly anything remained of the former social world they had inhabited—however confined and provincial it must have been here under the double-headed eagle—and that had been composed of more or less high-ranking government officials, owners of landed estates, officers of the garrison, university professors and like representatives of the so-called educated classes. Those who remained in Romania and did not return to the shrunken remains of the Austrian republic or emigrate elsewhere split into groups determined by nationality. The Romanians holding important government posts established themselves as the new masters under the aegis of the Romanian military establishment, which flaunted the brassy glitter of its fresh victory, and they remained largely isolated from those who spoke other languages and now were the new minorities. The so-called Bukovina Swabians—settlers who had established themselves in the region in the times of Emperor Joseph the Second—segregated themselves in a flag-waving Greater Germany clannishness, casting nostalgic sidelong glances at Bismarck's Second Reich. The Ruthenians refused to have anything to do with either former Austrians, who they felt had treated them as second-degree citizens, or the Romanians, who cold-shouldered them in return. Poles, Russians and Armenians had always congregated in small splinter groups and now more than ever kept to themselves. All of these despised the Jews, notwithstanding that Jews not only played an economically decisive role but, in cultural matters, were the group who nurtured traditional values as well as newly developing ones. But one simply did not associate with Jews — and thus obviated the danger of undermining credulously cherished ideologies or "bolshevizing" so-called healthy artistic canons through an encounter with what was regarded as too radically original and modern. We, as declared (and déclassé) former Austrians, were counted willy-nilly with the so-called ethnic Germans.

In a town that at the time had a population of some hundred fifty thousand inhabitants, it would have been possible, of course, to find a dozen or so like-minded persons to associate with. But this would hardly have allowed for the intoxicating illusion of a "grand life" (which in other parts, incidentally, had meanwhile also become tainted), certainly not in the company of the ladies and gentlemen of the ethnic-German singing societies at their summer solstice celebrations, with fiery pyres over which black-red-and-gold banners swirled in the wind while full-throated choir bellowed into the flying sparks: "Tshermany, o Tshermany, my lohvely faderland . . ." The person who saw through all this from the very beginning was my father, and he cared all the less for it since he was indifferent to anything that was not in some way connected to hunting. Mother thus was left all by herself. Her efforts to escape her growing isolation were pathetically touching; ultimately she became resigned and almost completely isolated herself and her children in the hermetic solitude of our house and garden.

Still, we children had that stereotyped experience of seeing Mother enter her bedroom, her deep décolleté glittering with jewels and she herself transformed into a movie star, followed by my father, who left it undecided whether the high color of his face was due to the tightness of the stiff collar he wore with his tails or to his rage at having to spend the evening on diversions he hated and in the company of people he despised. There existed in Czernowitz at that time a theater in which German-language plays were put on with "leading talents from the homeland," as it was advertised, until Romanian students ended these performances with a violent demonstration. This chauvinist manifestation sufficed to prompt my father never again to set foot in that theater. But other social events tempted—or repelled.

The Gay Twenties were upon us. From the illustrated magazines arriving at the house, we received graphic instructions on the fashionably updated life-style models, saluted by popping champagne corks. Even our unworldly mother knew enough of the world to recognize the difference in quality between these glittering images and the true level of the locally available entertainment. Father's ruthlessly acerbic comments the morning after such nights of revelry left no doubt concerning their real worth. Still, some romance remained in preparing for the hoped-for enactments of the great dream-life, however inadequate these might turn out to be. Whenever we found ourselves in my mother's dressing room, Cassandra would rummage with monkeylike curiosity in the costly fabrics of evening gowns and wraps from a more expansive prewar era, the heron feathers, diamond clasps, silk shoes, brocaded caps and other paraphernalia. But the atmosphere of real or imagined festivities was felt most vividly when the baubles had been put away and left once again gently to gather dust. And this happened soon enough: Mother's fairy-queen appearances at our bedside became increasingly rare and eventually ceased altogether. My father, once more in the best of moods, set out on his hunting trips and stayed away for weeks, while my mother again wrapped herself in manically conceived maternal duties. We children were her only connection to reality, her sole life possession, and she claimed it for herself alone. The shell around us closed hermetically while the years bypassed her life dream.

Nevertheless, the no longer so young woman—she is past the

"Balzacian age," *la femme de trente ans,* after all—is granted a short, late bloom after she separates from my father. For me it is a difficult time, for I am away from home and suffer much from homesickness. On the other hand, I too am given a new life, for I am freed of my sister's affectations of superiority; she is with our grandparents in Vienna and about to go to finishing school. I am almost nine and I am sent to Kronstadt (now Braşov), in Transylvania, to begin my education at the renowned Honterus Gymnasium there. Among strangers and released from Cassandra's guardianship, I am faced for the first time by the question of who and what I am. There is no doubt in my mind who is the steadying keel that gives me at least some self-assurance, which from the start had been weak and had been shaken further by the loss of my parental home: I am in love with my mother. Whenever she visits me, she is followed by glances of admiration, respect, desire. I find her at the Hotel At the Crown, an exemplary establishment of the old-fashioned Austro-Hungarian kind. The lobby with the deep leather chairs I founder in, the restaurant with its black-white-and-silver table settings and tailcoated waiters, the coffeehouse with its marble-topped tables and gypsy orchestra, the winter garden with its tropical plants and the diffuse light from its colored glass windows—all bespeak the elegance of a period about to vanish: the legendary luxury voyages on international trains such as the Orient Express and at palace hotels. We are privileged guests. The way my mother is treated by the employees, the waiters and the reception clerk makes me proud to be her son. The high regard and courtesy shown her by the men and the assiduity displayed by the women extends to me. I am spoiled because I am her child. I observe her sharply and compare her with other women, including the mothers of my school comrades, and the result makes me arrogant. The assurance with which she gives orders and makes her wishes known in her clear French to a chauvinistic assistant concierge at the hotel who alleges not to understand German and insists on speaking Romanian (which my mother never mastered); her girlish blushing when a gentleman of the old school who chances to witness this unpleasant scene (a typical one, incidentally, for the successor states to the Empire in those early years) compliments her for her fine bearing by a wordless bow—these are lasting impressions. In photographs from that period I see her gathering a fur piece around her naked shoulders in a gesture that nowadays is frequently imitated by transvestites; with her, it conveys an inimitable grace, seldom seen in the fatidic stars of the society sheets and the movies (beginning to flicker with their omnipotent promise even in those remote parts), who forfeited in the theatricality of their gestures a good deal of their ladylike pretensions.

It is difficult to reconcile this image of her with the last two-thirds of her life, when she increasingly distorted and coarsened herself. Two decades later she was so different that no one possibly could have recognized her, let alone have found in her the willowy girl with the grave and dreamy glance she had been prior to her ill-fated marriage. Perhaps someone might have realized, on the strength of faint signs—the claim to respect that betrayed itself in her bearing; a certain fastidiousness; her still well-formed hands—that what had occurred here was not only a personal decay but one of the countless individual destinies swept away and crushed by the eclipse of an entire world.

The surprising thing, given the rigidity of her character, was the pliancy with which she adapted to that fate. Her angry resignation somehow seemed like an act of revenge. She adapted to increasingly uncomfortable circumstances not only without resistance but almost with alacrity, as if she derived some perverse satisfaction from it. In her last years, she displayed a teeth-gnashing, reluctant submissiveness. By grimly bending under the blows that fate delivered to her, she could prove to the world the magnitude of the suffering for which she had been predestined. This psychological pattern must have had very deep roots, reaching back to her earliest days.

One of today's many overused words deriving from popular psychology is *frustration*. In the case of my mother this term is to be applied not merely in the figurative sense of bafflement but quite literally, as a castigation, a flagellation. In my mind rises a horrifying scene from her early girlhood that she once told me about, half in saddened forgiveness and half in awe of the pedagogic harshness it demonstrated with such naked brutality. The time is just after the turn of the century and she is thirteen or fourteen years old, on a summer afternoon bathed in a vine-green light that invades the house from the garden. She is doing four-handed piano exercises with her sister, younger by one year, and believes herself alone with her, for once unobserved, and so she begins to joke, to fool around, to laugh and to twattle—and is abruptly called to order by the biting stroke of a cane across her back. Her father stands behind her in all his mythic authority, as he towered all her life over her parental home, the embodiment of law and order in the entire world. When he punishes her he is not merely her idolized papa but the incarnation of universal law in all its inflexible severity. An irrevocable verdict has been pronounced: she is unworthy in her role as the oldest child and model for her five siblings, unworthy of the expectations placed on her, and of all those that will be placed on her throughout her life. . . . Never again will she regain full trust in herself. She was destined to fail, and she did not rebel against that fate but accepted it in smoldering rage and suppressed culpability, a self-lacerating readiness to suffer that she invested with the aura of martyrdom.

This anecdote did not make me fond of my grandfather. I did not at first understand how he could have been capable of so brutal an act. He was a man of the world with excellent manners and even a sense of humor. Photographs I preserve out of scientific curiosity show him in the smartly cut uniform of an officer in the reserves; as a culture-seeking tourist, clad in plaids and looking at some Near Eastern ruins; as imperial counselor in a frock coat. In all of them, a short-trimmed beard half conceals an ironic smile. He was known to be exceptionally stubborn. Molded by all the fatal preconceptions of the nineteenth century, he drew his overly developed conceit from contemporary ideas about one's "position in the world" and from related cast-iron moral and aesthetic principles, in particular those that were grounded in property. A pompous plush-lined Victorianism imbued him toward the end of his days with a cigar-smoking vulgarity in such sharp contrast with the elegance of his appearance that paradoxically—you see this in portraits of Edward VII as Prince of Wales—it became part of it.

He always impressed me as the prototype of the flourishing bourgeois at the turn of the century, during the so-called *Gründerzeit*. His well-to-do family was of Swiss origin; they had come to Vienna early in the eighteenth century and, together with cousins who also had emigrated from Fribourg, gained merit through their service with the then emerging Austrian tobacco monopoly. The cousins rose high in the world, they were made counts and married into the aristocracy. His branch of the family gained only a modest title of nobility, and whether there rankled in him some envy of those favored ones or whether the entrepreneurial spirit of his commoner forebears was reawakened in him is a moot question, but his life was that of an American-style self-made man. His admirers, especially his daughters, liked to retell with unquestioning adulation the legend of how, against the will of his family—but the why in this remains unfathomable—he turned his efforts to the lumber industry, how he became a leading figure in forestry circles and amassed a fortune that allowed him to marry the beautiful, well-born and well-endowed daughter of a general of Irish extraction. (That on her mother's side she had Greek ancestors who in the distant past had plundered some Wallachian fiefdoms increased her value—and thereby his reputation as a man who knew how to acquire the best on the most favorable terms.) This version of his triumphs, which surely in reality was not such a black-and-white thing, incensed my father, who never tired of stripping the mythic figure of his father-in-law of his nimbus; his scorn helped to set the seeds of my cordial dislike of my grandfather.

I saw him only seldom, though. My maternal grandparents no longer lived in the Bukovina. They too were part of what my father liked to call "cultural compost": envoys of the civilizing administration of an empire that no longer existed. Even before the First World War, they and my mother's siblings had returned to Vienna, whither we, who after 1919 were Romanian citizens, visited them at most once a year for a few days—usually when passing through on our way to the Carinthian lakes, where my mother dragged my sister and me for summer vacations, hated by both of us and clouded by homesickness for our house and our dogs. Eventually we came to understand that these "fresh-air resorts"—as if the Carpathians were lacking in fresh air and the fragrance of pine woods!—were a pretext for Mother to see her family and to afford one or another of her sisters a few weeks of relaxation. For those sisters had by then become impoverished and had to work for a living: the war and subsequent inflation, as well as some ill-advised speculations, had reduced my grandfather's legendary fortune to nothing more than its zeros.

So I never saw him in the fullness of his life, but only as a sick and broken man; and on the strength of my father's denigrations of the family myth, according to which he was the sole proprietor and protector of all civic and paterfamilial virtues, I thought of him as an unpleasant, despotic, petty, hidebound old man. He gave no evidence in his last years that contradicted this impression. He would sit immobile on a sofa in the drawing room of his apartment in Vienna, filled with heavy baroque furniture, family portraits, bronzes and layers of dark Oriental carpets, chin supported on his hands and lavishly beringed fingers clutching the ivory crook of an ebony cane. I fancied that this stick was the same with which he had thrashed my mother's back when she was a little girl. I was certainly not the only one who breathed a surreptitious sigh of relief when he died in the icy winter of 1927. In triumph my sister showed me one of the rings that had made his large pale hands, worm-streaked by thick blue veins, so especially repellent to me. It was given her as a reward for her skill in countering his temper tantrums with the slippery smoothness of her good manners. Strangely enough, an heirloom also fell to me, who was not endowed with such diplomatic skills: an intricately worked gold pocket watch with a dial in Arabic numerals which he had brought back from one of his trips to Turkey. It disappeared, like so many other things during my student days, at the pawnbroker's, never to be seen again.

·　　·　　·

I also have a picture of the young girl driven by that cane stroke from childhood ingenuousness into the baffling quandary of her being, to a realization of inadequacy in the face of the tasks with which life would confront her. In this photograph she stands, straight and lissome, in a high-necked summer dress in front of a bench in the parental garden—a large garden of the kind that even grandchildren, when told of its splendors, will dream about. Something of its freedom-promising green glory can still be seen in her eyes, but already it is tainted by the nostalgia of leave-taking. She is every inch the young girl brought up according to her social position—and at the same time she betrays the bedevilment of a young being imprinted by the stereotypes of convention. Her comeliness cannot conceal a puzzled consternation that has become second nature to her. She knows what's in store for her, as the saying goes: she foresees her future and the impossibility of coping with the demands that will be addressed to her—without conceiving for a moment that she might be able to change anything. The "grand life" belongs to the world of dreams: it may happen, but this will change hardly anything at all in her preordained fate as a woman. These are the sober facts: she will be married as well as possible, to a man in comfortable circumstances and not below her own standing; she will have children and will try to educate them according to the same stereotypes that marked her own education—verbal stereotypes, which she may even recognize as such but to which she has bowed without demur. She must live in accordance with the rhetoric of her caste and era, and if she does not succeed, her failure is her own and not due to the emptiness of the phraseology.

My father, to whom she was engaged shortly thereafter, following a tennis game, told us that she was an excellent pistol shot—under his personal instruction, it goes without saying. She rode horses well, though never without being accompanied. She cut a pretty figure as a skater and she loved to swim, though again always under supervision. The secretly entertained dream of becoming a pediatrician—after all, she had obtained a diploma—could not be realized by a girl of her class, which differed from the average philistines only through its greater pretensions. Instead, she attended in succession two well-known home economics schools, one in Bonn and the other in Lausanne. But the unrealized dream of serving humanity as a pediatrician curdled into a bitter residue at the bottom of her soul. Only her naiveté remained unaffected.

I have not forgotten the wistfulness of her look as she watched an ophthalmologist—a woman of eminence, a Russian and, so it was said, a morphine addict—the chief physician at the Czernowitz eye clinic, which, under her leadership, was recognized as state-of-the-art. This aristocratically thin-boned, eagle-nosed lady in a white smock was treating me after an accident in which I almost lost my eyesight. While examining me, she chatted of this and that. My mother's anxious, attentive, wistful expression as she listened changed to horror when the doctor said in passing, in her smoky, Slavic voice: "No woman who hasn't had syphilis can call herself truly a woman." No, Mother's notions of feminine self-fulfillment were less radically emancipated.

Shortly before her engagement, she danced at her first ball— one waltz too many—with a young lieutenant of the lancers, a golden-blond Pole with an interesting nervousness in his behavior, no doubt due to his being hounded by creditors. She was taken home forthwith. Decades later, when I had grown up, she confessed to me that she had fallen in love with him at first glance and irrevocably had dedicated her life to him. He remained the "great love" of her life even though—or rather because, although she could not admit this—she never saw him again. She still remembered his name but would never disclose it. "A name with a great many twittering sounds," she admitted with a bewitching smile and a surprising touch of irony. He cast a fair shade over her entire life: her sole, her lost great love which forbade her ever to love another man. The punishing stroke with the cane had been sublimated. After being sent home from her first ball after one too many waltzes, she knew herself to have been cheated of life's happiness.

And what about that other shade in the slouch hat and the artist's flowing lavalliere, on the sea cliff near Trieste? She never spoke of him and I never dared ask her about him; no doubt there is an unutterable reason behind both her silence and my discretion. So this man remained a mystery between us in a twofold way: as a sign of that most intimate core which every human being conceals in his innermost self, and as that undefinable and most private reserve which keeps us from penetrating the innermost self of another being.

Of her engagement with my father she told only horrifying stories. According to her, he was bent on hurting her by shocking the whole world. In the fashion of the times favored by lady-killer bachelors, he had shaved his head completely. She was too inexperienced to perceive that he was anything but a lady-killer. He was simply a man who lived a more full-blooded life than all the straitlaced people around them. He bubbled over with irrepressible zest and vigor—different from her stealthily tenacious vitality, which was to help her survive him by several decades. His overwhelming good spirits never failed him; he was always spontaneous, full of humorous notions and scurrilous ideas. Because only a very few could match his lust for life, he rubbed almost everyone the wrong way. Out of a puerile defiance that remained one of his distinctive features all his life, he took pleasure in his role as the philistines' bugaboo. No stranger to the accepted rhetoric of the day, he used it in antithesis. One of his favorite sayings was: *"Il faut épater les bourgeois!"* To my mother's Victorian soul, this was sheer blasphemy. She soon saw him as a true monster.

My father was a full fourteen years older than my mother; when she was eighteen he was already thirty-two, an age at which he could be expected to show a manly, staid character. Instead, he behaved as if he had just emerged from puberty. He joked frivolously with my mother's younger sisters, who were silenced, baffled, repelled by and, at the same time, hopelessly enamored of him. What they might have found amusing in a contemporary scandalized them in a mature man. He countered by calling them a bunch of silly geese and soon no longer spoke to them. He even dared to contradict their father—and had the additional temerity in proving to be in the right. Nothing like that had ever happened to my grandfather; he almost had a stroke and would have canceled his daughter's engagement forthwith if he had not feared the embarrassment this would have entailed. Meanwhile the son-in-law to be, from whom more respect was to be expected—after all, the bride had a quite considerable dowry—amused himself by composing a little song satirizing the arrogance of the propertied:

> *I own a theater box*
> *Where I'm seen in tails and high hat.*
> *I have servants and horses and cars,*
> *My money allows me all that. . . .*

The ditty bore the hardly flattering title "The Show-off."

Of his future mother-in-law my father asserted that, when preparing for bed, she wore white heron feathers in her hair along with her nightgown, and that when she wrote to her couturier in Paris everybody in the house had to walk on tiptoe. Instead of a bouquet of flowers, he presented his bride with a brace of freshly shot woodcock tied by a leather thong. His dogs attacked the idolized scion of the family (the only son and heir after five daughters), a boy of extraordinary beauty and equally exceptional stupidity, and almost bit off his nose, so that it had to be sewn on again; the scar remained visible to the end of his days. When the bride summoned up her courage to ask her maverick bridegroom whether he might not please let his hair grow again, he replied, smartly clicking his heels, that to his everlasting regret he unfortunately was totally bald but would see to it that the matter was redressed: henceforth, throughout the summer of 1908, except at meals, he wore a heavy woolen cap with a red pom-pom, headgear suitable for winter sports. My mother's grandmother was then still alive, over ninety and no longer in full possession of her mental faculties, but highly respected as was her due according to her rank in the family and her forebears in far-off Wallachia. During a tennis match, Father managed to smash an overhead ball straight in the face of the venerable lady— unintentionally, it goes without saying—and this did not make him more popular with the family, especially when we children learned of the incident years later and found it irresistibly amusing. "It's obvious they've taken after their father," was the tart comment.

And indeed this was true in that we could always see the grotesque or comical aspect of a situation and express our enjoyment of it in a rather exuberantly Rabelaisian way. My mother's legacy seems to me more dubious: from her we inherited irascibility.

In the myth that my mother created of herself, she ascribed her perennially smoldering rage to the disappointment in her marriage. It was not to be expected of her to recognize its other sources, least of all the helplessness implanted in her long before. She stubbornly stuck to the notion that all the shortcomings in her life originated in that period when she should have experienced her true flowering as a woman and instead, at the side of an unloved man—one whose undeniably lovable qualities she never appreciated—was confronted with inadequacy both as wife and later as mother.

I suspected at times that her anger had yet another root, namely in a profanation of her naive faith. She had been brought up in a thoughtless Catholicism that saw in regular religious practices— church visits, the telling of the rosary beads, occasional confessions and Holy Communions—a more than adequate fulfillment of one's duties toward God and His Holy Son, toward the Holy Mother and the Holy Church. This in no way equaled the self-evident reality of God's world as Cassandra saw it, though it was equally unquestioning—but unquestioning only with regard to dogma and mere theology: any discussion of the Pope's infallibility would have left my mother as empty of thought and as blankly incomprehending as an inquiry into the dual godlike and human natures of the Savior. As a Christian and a good Catholic, she lived in the innocence of ignorance, which unfortunately vouchsafed only a vulnerable and trivial state of grace. Her fiancé's booming atheism, with its bold Nietzsche quotations and Wagnerian background music (occasionally also bitingly ironic—still more disconcerting) was bound to throw her off the comfortable path of her shallow faith. He was destined to be her spouse, her lord and master, to whom on principle she was to grant the same authority as her father had, and if his views were shocking to her, they also opened up a confusing vision of a spiritual freedom in which she was anxious to participate so as to please him. Had her parents been aware of even a hint of this dilemma, they would gladly have allowed her to pursue the study of pediatrics. This, after all, was the direction in which the winds of the time were blowing. Meanwhile she thought to assuage her burgeoning doubts by reading Renan, and what in all probability remained concealed was a remnant of guilt, which she later attributed to her husband's subsequent misconduct.

Even decades later, the question whether she could not have refused to marry him encountered total incomprehension. How was that? It had been so decided, and therefore it had to be gone through. But hadn't her parents soon realized how little the two suited each other? Why, certainly, but who truly "suits" another? The miraculous power of love is precisely that it can overcome such discrepancies, and love is alleged to develop automatically — though not immediately — in marital life. All the external circumstances fitted well enough: it was a good match for both of them. Theirs was a life deep in the provinces, in the most remote crown land of the Austro-Hungarian monarchy; her parents too lived in the Bukovina, drawn there by the lumber of the Carpathian forests and properties inherited from their Phanariot ancestors (among these the Odaya, the house where my sister was born and whence we fled in 1914). Though it was true that the future son-in-law had no money to speak of, he was in a promising position in government service, he had a good name and high patronage, as well as an influential father in Vienna. Had there been no convulsions, no outbreak of the war and no collapse of the Austrian monarchy, had the Bukovina remained part of Austria, and had the fortune my mother brought to her marriage not been lost, it could have been for her, while not an ideally happy life, at least an acceptably pleasant one — but only with another man.

In his role as husband she found my father farcical, a parody of what a head of family was to represent; in his role as lover, outright repellent. When, after four years of her staying in various sanatoria and another four years of separation caused by the war, the two finally lived together in 1919 in a radically changed world, he showed no comprehension whatever for her desire, natural with a young woman, nevertheless to keep a house where an active social life would endow her with a measure of prestige. He was unable to understand that she expected the real (albeit not necessarily "grand") life of marriage to conform to a young girl's dream, to take place in an ambience of evening gowns illumined by glowing candlelight. Still less could he comprehend that this desire was not so much inspired by an urge to achieve social standing but, to her way of thinking, construed as a marital duty. She devoted much love to their house; at least it was in Czernowitz, and she could establish in it something of the solidly anchored family life she had known in her own parental home — though perhaps in a somewhat more relaxed atmosphere and without its draconian severity.

My memory places the house in a garden where beeches, birches and ash trees convey great airiness and luminosity; it is a two-storied neoclassical building similar to innumerable country mansions built in the nineteenth century throughout the Russian cultural sphere as well as in the American South; it has a colonnaded façade and a glassed-in porch in the back giving out to the depths of the garden. I need hardly mention that, were I to see it today, it would seem considerably more modest than it appeared to me in those far-off days. I had already experienced that shrinking of dimensions attendant upon any comparison between mythicized and factual past whenever I returned home for vacation from my various and dubious schools. Each time the house and garden seemed more confined, more trite, especially when, once my mother left, the familiar and beloved rooms assumed the gently run-down bohemian coziness of a bachelor's quarters.

During my childhood these rooms had embodied all the spaciousness and glamour of the entire world. In their furnishing my mother had shown that she was not, after all, entirely conventional. As her dowry she had requested, in addition to her inherited portion of baroque and Biedermeier furniture, pieces in the then fashionable Art Nouveau style. Since these had not been brought to the Odaya, they had escaped being stolen and vandalized by the Russians during the war. Among these furnishings—they could have been ascribed to Mackintosh or Hoffmann—we children lived and played, and then, as adolescents innocent of art-historical appreciation, we rejected them as unfashionable. We would have much preferred tubular steel furniture. Even more obsolete and precious seemed to us the wardrobes and chests of drawers, as well as my mother's Second Empire cherry-wood bedroom, heirlooms from our Greco-Romanian great-grandmother. But personally, I loved the bed. When recovering from some slight childhood ailment, I was allowed to wallow in it, huge as a blond galleon, and in its pillowed voluptuousness indulge my dreams of shimmy dances to the rhythms of the first black jazz bands.

It is but natural that nostalgia transposes this house for me into the perennial sunshine of a Bonnard painting. Yet I am certain the good taste of its furnishings favorably impressed our rare guests, who came at my mother's invitation. These were not just evening gatherings. We, the children, soon provided an excuse for these social events; our alienation from the world around us and our lack of contact with other children finally penetrated even my mother's consciousness and she recalled her duty to prepare us for life—though this too according to her own romantic notions. So as to bring us together with our peers, she arranged fancy-dress *fêtes champêtres* and pageants in which my sister, representing Titania, Queen of the Fairies, was drawn through the garden on a flower-garlanded carriage by some eleven-year-old maiden, both girls dressed in tutus and with dragonfly wings sprouting from their narrow shoulder blades, while I, together with two other boys (one of whom happened to be cross-eyed), led the cortege in page costumes, our locks crowned by wreaths, blowing on shepherd pipes. Such events were more entertaining for the mothers and governesses than for us, and they often deteriorated into brawls with my costumed coevals. Once my sister appeared as a *bayadère* whipped mercilessly with a cotton cat-o'-nine-tails by a fat man in a turban and Turkish breeches; this earned her such enthusiastic applause that she decided then and there to follow in Pavlova's footsteps and become a prima ballerina. When she glowingly informed my father of her intention, he commented dryly, "If your mother allows this to come to pass, I'll personally shoot you from the stage!" Eventually he brought a brusque end to those charades when he learned that because of them the whole town thought of us as wildly eccentric. (In Czernowitz, masquerades were thought appropriate, if at all, only at Purim.) At a house party where I enacted the role of sausage vendor, he doctored the sausages, generously offered to the assembled guests, with a potent laxative. The ensuing scenes of horror in the toilets and bathrooms remained a permanent obstacle to any further attempts to rescue his children from their isolation.

His other contributions to our social life were scant. All the men he brought to the house were rum birds: an alcoholic mathematics professor who was the only person with whom he could discuss higher mathematics (in which he was interested mainly in connection with ballistic computations); an old apothecary, expert in alchemical preparations, another of my father's wide-ranging, albeit almost exclusively hunt-focused interests; a painter and engraver who taught him the esoteric skills of dry-needle technique (he painted, drew and engraved dreadful pictures of mating capercaillies and rutting stags); or various of his hunting companions, who either were passionate ornithologists, botanists or armorers or lived reclusively in the forest, where they seemed to have grown mossy and, like Hamsun's Pan, exuded a pungent gamey smell. All efforts failed to awaken his young wife's sympathy for these cronies. To be sure, his attentions were directed not solely to these men. Quite the contrary, but the many more women than men who met with his approval did so in such an unequivocal way that Mother saw little reason to promote these friendships by extending the hospitality of her own house.

My sister was born on July 14, 1910. Partly to honor the coincidence of her birth with Bastille Day (though my father hated the French Revolution, he greatly admired French hunting traditions), and partly to accustom the newborn to the sounds of a huntsman's household, the newly baked father fired off a few shots under the windows of the young mother, whose delivery had been attended to at home. Mother suspected an attack by robbers and was close to fainting. A sympathetic physician declared her chronically ailing and toward the end of the year, when my sister could be entrusted to the experienced care of a nursemaid, prescribed a few months of rest in Egypt. The cure proved so salubrious that it was repeated each subsequent year until the outbreak of the war. Every year, after Christmas—a feast dear to my mother's family, celebrated with sentimental effusion, much to my father's distaste—my mother proceeded to Luxor, where she stayed until Easter. In July at the latest, she went to Montreux for additional recuperation. Whether these long absences had a salutary effect on her health may be doubted. I rather fear that the atmosphere of such resorts, so vividly described by Thomas Mann in *The Magic Mountain*, added to her remoteness; certainly they did not improve her marital life and her relationship with her infant daughter. All this was worsened by my own precipitate arrival in a coach in May 1914.

I cannot be certain whether Mother herself or someone else who was privy to such family secrets told me that I had not been entirely welcome. Because of her kidney ailment—which by then had become a devoutly believed fact not only for herself but also for all those around her—it was alleged that several efforts had been made to abort my burgeoning life, efforts which, however, I withstood with the toughness I may have inherited from her. One thing is certain: I had not been a child of love. She was more unhappy than ever in those years; and since she believed that the cause of this unhappiness resided not only in her marriage but also in my sister's increasing refractoriness, I soon became for her the most appropriate object on which to lavish maternal selflessness. Had I not been shielded by Cassandra during the early years of my life, her possessiveness would have smothered me altogether.

To some extent I played into her hands, inasmuch as from the very first I was a problem child. When, a few months after my birth, we had to flee the advance of the Russians, we were ambushed by a group of beggar gypsies at the top of the Bargău Pass. An old witch wished me a happy life, emphasizing this benevolent augury by spitting in my face, a politeness I acknowledged by developing a pink rash, whereupon Cassandra bathed me in an icy torrent. From Bistrice we continued by train to Vienna, where I arrived with pneumonia. My grandparents showered my mother with reproaches for not having taken better care of me and for having left me in the hands of "the savage one," thus starting a kind of battle between the two in which I served as the unfortunate shuttlecock.

When the Italians joined the war and we had to decamp from the shelter of my grandfather's summer house near Trieste, we stayed until 1918 in the house of friends in Lower Austria. It was located on a pretty patch of land but in what is known as a foul-weather corner: sudden storms made the aestival peace treacherous. In the middle of a storm that surprised us during a walk in the woods, I was soaked to the skin and came down with my second pneumonia. Then, at an unsupervised moment when I had scarcely recovered, I fell into a cattle trough. (Cassandra fished me out after my sister casually informed her of this mishap.) But pictures from those days show me as a robust boy: my mother's cannibalistic solicitude was probably motivated more by psychological reasons than by any frailty of mine. In a manner of speaking I was her only child; my sister rapidly outgrew her reach. Also the deprivation of our refugee life conferred a legendary aura on her maternity. That my boyhood was played out around the cow stables of Lower Austria with peasant yokels was due solely to the intrusion of the forces of history: in "normal" times, the scenery of this phase of my life would have been Luxor. The Madonna-like tone of her chosen role naturally also included a future *mater dolorosa*'s concern over the possible loss of this gift from heaven.

It would be hard to say who suffered more under this state of affairs, she or I. Her anxiety over me became manic and her concerns obsessive. My two pneumonias grew into a *menetekel*, warning of the ever present threat arising from her imagined wanton defectiveness. A doctor had told her that a third pneumonia would be fatal to me, and so everything possible was done to prevent such a recurrence or the onset of any other such life-threatening disease; eventually everyone got rather bored, when the intensely awaited catastrophe failed to materialize and I continued to exhibit red-cheeked vitality. Something of this disappointed expectancy always remained: when I had grown up and myself had become the head of a family, one of my aunts once asked me absentmindedly: "Weren't you a bit stunted as a child? or epileptic? How are your own children?" Though it may be perilously close to the bounds of good taste to say so, it seems a bitter irony of fate that not I but my sister died of a pernicious disease in the prime of her youth.

Thanks to the zeal, then spreading epidemically, to invest every moment with eternity by means of the camera, the early phases of Mother's maternity are fully recorded pictorially (an unfair advantage over Cassandra). The threesome always appears as the same little group in fashionably changing attire: my mother's hats draw in their broad rims, shrink in size and finally cling snugly to the head. The tight lacing at her waistline loosens gradually, and the skirts, instead of following the body's spindle form, are tucked up full in the seat and then fall to the instep of the high-heeled shoes. What remains unchanged is the young woman's countenance, looking straight at the camera: the eyes are of someone not entirely present in the here and now, of someone eager to recover reality. The plumb-straight posture indicates clearly that she is more than ready to present herself as the proud creator of two successfully produced children. I appear at first, cradled in one arm, as a truncated cone from which, as from the cotton of a Christmas-tree angel, emerges a crest of blond locks; soon I descend to earth, and my baby clothes are succeeded by sweet little sailor suits and folkloric costumes. My sister is ever the showpiece: almost too pretty to be true, her doll-face animated by a fresh awareness—open, trusting, precociously coquettish. In her sober school dresses she becomes grave, more maidenly, all the more lyrically beautiful, as if emanating an intimation of her latent frailty. My sister, of course, was embraced by Mother's neurotic and often domineering solicitude, but in contradistinction to my own experience, she was not used to it from the very beginning of her life. Father saw to it that she was allowed much greater freedom, but this did not make her relationship with Mother more tender.

Our childhood was befouled by two disinfectants: permanganate and Formamint. The first consisted of small purple hexagonal or octagonal rodlike crystals of hypermanganate acidic potash which dissolved in water to a kind of red-beet slop in which everything we came into contact with was washed: our toys, door handles that might have been touched by outsiders, all the table silver and any uncooked fruit—even from our own garden. My mouth still puckers whenever I am about to take a bite from an apple, in the unconscious anticipation of the insipid, tartly acidulous taste of permanganate.

The second disinfectant, Formamint, was a leftover from a pseudo-English governess (whose blessedly short stay in our house I memorialized episodically in a novel). It came in flat white lozenges with a sweetly sharp, somewhat alkaline taste. These were placed on our obediently stretched-out tongues like the host at Holy Communion, so as to guard us prophylactically against aspired or licked-up pathogenic organisms. Especially when we happened close to any gathering of people or, worse, when we passed a funeral procession, a Formamint was instantly slapped on. To be able at least to speak without obstruction, I was in the habit of storing my lozenge hamsterlike in the pouch of my cheek, where it dissolved not only itself but also my teeth. The enamel of the first tooth that I had to have filled and, eventually, pulled—in dentist's parlance the third right mesial—had been eaten away in my childhood by innumerable Formamint tablets.

The fright of the disorders that occurred in the Bukovina after the breakdown of the Austrian monarchy and before its occupation by Romania in 1919 remained with my mother for long after. She did not feel happy in a country whose languages she did not understand and to which she no longer had any ties after her parents had left it. She felt that she had been relegated to this exile by my father's passion for hunting, and she saw the deeper motive it expressed: his resolve not to return to a shrunken Austria and to her own family. She failed to bear in mind that he was being paid a salary in a relatively stable currency which would have been devalued by inflation in a matter of days had he returned to Austria and which, despite everything, assured us of a comfortable livelihood. The cheapness of food and services in Romania in those days, which appears today almost like a fairy tale, allowed her an incomparably more luxurious life-style than what she could have afforded in Austria after the loss of her own fortune; but she thought of herself as destitute and déclassé, and she transferred to her children the vulnerable pride generated by the myth of a grand and lost past. (No wonder that one of the favorite books of my sister's childhood was Brentano's *Gockel, Hinkel and Gackelaia*.)

Mother's arrogance, occasionally erupting from the constantly smoldering fire of her repressed rage, paralyzing her at such moments into a mute and rigid statue, did not improve her dealings with the people around her in a setting that was going to seed. Ever since the pillaging bands in the first weeks after the breakdown in 1918, she suspected the entire population in both city and country of waiting only for an opportunity to turn into marauders, to slit the throats of their betters, to skewer the children. It was obvious to her that this ragged and unwashed populace, coughing and spitting and pissing against the next-best fencepost, was composed of militant carriers of infectious germs. Any and all occasions for us to come into contact with ordinary people were restricted to an absurd minimum.

I know of no children who might have grown up in comparable isolation. We were never for an instant without supervision. When we played in the garden, the fence of which we were strictly forbidden to trespass, there was hardly ever another child present, and the colorful outside world was known to us merely through the images, rapidly flitting past our eyes, of animated street perspectives: an exotic travelogue through which we were transported in hasty processions of coaches, dogs, nurses and governesses from one enclosure to another, from the city to the country and back again to the city, shuttling between watchfully secluded confines. When a child did chance to penetrate our isolation, grotesque precautions were taken before and after its visit: Formamint and permanganate were lavished on us in extravagant profusion. Once an unfortunate pair of siblings borrowed some books from us and soon after came down with scarlet fever, whereupon the books, on their return, were placed in quarantine and we were not allowed to touch them for a year. I still recall my welcoming joy when once again I opened one of them, outside in the blazing sun, so that the sharp black print on the white page suddenly appeared grass-green to my eyes—and my ensuing alarm, for I imagined that the scarlet fever had poisonously discolored the lettering.

Yet all the images I have from that period are of an incomparable well-being—not a corporeal and even less an emotional one: we were more frequently unhappy than happy and more often rebelling against repression than enjoying a feeling of freedom. But even our unhappy times were filled with a self-assurance that I cannot ascribe to any other source than the innocence of life—not merely the innocence of childhood, nor the lighter emotional freight of an era not yet so guilt-ridden as the present, but rather and in large part the innocence of my mother. Her restlessness, her volatility, her occasional unfairness and even her rage and her almost vindictive manner in meting out punishments were all the result of a desperate attempt to realize an ideal, namely that of the perfect maternal head of family (irrespective of the fact that the paterfamilias refused to play the obligatory counterpart role), so everything she did, whatever its surface appearance, stood under a kind of ethical blessing. All her actions, even the most aberrant ones, were undertaken with pure intentions and to the best of her knowledge and belief. While in other households likenesses of the Madonna might hang on the walls—or nowadays portraits of Che Guevara, John F. Kennedy, Martin Luther King, Jr., or Pope John XXIII—our youth was dominated, so to say, by a lithograph of the categorical imperative. Our well-being was rooted in the security of ethical and moral incontestability, whatever objections may be raised to the methods used in our upbringing.

This sharp blade of pure intent was hardly ever wielded by my mother with unadulterated logic. Yet strangely enough, everyone submitted to her, even my father. Nannies and governesses were as powerless against her as we: they groaned and called on their maker to witness the extent of so much senselessness—her outlandish directions, her eccentric regulations regarding attire and nourishment—but almost always yielded to her. That one should not eat crawfish in the months whose names are spelled with an *r* is a generally acknowledged rule; but that in those months one was also prohibited from sitting on the bare ground or on a stone because vapors emanating from the soil generated infantile paralysis was a belief singular to our own family hygiene. Governesses with different notions about the physical strengthening of their charges either shrugged in resignation and conformed or were replaced by others who cared less for their own ideas than for gaining respite from their employer. To drink a glass of cold water when one was overheated was fatal. Melons and figs were the source of pernicious gastric fevers; we were allowed to eat them only when we had reached adolescence. Even when we thought of ourselves as grown-up, it would have been out of the question for us to drive even a short distance in an open car without wearing fur coats and hermetically fitting leather driving caps—and this too in the blast-oven heat of Romanian summers.

Little by little these quaint fancies, once seen merely as gratuitously imposed torments, began to erode the ethical and moral certainty of our world. In the face of one of my mother's extravagant fantasies, the commitment to the categorical imperative began to yield to a skeptical impatience bordering on cynicism. I recall a dramatic scene at one of the mountain lakes we used to visit for our "aestival recoveries." I was almost thirteen and had taken the liberty—imagine it!—of renting a rowboat on my own and of rowing out alone on the lake. When I returned to our hotel, my sister, with bloodless lips, told me that my mother had locked herself in her room to commit suicide.

I have to confess that this threat did not really alarm me. It had been used in the past—once, for instance, when I had come home from ice-skating after dark, even though I should have known that the most baneful vapors rose in winter after the setting of the sun; and another time when I secretly had acquired a magazine that today would be considered a harmless family journal but was then regarded as the vilest pornography because it contained drawings of scantily dressed ladies and photographs of bare bosoms. So I sat down quite unconcernedly on the hotel terrace and waited for the return of my sister, who had hastened to my mother's room and surely would be summoning me for sentencing. Half an hour and then a full hour went by without anything happening, and the fear rose in me that this time the threat might have been carried out. I could not stand it any longer on the terrace, but when I reached the lobby I was stopped by the concierge: my mother and sister had departed, he told me.

The embarrassed expression on his face was hardly needed to make me perceive the hoax. I calmly returned to the terrace. My earlier experiences had made me callous. The only thing that hurt was that my sister had allowed herself to be party to these shenanigans.

Occasional vacations on the Black Sea also offered opportunities for my mother's threats of self-immolation, her sharpest pedagogical means. The beach at Mamaia, where today a phalanx of horrendous tourist caravansaries of crumbling concrete provokes nature (only meagerly favored, as it is, with a bit of sea and sand and dune grass there) to lament her lost innocence, then—I speak of the end of the 1920s—was an empty expanse, excepting two or three bathing huts and a wooden pier, of miles of golden sand and tiny pink shells. This fine-grained sand, several yards deep, was blown landward into high dunes behind which lay the then still deserted steppe of the Dobrudja, and on the other side sloped imperceptibly into the sea, so that one waded for miles through shallows before the water reached one's navel. My mother nervously patrolled the glittering edge of the sleepily lapping waves. Her kidney ailment forbade her to enter the water. Our supervisory Cerberus of the moment, usually one of the dubiously English governesses from Smyrna or Gibraltar who were supposed to enrich our linguistic knowledge (the subtle differences in intonation of the English o in the sentence: "O Homer, what homage do we owe you!"), was sent out to the end of the pier to watch our doings from there. It would have been simpler had she come into the water with us to carry out this supervision, but my mother did not trust these ephemeral guardians, usually replaced after only a few weeks, to be conscientious, and believed they might not watch us if they were allowed to indulge in the pleasure of bathing. Posted as lookouts at the end of the pier, they were obliged to scan the sea while my mother, intent on protecting our books and toys, the beach umbrella, the plaids, the picnic basket and all the other paraphernalia from the thievery of roaming gypsies, ran to and fro, calling and signaling, all the more frantically the farther we moved out to sea: "a hen who has hatched ducklings," as she put it. Whenever she lost sight of us because we finally had reached water deep enough actually to swim in and when occasionally a wave covered our bathing caps, she alerted the miss or mademoiselle on the pier. If she was unable to obtain reassuring news of our condition forthwith, perhaps because Miss was engaged in a flirtation with a passing Lothario in bathing trunks, she sent the lifeguard to rescue us or, when he soon refused to pay heed to her repeated panicky alarums, the next-best complaisant bather.

In the weeks we spent at the sea, she surely must have become a locally well-known character, gently derided by all. Mamaia was anything but an elegant beach resort, yet she comported herself as if we were in Biarritz. She must have seemed a grotesque figure, running along the beach in her inappropriately elegant sleeveless bathing costume, between the puddles of seawater and the reeds, among the rinds of sucked-out watermelons and the spat-out sunflower seeds, protected from the burning sun by a parasol and a Florentine straw hat, legs singed to the same pink as the little shells crunching under her bathing pumps, in her arms a pack of magazines and bathing towels to have ready when we emerged. Years later an eyewitness described her for us, still shaking his head in wonderment: a maverick personality, indulging in bizarre gesticulations and signals, in calls, instructions and admonitions, in tweets and wails from a specially acquired marine whistle, in beckonings with bare hands, with a newspaper or towel, in the sounding of the ice cream vendor's bell—all in the forlorn hope of luring her brood back from the perilous watery element to the safety of solid ground. She made us so ashamed that we acted as if we did not belong to her. Ignoring her turmoil, we only increased it. We suffered from her ridiculous, irritating and pitiful appearance but could see in it only what was ridiculous and irritating without, in the cruelty of youth, feeling pity. The creature who was made to feel this most painfully was Bonzo, our mother's French bulldog, who could not console us for the separation from our own dogs. With his ruff collar of boar's bristles, he looked as pompously morose as a Protestant church deacon, and we baptized him in the highly saline waters of the Black Sea whenever we could get ahold of him.

At that time my mother was a fully blossomed and very attractive young woman, no longer slim and lissome, yet for all that the more feminine. This was the age of flat-chested flappers, smoking cigarettes in foot-long holders with their hair lacquered to their heads as tightly as our own rubber bathing caps; fads in Romania led to modish excesses only too easily imagined. She used to lament her own unfashionableness: "It seems my fate always to be out of fashion," she would say. "When Wagnerian Valkyries were all the rage, I was a slim slip of a girl. Now, among no one but nymphs and amazons, I am a full-bosomed frump." But she knew well enough that many appreciated this. I too found her highly attractive. I liked to be seen with her, for part of the flattering remarks directed at her fell my way. ("Who could have credited you with such a grown-up son . . . ?") That she would make scenes worthy of the stage because of trifling occurrences; that she threatened self-immolation because I had eaten vanilla ice cream when everyone knew it was toxic; that she was oversensitive, neurotic, prone to migraines and capable of imposing severe punishments, all this I found natural. It seemed to belong to the image of "the lady." A lady's original ethical qualities, as sketched by the medieval minnesingers, had long been supplanted by those nervously aesthetic ones defined by D'Annunzio (actually, their true prototype originated with Pitigrilli). Be that as it may, all kinds of pathos, exaggerations and idées fixes, emotional blackmail by means of ailments, suicide or at least expressions of deep grief, belonged for me to the vital signs of the species Woman; they probably had something to do with menstruation, which soon also became a concern of my sister. The concept of "woman" for me was synonymous with "crazy wrongheadedness," and it may well be that this had something to do with why, later on, love seemed to me the very essence of irrationality.

Love also appeared to me highly fickle and unreliable, not to be trusted, since it might be forfeited at any time by the slightest offense and bestowed instead on someone worthier. I once confessed to my mother that, until quite late in my life, I interpreted any love shown to me in this way and as a consequence had never been able to love in return, except in a provisional manner, revocable at any moment. And when I attempted to link this to the fact that in my childhood the usual punishment for misbehavior consisted in the instant withdrawal of love, she was deeply hurt—not because of the implied reproach but because she saw it as a degrading of her pedagogic ethos. Indeed, her way of punishing was infinitely more serious than the usual petty "Shame on you, you're a bad boy, Mommy no longer loves you!" Catholic as she was, she punished with a puritanically severe conscience. The emotional freeze into which even the most tender harmony could metamorphose from one moment to the next as the result of a childish misdeed was much more than feigned abnegation: it was the bona fide sentencing of a reprobate, the final verdict, like the stroke of the stick across her back in her youth. Behind it stood not only herself as mother and authority figure, but her own father, embodiment of all the ideals of family, caste and civilized human society.

Whatever wrong I did—a disobedience, an impudence against a governess, an assault against my sister or a failing in school—I was made to understand that a human being capable of such ignominy no longer could count on the indulgence of his fellow beings; he was to be expelled from their community. One of the worst offenses of which I became guilty also made me deeply ashamed of myself, albeit not as expected. Precociously engrossed in erotic dreams, I had been writing love letters to myself, as if these had been addressed to me by various girls. My mother, who felt duty-bound to check on everything, managed to find the letters in their hiding place and was outraged. She believed me capable of leading the double life the letters suggested, in which I indulged — God alone would know how, when and where — in lively sexual activities. As to me, I was mortified by this revelation of my secret inner life. She had found me out as an ignominious fraud. I do not exaggerate when I declare that, barely ten years old, I already was considered a failure and felt myself as such; I was all the more crestfallen since, even as a monster, I could not achieve anything so remarkably wicked or loathsome to warrant a *real* suicide.

As children and even more so as headstrong adolescents, my sister and I were of course unable to grasp that what, between us, we bluntly called Mother's "nuttiness" was in reality the tragicomedy of an obsolete pedagogic principle. The strictness of her own upbringing had established for her a world cast in primer-like simplicity, which contained no real human beings but merely standard roles whose comportment was assigned irrespective of individuality, character, temperament or nervous disposition. It was the world concept of a stable social order, a world of stereotypes: a peasant was unmistakably a peasant, a sailor a sailor, and a privy councillor was forever nothing but a privy councillor; any deviation into the specifically individual was a step toward chaos.

Especially in the picture of the family, which was known to be the germinal nucleus of all civilization, the stereotypes stood in firmly ordered rows. What a "father" or a "mother" had to be, or a "sister" or a "brother," or a "husband" or "wife," was rigidly determined; it had its own costume and certainly its own prescribed text, just as in a stage play. Whoever deviated from this predetermined role, a role reduced to its most essential or trivial elements, or whoever went so far as to forget the assigned role altogether, was not merely reprehensible but downright evil. This was the case with her own husband, who refused to play the role

of the competent and kind, affectionate and considerate paterfamilias, and therefore took on for her all the characteristics of an
egocentric and inconsiderate, beastly and lustful proprietor of a
conscripted slave wife. Paradoxically, this nonconformity extended to herself, for she recognized her own failings. She felt
only too acutely that she was no match for my father's full-
bloodedness and consequently that she was a failure as his "life
partner," as much as in her hackneyed notion of the role of
mother, in which no one, least of all we children, took her
seriously. The harder she tried to embody the image of the heroic
mother (heroic pediatrician sacrificing herself to shield her brood
from the diabolical perils of disease, death and moral decay), the
more piteously her efforts miscarried.

Yet there was often something deeply touching about these
efforts. Decades later, as a grandmother, she still could not desist
from her heartrending solicitude. She showered on my youngest
son all her nurturing and pedagogic instincts, which his brothers
had repelled as meanly as I myself had disdained them toward the
end of my childhood. So that he would not sit on bare ground
while playing, she had the carpenter of the village where we
happened to be living at the time—once more as refugees—
fashion a diminutive stool that she then carried faithfully after
him whenever she could not persuade him to lug it himself. His
playmates' derision may have strengthened his personality but
certainly did not contribute to making it more affectionate. For
my sons, especially the youngest one, she resurrected many aspects of her relationship with my father, and they were pathetically moving, for example, the darning of their clothes: she
had always been shocked by the heedlessness with which my
father wore his hunting clothes, and she would secretly weave and
repair, as invisibly as possible and with her own hair, the rips in
his rough tweeds and donegals. She certainly did not love my
father, but this gesture of almost medieval marital devotion
expresses her ineffectual conception of her supposed duties, even
those she assigned to herself like a curse.

．　．　．

Ironically—if one cares to impute such literary subtlety to the existential drama—the years of her unhappy marriage and anxiety-ridden maternity may well be counted as her most fulfilled ones. She had not yet quite lost her girlish charm and she preserved something of that magic of vulnerability which disarms criticism. "She is ailing, after all," it would be said. Or, "She just takes everything too seriously; she places everything in a tragic light; she is haunted by her sense of maternal duty"—all of which was true. Whenever she managed to loosen the desperate grip of her conscientiousness, when she was abandoned in thoughts of something outside her rage-distorted imaginings—especially if this something would bring pleasure to us children—her forlorn poetic inspiration would reappear. No one knew how to give presents as well as she, showing moving empathy for the most secret wishes, dreams and fantasies of the receiver, and each of her gifts was a truly treasured thing. Festivals like Christmas, Easter or birthdays were so blissful in my childhood they could never be reproduced in later years. Her benevolent spirit also carried over to everyday life: the memory of our nursery is filled for me with a sensation of freshness and luminosity, a fastidious cleanliness and restful quiet, broken only occasionally by happy or belligerent noise, a combined sensation which even today represents for me the incarnation of all desirable well-being.

In her lovable moments she was as seductive as the most supportive woman could ever be. Once, on one of our confused summer sojourns on the Black Sea—we were alone together, as my sister had been allowed to go with my father to the Moldavian monasteries—I found myself in Constanţa in front of a shop window that displayed the embodiment of all boyhood's longings: the model of a steamboat, accurate in all its details, with tiny life buoys hanging on its dinghies, innumerable portholes between the decks, a captain's bridge with lifelike miniatures of the rudder, binnacle and other technical sophistications—in short, perfection, the faultless reproduction of reality on a reduced scale. I was ready to give my life for it. I promised anything that would ever be requested of me: limitless consumption of Formamint and permanganate; ready acceptance of wool scarves and coats for the evening breezes; stringent respect for the pre-scribed limit beyond which I was prohibited to swim; even the renunciation of a white-bordered navy-blue blazer with brass buttons, the promise of which I already had wheedled out of my mother; generally, total future obedience if only I could call this model ship my own. Unfortunately it was not for sale; the display window in which it stood was not that of a toy shop but that of a steamboat agency.

The two Levantines who managed the agency—two olive-eyed gentlemen with remarkably heavy black moustaches and sim-ilarly luxuriant black hirsute growths on the back of their hands—had not counted on my own and my mother's per-sistence, however. For a few days I behaved like a howling dervish (I must have been a brat, incidentally), and for a few more days my mother exchanged telegrams with the steamship company. Shortly thereafter I paraded down to the pier, flushed with vic-tory and clad in a white-bordered navy-blue blazer with brass buttons, the model ship clutched under my arm, accompanied by my indulgent mother, who allowed that for the price of the toy she could have bought herself a diamond ring. Held by her so as not to fall in, I lowered the precious model into the water—and watched with horror as it forthwith disappeared under the sur-face and sank like a stone, glugluglugluglup, right to the bottom. When I straightened up and met my mother's eyes, something totally unexpected occurred: she burst into relieved and happily liberating laughter. Closely holding each other, we walked back to the casino esplanade to enjoy some ice cream. Decades later I tried imagining how different life for all of us might have been if only once she could have laughed like that with my father.

He may scarcely have known that facet of her nature—and, if at all, only in fugitive moments; the futile hope that these might occur more frequently could serve only to accentuate her less attractive qualities. Because his constant high spirits and his playfulness irritated her, her behavior with him emphasized her worst traits: harshness, triggered by mimosalike sensitive pride; intolerance, jaggedly sharpened by her grinding subterranean

rage; jitteriness, grounded in her obsessive assumption of responsibilities and simultaneous dread of failing them; rigidity. I enumerate these features as if they made up a single, coherent
character bundle. But this was not the case. It was rather as if, in
response to a given irritant, she recovered one or another response from among the broken pieces of what once had been a
homogeneous whole, an otherness shattered by a misspent life.
Her harmonious and pleasing moments were its far-off echo; her
harsh explosions stemmed from despair over its loss. At times,
when she sought to take revenge—that is, when she punished—
there emerged something truly diabolical in her.

The experience that made me callous enough to bear with
pretended stoicism her suicide threat and the subsequent make-
believe scenario of an alleged departure from that hotel in
Velden, in Carinthia—a situation more likely to occur between
lovers in the dramatics of D'Annunzio—that experience had
occurred much earlier. She had experimented with this shock
treatment on me in the first years after the war. In those days her
anxiety for her children was at its peak, and she incarcerated us in
the garden with corresponding severity. One time—and only this
one, fervently enjoyed time—I found myself there without supervision. My sister was inside for lessons and even Cassandra was
not close. I had been playing with an especially beautiful ball,
decorated with circus scenes, given to me for my birthday. As a
result of a clumsy throw, it rolled through the bars of the garden
gate. . . . Outside stood a boy, older than I and—so it seemed to
me—with the seductive mien of the street-wise urchin, holding
the ball in his hands. It was useless to ask him to return it to me
through the bars. "Come and get it," he said, "then we'll play
together."

What he expected of me was monstrous. Was I to leave the
garden and go out into the street to play there with this stranger,
unkempt and so obviously irreverent? No doubt his games would
be wilder—and more temptingly adventurous—than my own
tame hopping around with a colored ball. But to give in to this
temptation would be not merely to transgress a rigorous prohibi-

tion, but openly to rebel, wantonly to disavow the authorities safeguarding the laws of the universe. I felt my pulse hammering in my temples.

Derision glittered in his eyes. He doubted I could muster that much courage. I flung misgiving to the winds and slipped out. Immediately he dropped the ball and kicked it some hundred yards down the road. We ran after it. Of course, he reached the ball long before I did, and kicked it even farther away; when I finally caught up with him, only because he had waited for me, he dribbled the ball over my feet and sent it flying away in a flat curve. Thus we played—if one can call this a game—until we reached the edge of the city proper and its more populated streets. He continued to "play," and soon I had lost all sight of him. I went on running desperately. I loved my ball: its vivid pictures of clowns and trained poodles, acrobats and jugglers inspired my fantasy, and it had been my mother's birthday gift to me. I dreaded to lose it. Almost worse was the disillusionment that I could have been betrayed so blatantly—for the first time in my life and obviously as punishment for my disobedience. In vain I searched for my treacherous playmate among the crowds and in the flow of vehicles. Soon I found myself in the center of Czernowitz on the Ringplatz, my heart filled with all the bitterness of the world: grief over the loss of my ball, dread of the evildoer weighing on me, and now, in addition, the fear of having lost my way without hope of return.

I must have been a pitiful sight. My long locks and velvet suit with lace collar—my much hated daily attire at the time—together with my tears, could not remain long unnoticed among the Jews in caftans, the coachmen slouching against their fiacres, the spur-jingling Romanian soldiers, the colorfully dressed peasant women with baskets of eggs on their heads, the rabbis and solid ethnic-German burghers in their stiff shirt-collars worn, according to local tradition, with wide knickerbockers and Tyrolean hats. Czernowitz was a city in which everyone knew almost everybody else. A gentleman who saw how obviously lost I was rescued me by putting me in a hackney coach and sending me home.

I found the garden empty and the house closed. All was silent; there was no sign of life. I knocked, I rattled the main door and hammered on it; all in vain. I ran around the house several times: all the doors were closed, the shutters were shut, and the Venetian blinds on the porch were lowered. I stood before each of the windows and called and called. For an instant I thought I saw the pale mask of my sister through the blinds of the French doors on the veranda, but it disappeared in a trice and must have been only an illusion. Desperately I called for my mother, Cassandra, the housekeeper Mrs. Hofmann, the maids and my dog Rauf. Silence. I was in a panicky sweat. Any neighbors were quite far off, and of those I knew only a Polish surgeon by the name of Dr. Buraczinsky. For some time I had been allowed to play with his son, but our friendship had fallen apart over a toy: a tin armored cruiser that ran on wheels. That something that belonged in the water should move on dry land by means of small concealed wheels as if it were on the high seas seemed to me as running against nature and worse than a fraud. Miroszju—the name of Buraczinsky junior—declared I was merely jealous. This was what had caused our breakup and since then we hadn't seen each other.

It was true I was jealous, though not of his fraudulent ship but rather of the freedom he enjoyed. He was allowed to play with other boys in the gardens of our district without having to fear that this would mean the end of the world. Yet he was well brought up and always kept within calling distance from his house: when, in the evenings, Mrs. Buraczinsky would pop out her head from the dormer window of their small villa and let a long-drawn-out "Mirooohszju!" reverberate in the smoky turquoise of the darkening summer skies, an obedient *"Proszju!"* ("Yes, please!") could be heard from far away in reply, an exchange that, in my loneliness, always left me forlorn. The dutiful answer to the call for homecoming seemed to attest to a day's work done; I heard it as one condemned to idleness, excluded from the world of connecting activities and affectionate relationships that find expression in the interplay between a name and its echo. It was this that now came to mind in my moment of dire need. I ran to the Buraczinsky house, pushed Madame B. aside, scaled the stairs to the top floor, stuck my head out the window and yelled all the names of my missing family into the countryside. In my innermost core, I may have known, of course, that their disappearance was make-believe, but greater still was the fear that it was otherwise and that they had actually left house, city and country, forgetting me. I was only six years old. Madame Buraczinsky took me by the hand and led me back to our house, where she energetically rang the bell at the entrance; when it was finally opened, she delivered me to my mother with the strong recommendation not to play such jokes again at the expense of a child.

But my mother did not mean it as a joke; it was a punishment that was supposed to teach me a never-to-be-forgotten lesson. She achieved that goal — though probably with corollary effects that invaded my whole nervous system with fine-webbed ramifications. My father never heard of it. If he had, he surely would have dampened, in this one case, the jocularity with which he generally commented on my mother's pedagogic measures.

They separated after thirteen years of marriage, in 1922. It happened rather precipitately. One day our mother packed up her things and her children and brought us all to Vienna. Those came with us who, in any case, had been eager to leave the household in Czernowitz: her erstwhile and presently our own governess, Miss Lina Strauss; Mrs. Hofmann, our housekeeper, who for reasons of age returned to her native Bohemia. Cassandra remained behind, for my mother intended henceforth to keep me for herself alone.

My father let us leave in good faith. He expected us home after a few invigorating weeks at the Carinthian lakes and after some spiritual regeneration at the hands of our Viennese relatives. He was to be proven wrong. The choir of my mother's kin, which had always provided the tonal background for my mother's tribulations, as is traditional in tragedies ("exile under the yoke of slavery"), was jubilant: her sisters, whom the war and the hard years thereafter had made independent and self-sustaining, notwithstanding their consonance with the collective spirit of the family, had adopted the rhetoric of the new era. (Most of the catchwords so freely used by feminists today had already been hatched at that time.)

My mother considered the war, the uncertain postwar period, the disintegration of the old world and the dawning of the new (from which, up to then, she had felt excluded) as penal extra aggravations to her imprisonment in marriage. She now heard this awakening call of the new spirit of the age from the mouths of her younger sisters as a clarion call promising final freedom. These nestlings seemed to her to be taking wing like a covey of larks flying toward the sun. That her barely grown-up youngest sister was to become an artisan in the newly formed Wiener Werkstätte seemed to her as bold and spirited as that the next youngest professed herself a theosophist; that the third youngest was a pioneer of women's rights; and the fourth, the eccentric bluestocking in the family, went so far as to endorse socialism. All these fresh, confusing breaths now blew in unison into the horn of emancipation, particularly that of the liberation from the marital yoke. A sensitive, high-minded and physically frail woman had been deprived of her right to a fulfilled emotional life and to social evolution; moreover, a passionately self-sacrificing mother had been saddled by a mentally unbalanced (the woolen ski cap!), monomaniacal (the hunting!) and amoral (lack of respect for his father-in-law!) egotist and brutal sensualist.

My grandmother somewhat reduced the ideologically high-flown polemics against the fiend who held her oldest daughter under the yoke of serfdom, by declaring that, yes, she too never had liked him but that, as a Catholic, she had to exclude any thought of divorce. My grandfather, on the other hand, already then in the habit of commenting on events around him only with abrupt barks, his decrepit head leaning on the spastically clutched crook of his cane, asserted bitterly that in view of the present proletarization of the whole world and the general decline in manners and morals, "nothing matters a damn anyway," and everyone should do whatever he felt like doing or not doing. This was the backing with which my mother sued my father for divorce. With great understanding, my father did his best to facilitate the proceedings. The marriage was annulled with the provision that both parents were to share equally in the rights to the children. My sister and I coped with the confusion ensuing from this arrangement in the years to come with the patience of the much tried and with, of course, occasional outbursts of laughter.

It would have been understandable if my mother had used her freedom to start an entirely new and, if possible, active life in Vienna. But Vienna was desolate for her in those years; her parents, distraught over the loss of their fortune and the proletarization of their world as a result of war and inflation, led a very secluded life. She had grown out of her own family and had become alienated both from her parents and from her siblings, who were trying to adapt themselves to the times to an extent beyond her own capabilities. Also, she may have had already some inkling of what, twenty years later, was to become bitterly evident—namely, that her family's vaunted cohesion was merely rhetorical in nature and the cohabitation of all its members under one roof did not go as smoothly as one would have hoped in the case of like-minded, devoted kinfolk. Just about everyone in the family had either inherited or acquired by imitation from the head of the tribe his inflexibility, foremost his eldest daughter, our mother. Although forever conscious of her inadequacy, she, after all, had managed her own household for thirteen years, and it was unthinkable that she might conform to the stiflingly conventional concepts and customs of her family; even less was it to be expected that she could adapt to the radical new notions inherent in the spirit of the times. On the other hand, it was also out of the question for her to live alone. All unmarried daughters lived as a matter of course under the guardianship of the family and under the parental roof; now that she was once again unmarried, she was counted among them: the independence of a young divorcee—she was thirty-two at the time—was considered as something shady, almost disreputable.

She got off the horns of this dilemma by returning to the Bukovina. An admirer, the same who years later told me of her peculiar fascination, placed at her disposal a quaintly but tastefully furnished peasant's house in the midst of a magnificent landscape an hour's drive from Czernowitz. It was distinguished by an attractive collection of Romanian folk art, leather and ceramics, roughly woven rugs and hand-carved wooden table utensils, and by a total lack of bodily comforts. Even today my bones ache from the unforgivingly hard bedsteads, and I still can smell the sharp fumes from the hearth and the sooty clay of the open fireplace, the odors of rancid mutton fat, charred thyme, and garlic, and I am haunted still by the fly-infested lapidary hole provided in a wooden plank over the cesspool. But to my mother the little house, with its thick straw-covered roof, its crooked whitewashed loam walls, the rural knickknacks in the three small rooms, may have appeared as something playful out of a fairy tale, maybe even as an expression of emancipation, given the newfound taste for folklorica.

She could have moved to the Odaya. The rural property, from the estate of her Phanariot great-grandmother, belonged to us all—to her mother, to her and her siblings, and to all the grandchildren—and thus to no one in particular. Because it was in a remote location on the left bank of the Prut River and was not productive—a few Easter lambs and some Christmas carp from a muddy pond were among its meager farm produce—it was despised as not worth the price of its upkeep. All the same, the house was there, on the estate that in 1909 had been intended to shelter my mother's new family and whence we had fled the Russians in 1914. In Romanian, *odaya* means "room," and I did not know that the word derives from an older one meaning "estate," or "property"; I didn't understand why such a fairly spacious building and the holdings around it had the name. Perhaps it was a term used only within the family, but in any case, the factual anonymity indicates how little pride of ownership was involved when we spoke of it. Even my father did not think much

THE SNOWS OF YESTERYEAR

of it: as part of his bride's dowry, he had considered it almost insultingly puny, even though he liked to shoot hares and ducks in the wetlands of the Prut. Mother's hatred of it was unconcealed; for her, it represented exile, the scene of all the horrors of her first marital years, whence she had fled as often and for as long as possible to Switzerland and Egypt. It was there, in the Odaya, that, in danger of her life and under great pains, she had borne my sister and, in the attempt to avoid repeating that ordeal, had almost lost me. She had never thought it worthwhile to bother about its furnishings.

Nowadays interior decorators seem to be inordinately stimulated by the chance to modernize old barns, attics and warehouses. This was not yet the case either in 1909 or in 1923, at which time my mother—even though she was homeless—ruled out the Odaya as a possible residence. The building, originally constructed as a cloister and later converted into a rural mansion, stood like a forbidding fortress on the flat steppe, and it included stables, barns, granaries, carriage houses and living space all under a single roof. Before us, generations of predatory estate managers had lived there and only a few rooms had been reserved for the masters. Their furnishings may have been fashionable in the time of Cuza Voda, the first elected Prince of Moldavia in 1859; since then, mice had nested in the tasseled plush of the neo-Gothic furniture; moths swarmed from the sun-bleached taffeta curtains; the dried decorative flowers sprouting in discolored bunches from gigantic Manchu porcelain vases, edged in brass in the fashion of the Rococo period, were crumbling to dust; the mirrors were blind; the steel engravings on the walls were foxed by brown mold; and cracked oil paint flaked from the portraits of genealogically unidentifiable forebears. There was no plumbing of any sort: one bathed in tin tubs, filled with innumerable pails of heated well water, and performed one's other elemental needs in oriels, glued like swallows' nests to the building's outer walls, from which pipes led directly down to the dungheap of the stables. That my mother had preferred a house in town to such discomforts after our return to the Bukovina was readily understandable, and even now it was comprehensible that she felt little attraction for the place. Yet in a sense it was her ancestral home, and it seemed astounding that now she would swallow her pride and accept an even more primitive shelter from friends.

It was the first of a series of undertakings that were acknowledged by those who wished her well, including my father, with an uncomprehending and somewhat ironical shaking of the head; but the motivation was fairly transparent—they were attempts at ultimate liberation, trial flights to escape the cage of convention and lead a life according to her own notions. Unfortunately, the fact that she had no self-evolved ideas and that she merely adopted others'—usually the most prevalent and hackneyed—soon brought her enthusiasms to a halt. At the same time her maneuvers camouflaged some quite purposeful strategies: she managed to rid herself of my sister, as well as Cassandra. Without any objections on my father's part (he favored a German education for us), my sister was placed in a boarding school in Vienna while I was to be sent, at the end of the summer vacation, to the German-language *Gymnasium* in Kronstadt. I was removed from the care of Cassandra and yet remained within my mother's easy reach.

At school I was entrusted to the guardianship of the father-in-law of one Dr. Viktor Glondys, then municipal vicar of Kronstadt and later bishop of all Transylvanian Saxons. My house warden, the long-retired Court Counselor Meyer, was a wiry little man of some seventy years, spartanically tight-lipped and of patriarchal sternness. I have carried in me for a lifetime the gloominess of the untold hours I spent behind the gray walls of that massive vicarage, but Kronstadt itself was another matter: it seemed to have emerged whole from a toy shop, a fairy-tale German enclave in the elemental Romanian countryside, spanned by a cupola of boundless blue skies.

Kronstadt lies in a hollow surrounded by steep hills, still medievally walled in and clotured, its little gingerbread houses and ancient trade manses angled narrowly around the church and town hall square. The Transylvanian Saxons had become Lutherans during the Reformation: in front of the massive Black Church—so called because it once had caught fire and some of its

Romanesque brickwork still bore the blackened traces of that conflagration—stood the bronze statue of the churchman Honterus, in Faustian pleated frock with ruff collar, capped by a floppy hat shaped like a champagne cork, and pointing an admonishing outstretched arm to the old vicarage, where I, under the laconic supervision of Court Counselor Meyer, had ample opportunity to ponder what ill wind had blown me into this confining, hidebound community, which seemed to have retrenched in an act of stubborn self-protection against scimitar-swinging, slit-eyed, rattail-moustachioed Mongols.

Court Counselor Meyer's pedagogic qualities resided solely in his persona and not in any educational method. His entire being breathed discipline. He was so small that even when I was nine I already equaled him in height: a ramrod-straight old gentleman whose head, with its spare bone structure, short-trimmed gray hair and neat short beard, bore a striking resemblance to Joseph Conrad's. Indeed I found in his library bound issues from the 1870s of the periodical *Über Land und Meer* (*Over Land and Sea*) from which, it seemed to me, emanated as from a whiff of tar all the romance of the Tall Ships. When I later read Conrad, it was as if on the bridge of every one of his ships a youthful Court Counselor Meyer were standing in full command.

I had plenty of time to spend with books. In the mornings, while Court Counselor Meyer, who was by no means ready to resign himself to idleness, labored at some honorific bureaucratic activity at the municipal consistory, I went to school—first a year at primary school, then two years at the Honterus Gymnasium. Both of us returned home for lunch, washed our hands at a foldout washstand as thoroughly as surgeons scrubbing up for an operation and sat down to our meal. This was served by a Polish housekeeper, who occasionally would teach me some Polish words by the tersely rhymed method favored by the Court Counselor (whom she worshipped): "*Koza*—goat; *suknia*—coat; *krzeła*—chair; *włos*—hair." At table she served wordlessly, and neither the Counselor nor I uttered a word; we mutely faced each other, he sitting bolt upright and handling knife and fork noiselessly and with a minimum of motion, I trying desperately to imitate him. As we ate the simple but filling dishes, we both would sip from glasses of water. After the meal I thanked him with a formal little bow, and then we walked in the garden in accordance with the dictum "After dinner walk a mile—or be sure to rest awhile."

The garden was a tiny square squeezed in between ivy- and vine-choked walls, with beds of leathery purple and yellow pansies and sky-blue forget-me-nots edged by miniature boxwood. A narrow gravel path crossed the flower beds diagonally in both directions and ran along the four sides of this diminutive horticultural plot. That is where we paced our postprandial "little mile," the Counselor ahead, I following, both straight as guardsmen, arms crossed at the back, audibly breathing in through the nostrils with the mouth closed during three strides, and then breathing out through lightly parted lips during four strides. Every hundred paces or so, the Counselor would voice without further elaboration some gnomic adage, as for instance: "Cool the head and warm the foot, stomach full but empty gut!" Or: "One single friend is better than the many you may lose; therefore be careful whom you see and wary whom you choose!"

When we had done our "little mile," Counselor Meyer would rest for half an hour—a concession to his age which, he said, I too could expect after another sixty years, but for now I was left with my homework. Once it was finished—it wasn't very hard usually—I was free to do what I wanted. And what ordinarily I liked best was to scan through the old and crumbly issues of *Over Land and Sea*. There wasn't much else for me to do. I had trouble adapting to my new environment. I had no friends. My all too solicitous upbringing had not accustomed me to unconstrained intercourse with coevals: I was timid and felt awkward. In addition, I suffered much from homesickness.

The monastically labyrinthine vicarage was deathly still in the brooding Romanian summer afternoon. In the main building—the Counselor's small apartment and my own little room were located in a side wing—Dr. Glondys might be preparing one of his famous sermons, and in view of this awesome possibility everyone naturally was tacitly enjoined to be as quiet as possible.

Dr. Glondys was an important man and was granted special status among ordinary humans on the strength not only of his ecclesiastical office and the prestige that devolves on patently large talents and responsibilities, but also of his awe-inspiring appearance, his manly handsomeness. Tall, slim and of innately dignified bearing, he carried on his broad shoulders a head that was the image of the classic portrait of Goethe. It had become known that he was a neo-Platonist—the term obviously drew a blank with most people, but nevertheless prevented one from raising one's voice, slamming a door or, unimaginably worse, engaging in guttersnipe whistling. Therefore not a sound was heard throughout the vicarage; the square in front of the Black Church, where the harshly imposing Honterus drilled his accusatory index finger into everyone's guilty conscience, was deserted.

My little room was confining and rather gloomy. So as to have better light, I sat in the window recess, cut so deeply into the building walls that I felt as if I were sitting in a cell. The window, with a view of the tiny garden, was closely framed by an ancient vine, its trunk as thick as an arm, which wreathed it with leaves like Silenus's head—a very drowsy Silenus, for the whole world dozed in the wine-hued afternoon light. The confused buzzing of summery flies threaded the hour, sluggishly trickling away. Across from me, among the leaves on the ledge of a wall, a cat slept rolled up into a furry black and white ball, and up above, in the high skies—those spanking blue bright Romanian June skies—swallows tweeted.

I had before me an 1873 issue of *Over Land and Sea*. From its yellowed pages rose a subtly musty whiff. A foxed steel engraving of a three-master with reefed sails in a small palm-fanned harbor in front of a background of steep volcanic cones—this lured my imagination into the airy remoteness of spiced shores. But there remained a floating core of consciousness filled with nothing but a transparent void—I would have called it my "I," had I been asked—that was neither here nor there but, instead, in an anguished and tormenting nowhere.

The bright light falling through the vine leaves drew serrated curlicues on the magazine pages, and the brownish-black letters of the old print took on a green hue, as in the scarlet-fever book of my early childhood. As if the paper bore a visible watermark, another even more remote vision was superimposed on the picture of the exotic harbor with its bare house-cubes, zebra-striped awnings over the windows and corbeled balconies under the palm fronds through which the spice winds blew. It was a vision so dim and fleeting that not even its outline could be perceived: more impression than image, more remembrance of a mere echo than an actual sound, more a hint of a feeling than a feeling itself. And yet it could be expressed in words. It was a vision rendered in the pale color-tints of English children's books, with the changing light coming through curtains barely moving in the breeze, between which the eye could follow, over massed crowns of trees, a row of poplars lining a country road that extended all the way to the darkly purplish mists of a faraway horizon—a vision that for me contained all the sweetness and warmth of my parental home, all its luminosity shimmering through the birches and rowan trees, the smell of baking, the sound of my mother's voice. It all now seemed more remote, more fanciful and more inaccessible than even the three-masted earth-circling schooner of a bygone era, and much more irreal and incredible than the medieval surroundings in which I found myself transposed as if by a spell, sitting between these thick walls, entwined by thick creepers, with a thick book on my knees.

I looked up. Over the heavy roof of the vicarage, the steeple of the Black Church rose heavenward. The blueness into which its pointed spire cut like the prow of a large vessel was swarming with swallows flitting hither and thither. Among them also hovered falcons around the spire; at times pigeons threw themselves from a ledge with a splattering of wings, circled the church tower, then dropped down on its roof like a handful of snow, or they slipped into holes in the brickwork that had been put there to hoist blocks of stone when the church was built. I had been told that falcons sometimes pounced on the pigeons with such wild impetuosity that they shattered their own heads against the stone whenever the pigeons managed to escape into those flight holes. I didn't like to hear such stories, for my heart was on the side of the falcons, but I believed them. Just now, a swallow swung from a hole and rose vertically, as if drawn fluttering along an invisible string, in total disregard of the falcons and in an apparent enraptured longing for heaven; it alit on the uttermost extremity of the minute hand on the tower clock. It was a quarter to three.

I waited for something to happen, but nothing happened. The falcons kept on hovering and the pigeons flitted to and fro in passionate hunting. Nor did the minute hand of the clock continue in its upward motion. The weight of the swallow was enough to keep the pointer horizontal. (Thus, another story also was proven a lie—to wit: that the hands of the clock were so heavy and the strength of the clockwork correspondingly so powerful that once, when an incautious sexton had looked out through the peephole in the dial as the hands were pointing to five minutes before twelve, he got his head wedged between them and cleanly cut off as by scissors.)

The skies were a piercing blue. From afar, coming from the hilly slopes beyond the town moat, could be heard the cheerful noises of a bevy of boys—lost in the wind and as if shrunk and made transparent by the distance: a sound merely dreamed, possibly. And indeed, the reality it evoked for me was totally abstract. I imagined those boys as being lively, but they were also abstract to me, like the sailors from the schooner pictured in the old magazine, whom I fancied roaming through the streets of that exotic harbor town. The boys were surely engaged in wild games, and I almost could feel their hot breath; at the same time a sense of being excluded from the rich stream of life cut deeply and painfully into med, whether at a remove of a mere hundred paces or of thousands of miles overseas. I was overcome by a fear I had hitherto not experienced. The world around me split up into imaginings, illusions and lies—and I was no longer one with the world. The tangible world around me—the book on my knees, the gnarled tangle of vines along the wall and even the wall itself, the vicarage wall in front of the mighty Black Church of Kronstadt in Transylvania—all this no longer truly contained me. The core of my being had been left behind in a lot, homefelt at-homeness in Bukovina, remembrance of which I could no longer summon up; even less could I have demonstrated that it was more than a phantom, an illusion, a myth of myself. I was in the Bukovina in as abstract a way as I was in that far-off exotic harbor or with the boys playing games. I began to doubt my own factuality. I could not have given my name with any kind of conviction; it would not have sounded as if it were my own.

The swallow sitting at the end of the minute hand of the tower clock did not move and the hand itself stood still. Time stood still. The sound of the children was lost in space. The tweeting of the swallows fused into a single piercingly high note like a thread spinning away into the skies. The deep blue of those skies, in which thousands of swallows were scattered like tiny playing-card clubs, seemed all at once transformed heraldically into a reverse ermine: a black sky seeded with swallows of a forget-me-not blue. And thus it became transfixed. The whole world stood still.

Then, quite suddenly, the swallow flew away and the minute hand snapped over to show a quarter past three. Barely a half-hour had elapsed; the sky was blue once more, and the swallows were once again black, like tiny fork prongs flitting to and fro. Once more their tweeting was intense and relentless and once again the sounds of the children could be heard from afar.

My mother visited me at Christmas. She had given up her rural cottage and was vague as to where and how she lived. By means of a small Christmas tree made of green-enameled wire with glued-on green paper needles, which folded out like an umbrella and was decorated with innumerable small candles and lavish silver tinsel, and with her typically thoughtful gifts, she managed to arrange a true Christmas Eve in her hotel room, even though it served only to sharpen more painfully my longings for the festive atmosphere of Christmas celebrations at home. She promised to come back at Easter but in fact came much sooner, this time accompanied by a gentleman with neatly parted flaxen hair, of careful manners and impeccable attire, who attended to her with utmost, even adoring politeness. Upon my suspicious question of what role he was to play in our lives, she disclosed that she had remarried and that henceforth I was to consider him my stepfather.

Then a strange thing happened. Whenever one spoke of family spirit and tribal solidarity, one referred only to my mother's kin. My father became an outsider, personally related to and loved by no one but my sister and me. But now our solidarity with him manifested itself with an intensity that my mother may hardly have anticipated, at least in me; that my sister would take his side unconditionally was to be foreseen, but my own reaction was equally strong. I would rather have strangled the stranger escorting my mother than concede to him even the smallest of the rights over me belonging to my father. I refused to call him anything than by his family name, persistently addressed him ceremoniously with *Sie,* the formal third-person plural, deliberately ignored his requests though these were polite and never peremptory, and followed them only when my mother transmitted them as her own. I overlooked his acts of kindness, especially any demonstrations of his almost reverential love for my mother—in which, I assumed, I was included merely to please her. How much I wronged him I perceived only gradually and much later. It took years before I learned to like him truly and before I came to realize that no one could have been more patient, correct, tactful and kind than he showed himself throughout the time we were together. Once, while I was home on vacation, I flew into an uncontrollable rage when Cassandra told me, not without impishly malicious intent, that quite probably I would soon be granted the joy of getting a little brother or, better still, sister. My mother heard of this, and I'm afraid it did not have a salutary influence on her willingness to conform in her second marriage to the rightful expectations that my father's successor may have placed in it.

He was a well-to-do, highly respected man, in most of his character traits the exact opposite of my father: restrained and dry where the latter was expansive and blusteringly humorous, deliberate and composed where the latter was inconsiderate, spontaneous and gruff. He loved my mother with a shy devotion that never turned into bitterness but merely lost its light, became vesperal and eventually was extinguished as he came to perceive the inherent hardness that made her sweetly evanescent smile so brittle, the underlying violence that suddenly could break through her inner-directed dreaminess and the scornful arrogance that hid beneath her vulnerability. Yet at first she revived under the warmth of his devotion; to begin with, her second marriage seemed incomparably happier than her first. Even though I did not care to acknowledge it, she radiated a kind of nuptial transfiguration: the self-assurance, greatly enhancing her beauty, of a woman who knows herself to be loved and desired and—last but by no means least!—economically secure. It was to remain but a short afterbloom.

We were still in the much vaunted 1920s. In our own Bukovina and in other similarly remote corners of the world, filled by the rustling of corn leaves and the shrieks of buzzards, the decade was dominated less by the art-historical developments of Dada, Expressionism and twelve-tone music than by the triumphal appearance in the Old World of the American life-style. It was the sounds of jazz and the vogue for pageboy hair rather than the Blaue Reiter that penetrated the melancholy spaciousness between the Siret, Prut and Dniester rivers. Movies served as the prime mediator of cultural trends, and the fops of the *jeunesse dorée* in Czernowitz, Radautz, Suceava and Sadagura even then (when men's fashions were not yet as parodistic as they are nowadays) liked to dress like silver-screen Chicago gangsters. With their fedoras worn low on the brow and their chalk-striped suits with square shoulders and bell-bottom trousers, their black shirts with candy-pink and pistachio-colored ties, they brought the true spirit of the twentieth century to the idyllic land of pipe-tooting mountain shepherds, perfumed and garlic-chewing operetta officers, and Hasidim sprung from the pictures of Chagall. The house my mother moved to with her second husband—it stood, surrounded by old cherry trees as gnarled as oaks, in one of the last large gardens in the center of Czernowitz—contained the first privately owned radio; its acquisition had required the authorization of the Romanian military authorities. There, amidst static whistles, chortlings and growls mingling viciously with syncopated rhythms, occurred my first love encounter with what, ten years later, was to be given the derogatory term "nigger music" and included in the category of "degenerate art": American jazz.

The power of the media—foremost the motion pictures and illustrated periodicals—made itself felt in full force. Following the example of the Americans blithely ignoring their own Prohibition, people took to drinking cocktails; the men who mixed them wore with their dinner jackets small white boaters on their smoothly oiled-down hair. Dream cities in futuristic styles evoked the vision of a golden future in a world-spanning metropolis, enjoying freedom of religion, the equality of all races and social justice. The mood ran high in those years right after the first suicidal bloodletting, and the promise of an earthly paradise and the New Jerusalem arose once more as fresh winds of youthfulness blew across the Atlantic. The American life-style was as enticing as the American optimism it sprang from. Bare of scruples, people set out to make money and, without much regard for obsolete conventional hierarchies, blithely considered a fellow man either a "pardner" or a "sucker." Girls cropped both their hair and their skirts. People who never would have done such things a few years before danced the Charleston to the tune "Knock on wood that in this life I still have a faithful wife," speculated on the stock exchange and associated with Jews.

My mother followed these innovations reluctantly. It is true that the long-dreamed-of moment arrived when she was in a position to open her house to a glittering social life—or at least to the backwoods notion of what this would be: shimmering candlelight on the bare shoulders of glamorous ladies, melodic laughter and the tinkling of champagne glasses, and what have you—without having my father appear, to the horror of the assembled guests, surrounded by a pack of baying hounds and dragging behind him through the festive crowd a freshly shot wild boar, all the while repeating an apologetic "Not to mind me, please!" on his way to his room, where, much pleased, he would throw the piece of game out the window. She was now in fact the respected mistress of a house, though a more modest one, and open it she did, though only to learn soon enough how right my father had been not to lend his own house to such diversions.

Her sense of social duties drove her in the direction in which her emancipated sisters in Vienna pointed her. A lady from the German circles in Czernowitz was an active promulgator of women's rights, and my mother joined her in these strivings. The activities of these johnny-come-lately suffragettes hardly went beyond some inspiring speeches and various meetings with feminist pioneers from abroad over tea with thin slices of lemon, rum in crystal decanters and petits fours. My mother was given the honor of leading a delegation of ladies from Czernowitz to a congress in Reps, an idyllic small town in Transylvania. She took the opportunity to pick me up in Kronstadt on the way and take me along for the three days of meetings; as a result, I owe to these feminists one of the most enchanting memories of my early life.

While the amazons worked, a playmate was assigned to me, the son of a physician, if memory serves: I no longer remember his name, although I count him among the best of the hardly numerous friends from my youth. It was one of those fortuitous encounters between two boys that represent love at first sight in its purest form and last not long enough to be destroyed by the usual puerile quarrels. He led me to the ruin of a castle on a hilltop near the town, from where we had a fine view of the magnificent countryside all around: a landscape richer and better cultivated (so to say, more German) than my native Bukovina but of equal spaciousness under the deep blue of the Romanian summer skies. Swarms of pigeons circled around the gabled roofs of the town at our feet, and above our heads falcons hovered in the wind that drove the sailing clouds and bent the high grass on the slopes. We chewed on juicy stalks while we lay stretched out next to each other, our arms crossed under our heads, looking up into the clouds, chatting of this and that; then we would jump up and run until our cheeks were aflame, climb over the remains of the castle walls and fill our fantasy with images of a militant past. . . . I tasted a freedom never known before. As a farewell gift my new friend presented me with a collection of bird eggs, from the magpie to the sparrow hawk, from all the species of finch and titmouse to those of the cuckoo, from the quail to the brown owl—an inexhaustible delight in its wondrous completeness. Blown out, weightless and brittle, they reposed, speckled sky-blue and greenish-gray, doe-brown and ivory-colored, in the fine sand of three neatly carpentered, stacked wooden boxes which I lovingly preserved through many years until, together with untold other things, they fell into the hands of the Russians during the Second World War.

My mother repeatedly apologized that, because of its fragility, she could not include them in her relocation baggage in 1940. No utterance could have been more revealing: it expressed her fundamental guilt feelings as much as her capacity for a lyrically loving empathy. But something else also showed itself in her in those days in Reps, to wit, her egocentrism. Women's emancipation was not a cause that recommended itself to her because of her own experience and conviction; rather, its impulse was bred in the disappointment of her first and—soon—her second marriage and was too intimately related to the offending husbands to allow her to draw any valid ideological points. For her, women's rights meant maternal rights, and since no one spoke of these in Reps, she didn't open her mouth. With a lady's drawing room smile, she clutched and shook hands, nodded acknowledgment to the sororal militants when they were introduced, replied politely and listened with glazed eyes to speeches and lectures. The congress took place in the auditorium of some public building—I no longer remember which—and during its closing session, I, together with my beloved newfound friend, managed to sneak in. My mother sat with the other delegation heads on the rostrum facing the audience. Under their hats laden with bird wings and fruit clusters, the ladies were of defiant mien, while my mother under her fashionably sober "pot" looked paradoxically frivolous among the others. A lady lecturer pilloried the despotic rule of men—a scrawny person, in type resembling the charmless piano teachers who had instructed my sister without much success;

when reaching key dramatic points in her delivery, her voice would break into descant. Some solid male notables of the town were seated alongside us in the last row, and since they did not know to whom we belonged, they neither suppressed their amusement nor minced their words about the pioneer feminists. Of my mother, one of them said: "Picture that one in a motorcar and furs arriving at some peasant hut and preaching rebellion against the peasant husbands! At least she looks as if she had her mind on other things—by the end of her crusade she'd probably have forgotten why she came." Admirably sharp! Reps marked the term of my mother's role as a feminist and, at the same time, put an end to her social activities.

From her second husband's relatives my mother held herself icily distant. Friends from her youth who had remained faithful to her despite my father's derision toward them now seemed to her as trite as he had claimed. Soon she lived as isolated a life as ever, no longer as a romantic prisoner but merely as someone known to be difficult, haughty and moody.

The only ones with whom she could thus comport herself with impunity were her children. We bore the brunt of her exhausted and jittery inner emptiness—at times in resignation but more often with the helpless laughter that alone made life bearable. We still accepted her behavior as inspired by our alleged needs and endured it with the submissiveness that in those days was regarded as a matter of course toward one's parents. With acute envy we occasionally noticed how the mothers of our coevals understood their adolescent wishes, dreams and anxieties and made themselves into well-meaning helpmates, instead of acting merely as the taskmasters of a nutritional and pedagogic program. But we overlooked the essential fact: her exclusion from the world around her. Nothing connected her to Philip, her second husband, whose adoration she accepted only as long as her resentment against my father was unassuaged and until she was accustomed to it, after which her irritability once more regained the upper hand. Her maternal militancy allowed him no place in her emotional life. His professional existence did not concern her. According to her concept of how life's roles were assigned—a concept in no way shaken by new emancipatory ideas—women had no business getting involved in men's affairs. For her, it was enough to know that his work would ensure a comfortable support for her and for us. (In her eyes, my father was a penniless and irresponsible spendthrift with whom she had always feared impoverishment.) Philip appeared not to have any so-called spiritual interests, and if he had, he would in any case have expected her to take the initiative in fostering them, since he looked up to her in all cultural matters. But to set up a literary salon or offer musical events (thanks to paternal severity, she played the piano well), of that she was incapable. More and more she withdrew into the rusting shell of her unapproachability.

Soon there was no room left for the exercise of her maternal role either. Most of the year now, my sister and I lived away from home. After some youthful misdeeds which prompted the aging Court Counselor Meyer to suggest to my parents that I should better be placed in the hands of a more energetic tutor, I was removed from Kronstadt and placed in a boarding school in Austria. The happy hours spent with my mother in the discreetly lush comfort of the Hotel At the Crown—almost like two lovers—were over. (Whenever we went to the coffeehouse for a hot chocolate, which I enjoyed with an eleven-year-old's greedy delight, the first violin of the gypsy orchestra that entertained there in the afternoons would play for us, an obsequiously effusive smile on his purple lips, the tearjerker tune "Ay, ay, ay," supposedly a South American lullaby; in the dining room we were served personally by the maître d', who in return would ask for one of my caricatures, for I constantly doodled; the lobby boys, with their little kepis held by chin straps and worn on a slant on slicked-down hair, their white gloves stuck military-fashion under their shoulder tabs, dared not respond to my banter, and only when my mother feigned not to notice did they drop their sternly stylized self-restraint and show natural collusion—after all, we were almost the same age.) All this now lay in the past. My sister would soon be sixteen, almost grown-up. When we came home for vacation, we shuttled between the houses of our separated parents; my mother arranged the summer sojourns at the Carinthian lakes so as to have us alone, at least for a while—but we escaped her even more irrevocably there. School had broken the fetters that had bound us. Now we had friends with whom we were on much more intimate terms than with her. With them we could prove how absurdly exaggerated both her anxious solicitude and her ensuing claims for absolute obedience really were. Increasingly helpless, she could do nothing but watch us take flight.

She did not give up easily, however. When we were apart, she attempted—sadly and unilaterally—to keep in close epistolary contact by bombarding us with admonitions, sartorial instructions and hygienic advice, requesting full information on everything we did, even mobilizing supervisors, spies and informers from afar. This abstract and vicarious sharing was as futile and tormenting as her helpless attempts at the Black Sea to control us from the remoteness of the shore.

The more independent we became, the more nimbly we eluded her remote-control guardianship. Now she was reduced to imagination, which had always fostered panicky alarms. The perils to which she presumed we were now exposed greatly increased. Permanganate and Formamint alone no longer sufficed. It was no longer a matter of guarding against scarlet fever or against polio. Much worse now threatened: syphilis! The danger was not so acute for my sister as for me. In theory, young ladies educated at Sacré-Coeur were chaste and shielded from the pernicious insinuations of free spirits like the Russian ophthalmologist. Moreover, the danger of infection from drinking glasses or toilet seats was small. I, however, had reached the difficult stage of puberty and had entered the zone of immediate sexual temptation. More and more often I would find sex-education material in the mail or on my bedside table, strongly recommending total abstinence as the only safe protection against lethal venereal diseases and the loss of sight as a result of masturbation. ("Young men, rejoice in your full testicles!") However, it was possible that I had been infected long before without knowing it; after all, primary symptoms are easily overlooked at the pimply age. To determine whether I had dallied in more than innocent play with one of the maids, my mother alleged that she had had to fire the girl because she had been found to be contaminated. I gave no sign of blanching terror at this news and condemned Mother to continued uncertainty. She was equally helpless with regard to bronchi, flat feet, the people we associated with and the abominations with which we were threatened by professional perverters of youth. Half a continent away, she hotly fussed about our woolen underwear, while her own life trickled away.

The halo of her martyrdom gained one more prismatic color ring. She disliked her new house; its confined middle-class setup gave her a feeling of social *déclassement*. She had brought with her most of her own furniture, including the blond galleon of the Second Empire bed, as well as the baroque chests of drawers and Art Nouveau chairs. But the rooms in which this recycled dowry was placed were too small. The tiny windows were positioned so low that on the garden side their lintels were at chest height. ("If you bend your knees," said my sister, "you can stick your head right into the house.") Nor was it any consolation that there was so much greenery around that the house resembled one of those quaint ivy- and dog-rose—covered cottages in the English style, dear to us from the cocoa tins and puzzles of our childhood. Unfortunately, it was located not in the Cotswolds but in the very heart of Czernowitz, a remnant from the city's founding period, less than a century before.

All too rapidly Czernowitz, built in the time of the Emperor Joseph II, had grown into a provincial capital. Around the house, originally a farmstead, five- and six-story apartment buildings had mushroomed. The garden with its old fruit trees and mighty acacias was enclosed on three sides by forbidding gray fire walls; an oversize wooden fence separated it from a heavily frequented street, its boards covered with circus posters, announcements of meetings and soccer games, political manifestos, official decrees and proclamations, and the homemade ads of job tailors and matzoh bakeries. At the entrance to the garden stood a kiosklike gatehouse, through the perennially open door of which an old Ruthenian hag, Mrs. Daniljuk, watched over anyone who entered and left. Across from it stood Fieles Court, a complex of low buildings in which, in the days of the Austrian monarchy—nowadays it is hard to believe—a fashionable dance school had found its customers among the *jeunesse dorée* of Czernowitz. A passageway connected it to the city's main thoroughfare, Transylvania Avenue. All these buildings, including the high-rises, were occupied by Jews, and one of them was a prayer house from which on Friday evenings a stream of bearded Orthodox clad in black caftans, with long side-locks under their broad-rimmed black hats, and black-bordered white prayer shawls around their scrawny or stocky shoulders, swarmed out in order to greet the first star on Friday evening, which initiated the Sabbath. During the week it was the playground of hordes of motley-colored cats, who bred in the nooks and crannies of the district, which they permeated with the biting reek of their urine. Commingled with it were many other odors—the fumes of the horse apples on the bumpy pavement, the smells of onions from kosher kitchens, odors of spices and herbs, the vapors of cow and sheep dung from the neighboring Hay Market—together forming a rich broth of miasma-laden vitality, to which audible expression was given by the twitterings of myriads of sparrows, lending a phonetic background to the soundless scrabbling of lice in the sheepskin coats of the peasants who came to town on market days.

Even though all this was only a few hundred yards from the city center—the Ringplatz, with the city hall; the line of dozing hackneys in front of the Liberation Monument, on which an aurochs, heraldic animal of the Bukovina, thrust its forehooves into the breast of a fallen double-headed eagle, symbol of the vanquished Habsburg domination; the hotel that unconcernedly continued to be called At the Black Eagle; the Byzantine dome of the Great Synagogue; the half-dozen shops that brought to Czernowitz a whiff of Occidental luxury—it nevertheless had the slovenly, deeply backwoods, leadenly nostalgic character, heavy with empty longings, of the no-man's-land between the cultures of West and East. My father, when speaking of my mother, never missed asking maliciously, "Well, is she comfortable in the Yiddish shtetl?" But for myself, I liked staying in that house when I came home from school.

At that time, city noises had not yet fused into a single continuous and deafening shriek of machines and roar of engines. Urban noise still had a kind of human dimension, composed of voices and natural sounds, the rumble and rattle of peasant carts, the crack of whips and the warning calls of coachmen, the clip-clop of the horses' hoofbeats, all of them ebbing away at eventide to make room for the great silence of the night, in which one could even hear chirping crickets and croaking frogs in the wide-open land all around.

Almost as quiet were the long Sundays; only in the afternoon could one hear, at times, rising from one of the backyards beyond the walls, the tenor call of a trumpet signaling the startup of a band accompanying the heavy, hopping dances of soldiers with their girls, mostly maids in service dressed in their colorful rural garb. It was as if life's melody penetrated the space of my solitude only from very far away; it is probably the special elegiac magic of such hours that contributed to making me a melancholy choleric.

I was still forbidden to leave the garden without a very good reason. I had no friends. I wasn't bored—and I still don't know what boredom is as long as I'm left alone—but I suffered a kind of poignant pining when I heard those Sunday hummings and fiddlings and poundings from the walled-in chasms beyond the roofs, so near and yet so far; time and again the voice of the trumpet would rise to carry, alone and undaunted, the simple melody into the empty afternoon. . . . I simply had to find out what these backyards were like, where the homesick boys and girls, cast off in the city, danced as if they were still back on the village threshing floor.

In our garden, surrounded by a group of gnarled acacias, stood some old and now disused stables and carriage houses, adjacent to buildings that opened up to another street. It was not hard to climb the trees, reach the stable roof and then continue to the roofs of the neighboring buildings. From there I still did not have a view into the backyards, but I could see into the back apartments, their windows opening onto narrow light shafts.

My unexpected appearance occasioned some scared surprises and occasional scoldings from those windows. But once it became known that I was not a burglar but simply the harmlessly venturesome child of well-known parents, everybody got used to the strange roof-roaming tomcat. I did my best not to seem indiscreet. I would creep over the hot tin roofs to some shadowed corner against a chimney pot or a high wall, glance through the mildly titillating magazines I had secretly obtained, which were safe from my mother's methodical searches only up here, or simply crouch in my nook and watch and listen.

The dwellers in those rear buildings were almost exclusively lower-class Jews, and what I saw and heard was the very core of their lives. I watched as the women cooked and laundered and sewed—women who almost always had a cheerful word for me or implored me to be mindful of the dangers of my mountaineering expeditions; I heard them scold their children and joke with their men; I saw them air their bedding and feed their cats; I heard their fathers pray and cough; I looked into the sickbeds of witchlike old grannies. Weekdays, when there was no dancing in the backyards, the old trumpet phonographs would tootle Yiddish pop music—"Yiddl mit san fiddle" and "Iach bin der Doktor Eisenbart" or "Du bist schain in maine oigen" and the like.

One of the windows—they were, incidentally, open day and night, for the summers in the Bukovina were warm—was of special fascination to me. A lad of about sixteen sat and read there day in, day out. I don't know whether he was sick, but he certainly looked it, with a highly sensitive, pale face under smooth black hair. He didn't wear the usual *payes*—the curly side-locks—of Orthodox Jews, but he was always clad in dark clothes like a rabbinical student and usually had a blanket wrapped around his knees. He would sit immobile and read, turning pages with a sparse motion of his thin hand.

He took no notice of me, barely looking up when I first appeared before him. The roof I crawled on was more or less at the same level as his window: only a narrow light shaft, four

stories deep, separated us. The arrogance with which the lad
ignored me was a challenge. I reacted very childishly: I brought
my own books to the tin roof, sat down facing him and read in
imitation of him.

As I have mentioned already, I was no great reader—probably
in protest against my sister, who devoured whole cartfuls of
books. What I had read up to then had been simple fare: Cooper,
Kipling and—secretly—King Ping Meh, in addition to any
amount of hunting literature. Occasionally I borrowed books
from my mother's library: Thornton Wilder's *The Woman of
Andros* (which bored me and which I found incomprehensible),
Claude Anet's *Ariane, jeune fille russe,* or books of my sister's—
H. G. Wells's *The Time Machine* and *The Shape of Things to
Come* (my sister, by then sixteen and intellectually and politically
"engaged," had long before switched to the diaries of Lily Braun).

So I dragged these books to my aerie on the roof, where I read
against the young Jewish scholar, so to say, in mute competition;
a duel in which, however, he refused to participate. Only once did
he raise his head—eerily, on the very day I dared to get a volume
of Dostoevsky from my mother's books.

"What's he reading?" he asked without so much as looking at
me and with only a trace of a somewhat contemptuous smile.

"Dostoevsky," I replied casually.

"A step forward, I'd say," he commented with cutting irony.

That was all. Nothing more; no word, no further sign of
noticing me.

Soon my roof expeditions were found out and placed under
strict interdiction. I never again saw my reading companion, but
our encounter prompted me to read all of Dostoevsky.

My mother would have been much too proud to admit that she
felt hopelessly exiled in the middle of Czernowitz, in a place cut
off from possibility, unable ever again to participate in what
elsewhere appeared to be the "real" life: a life of ineffable fulfillment, for which the slowly fading memories of Montreux and
Luxor and the pictorial reports in the magazines' society columns
were only vicarious evocations, feeble aids to an inadequate
imagination that had to make do with atmospheric inducements

of what, more or less, young Hans Castorp's snowbound dream in Mann's *Magic Mountain* was: a mixture of an Art Nouveau version of exalted human existence, clad in Isadora Duncan's Greek tunics, and the bourgeois idea of courtly society in now vanished principalities, with its puffed-up, chest-swelling German self-confidence. A mundane surrogate for this could have been reproduced, after a fashion, even in Czernowitz; but she was too disappointed and too fatalist to transform these wishful images into a living "as if" reality, as those who dance at New Year's celebrations, amidst colored balloons and paper streamers snaking through champagne giggles, like sleepwalkers waltzing to the choreography of the "grand life." She did not follow the fashion. She became plump, neglected her good posture and let herself sag into a housewifely pelvic slouch. Her preoccupation with her children's physical well-being began to impart to her entire bearing and behavior a prosaic obsession with the tangible everyday, a manic concern with triviality.

As she had kept us prisoners in our garden in the past, she now exiled herself to the enclave between the fire walls of the Jewish tenements, in which roses and dahlias granted her the illusion that the outside world, replete with unfulfillable promises and unnamable perils, could be shut out and a kind of retreat be established here for herself, in which Czernowitz was banished from view, sparing her any direct contact. She hardly ever ventured into the street beyond the garden's enclosure. All the more reverentially was she regarded by her neighbors. Out of duty but also out of kindness she had always an open — albeit stern — heart for the needy, who, as a result, habitually crowded around her. Beggars or handicapped petitioners never left her empty-handed; that she never discriminated against any ethnic group or religious affiliation in her charities — a virtue rare in a town in which the conflicts among these were sharpening — was greatly appreciated, especially by the Jews in her neighborhood. I still can see those white-bearded heads under their fiery-red rabbinical hats trimmed with fox pelts, telling me with approval, their eyes half closed and swaying from side to side: "The lady your mamma, *emmes,* she is an exceedingly kindhearted lady, may God protect her." It did not matter that her benevolence was of the institutional, Salvation Army type: warm soup and bread for old rummies, who would rather have had a few pennies to buy themselves a shot of booze and a few moments of bliss; old clothes for camouflaged rag women, who would make her believe that they had half a dozen children to clothe; handing out of alms only on fixed days and never without admonitions to turn to more honorable occupations than begging. In the Fieles Court she was considered a saint. The one who benefited most from all this was her French bulldog, Bonzo, who took every opportunity to slip through the garden gate and yap after the hundreds of roaming cats, to be spoiled with kosher tidbits and to help out every randy bitch in the neighborhood, much to the delight of the respective owner. ("Oy, what a cute little doggy, pretty as gold!" "The young gentleman won't know me, but through my little Fifi I am, in a manner of speaking, the father-in-law of the *khelev* of the lady your mother.")

The turn from the 1920s to the 1930s, turbulently marked by the crash on Wall Street that led to a world economic crisis and by political events in Western Europe (among which Hitler's seizure of power in Germany was the one with the most far-reaching importance and the one that most radically separated people), went by without diverting my mother's attention from the immediate obligations to watch over the physical well-being of her children and her needy charges (for us wool caps for sudden cold snaps, superfluous arch supports, repeated written and verbal prohibitions against visits to the public baths where skin diseases were allegedly rampant; and for the beggars the distribution of pearl barley, bacon rinds and sausage ends—insofar as these did not contravene religious nutritional proscriptions). In this tightly woven, prosaic web of perversely conceived maternal obligations and miserly charity she lived as isolated as a spider under water, snared in her notions of duty, her worries and anxieties. And there she also experienced her greatest personal tragedy. What she had always feared with the greatest anguish—

and thus expected—occurred in 1931: my sister fell sick with lymphogranulomatosis and died after a year of suffering. All the means at the disposal of medicine at the time were applied to save her life. Through the mediation of our theosophically and spiritistically active aunts (the Wiener Werkstätte and socialist ideas meanwhile had expanded into the transcendental), every kind of arcane force was also mobilized and proved equally unavailing. Death came to my poor sister as a welcome release.

My mother went about as if blinded. In arduous self-devotion, she had never left her sick child alone for a moment. All her physical and spiritual forces, but unfortunately also her intellectual powers, were exhausted. She became oddly and totally cantankerous. Each evening she held a kind of devotional service in front of a picture of my sister during which she was not to be disturbed by anyone. She was not burdened by remorse that she had made her daughter feel she was not her favorite child, for she had expiated that wrong in a year of almost medievally devoted nursing care. Instead, a kind of transfiguration of her daughter into an angel took place, and simultaneously the image of the mother-daughter relation was retouched.

From an ethical standpoint, this put me at a severe disadvantage. It was not I, the predestined problem child, who had transformed her factually into a *mater dolorosa;* rather, the angelic being whose picture she now caressed nightly as if this might alleviate her sufferings had sacrificed herself and taken my place. Whenever my mother glanced at me through her tears, I felt that my healthy sturdiness mocked her solicitude, was sardonic proof of the purely random efficiency of her lifelong care and all her precautionary measures for our protection. I embodied the injustice of fate and its cynical remove from influence; against this her rage was sublimated into gnawing, persistent demands of me—verbally expressed in the behest not to wreck her "ruined life" even more by my insubordination and, at a deeper level, shielding her subliminal wish that I would crown her even more definitively as Our Lady of Sorrows.

Meanwhile her second marriage fell apart. Even though Philip dealt with her most solicitously, she had begun to foster an animosity against him that burst into open ugliness at the first plausible excuse. It erupted after one of her spontaneous initiatives, which my father acknowledged only with an uncomprehending shaking of his head, even though he himself was involved, albeit involuntarily.

This had to do with someone's scheme to establish a sanatorium in the Carpathian Mountains. My father had been approached with the suggestion that he provide the capital—a ludicrous idea, for he didn't have any money and if he had he would have known at best how to spend but not how to invest it. There were many other reasons why he refused. Meanwhile, however, my mother also had heard of the project—possibly via me and my sister—and threw herself into it with the keen fervor that the almost irresistible spirit of the time dictated to her, she who had been so unpardonably late in her economic emancipation. At first Philip cautiously advised against the project, but soon and as usual he yielded to her will and contributed the lion's share of her investment—which represented all the money she had. The enterprise not only ended catastrophically as a business venture but also led spectacularly to a murder. I shall tell more of it in connection with my sister, since it was one of the reasons she hated what she called "our Balkan origins," and it contributed, if I'm not mistaken, to her early death. While alive she was tormented by the violent quarrels between my mother and Philip that were the most deplorable consequence of this wretched undertaking, and after her death the dispute continued with ever sharper acrimony, of which I am ashamed for all of us to this day.

The question at the heart of the matter was whether the Odaya could be sold to make up for the loss they had suffered. This old rattletrap, set where the Prut's murky waters flowed most sluggishly through scruffy stands of trees, spookily denuded and whitened by the guano of thousands of herons that bred in the endless marshes, impassable because of the shoulder-high nettles—this place suddenly gained an importance, as if it were the ancestral seat of some historic dynasty. Its sale would have been complicated in any case, since consent of all members of the family would have been required, with the unforeseeably awkward discussions as to how and to what extent each would be compensated. I, as the sole male descendant at the time, was called upon to defend this common inheritance against Philip.

My efforts were lame. All my life my ties to property have been very loose, and Philip made it hard for me to develop stronger ones at this juncture. He could not have acted more generously, particularly when I found that I could not defend my mother's cause with any true conviction, though loyalty prevented me from taking his side openly. He showed an understanding so delicate for my dilemma that I count it among the most edifying experiences of my life: the revelation of a humane, considerate magnanimity that hitherto I had not encountered or to which perhaps I had been blind. My mother was not receptive to it. I, now her only child, was no longer her ally. She regarded me as her enemy. The insidious tragedy of our alienation had begun.

In those days, however, dramatic events took place also outside the private sphere. Adolf Hitler had come to power in Germany — an occurrence that occasioned many ardent though tragically futile prayers at the Fieles Court. We ourselves did not share in these at the time. From our viewpoint, the developments in Germany were welcome: a profusion of optimistic images of youth bursting with health and energy, promising to build a sunny new future — this corresponded to our own political mood. We were irked by the disdain with which we as the German-speaking minority were treated, as if the former Austrian dominion in Romania had been one of Teutonic barbarism over the ancient and highly cultured Czechs, Serbs, Slovaks and Wallachians, as if these had freed themselves from their oppressive bondage in the name of civilizing morality. The bitterness of the defeat suffered with Germany rankled in us, and we felt good when we saw that in Germany, a new self-reliance refused to accept that a people vanquished was a people despised. At the same time, the threatening, even criminal aspects of socialism seemed to be averted; socialism confronted us at all times in the frightening mask of close-by Communism. "Reds" were the enemy per se, throughout the world, and the Germany of the valiant Brownshirts stood as our protection against them. Nor were we alarmed by the adjective *socialist* in the name of the National Socialist German Workers Party. The commonweal objectives of the National Socialist movement did not fade into abstract ideologies, we thought, which in international Marxism ended up in a general disintegration of values, but instead bound the nation together on behalf of the people's welfare. This could be equated with the welfare of the individual, and instead of the disastrous leveling of materialism, varied individualities could join in a common ideal. As to the anti-Semitism of the upward-striving Third Reich, it was the generally accepted wisdom among non-Jews in the Bukovina at that time that, irrespective of all tolerance and even close personal relations with Jews, it could be only salutary if a damper were placed on the "overbearing arrogance of Jewry." That this "damper" would bring about the murder of six million Jews no one could foresee.

In a nutshell: The ascent of Nazi Germany, with its thunderous marching columns and wheat-blond maidens, concerned us infinitely less than the abdication of the recently crowned King of England in order to marry Mrs. Simpson. And in this act no one could have recognized that not merely was it symbolic of the decay of venerable traditions and values but it signaled the final decline of the Occident as we had known it, a decline that was eventually sealed by another marital bond: to wit, the one between Adolf Hitler and Eva Braun in the air-raid shelter of the Reich chancellery in a dying Berlin.

Almost without anyone noticing, the years of illusory peace between 1919 and 1939 were suddenly gone; they turned out to have been but a truce between two phases of the European suicide. When the Second World War started, Romania at first remained neutral, but it was only a question of time before it too was drawn into the conflict: as a reward for the Russo-German nonaggression pact, the northern parts of the Bukovina and Bessarabia were ceded to Russia, but the Romanians harbored hopes of regaining these two rich provinces—paradoxically, by fighting on the side of the covenant-breaking Germans to whom they owed their loss in the first place. In great times the paradoxical becomes the usual.

I learned of the occupation of the Bukovina when I was in a moviehouse in Vienna, where a latecomer in the row behind me whispered the news to her neighbor, accompanied by the cynical giggles reserved in those days for imparting reports of dire catastrophes. I did not yet know that it had been agreed to have the German-speaking populations in the ceded territories, the so-called ethnic Germans, repatriated to the German "homeland." Nor did I see any reason why the Russians in 1940 would comport themselves differently toward the *burshchuj,* the bourgeois, than the Bolsheviks of 1917. I knew my father was safe. He had smelled a rat and had relocated himself in Transylvania three years before. But my mother was in Czernowitz. Only later did it become known that former Austrians (now also "ethnic Germans," for the shrunken Austria in 1938 had become the Ostmark of the Third Reich) were also to be "repatriated." For my mother that meant that—just as in 1914—she had to leave her house and her adopted homeland, this time forever.

I tried to imagine her leave-taking, for she must have realized that it was the farewell to her entire past life, and though she considered it misspent, it had at least been comfortable. Henceforth it would be an existence in uncertainty and deprivation among strangers, a refugee life much worse than during the First World War. I could not feel what she must have felt, but an image took hold in my fantasy as if in a dream: she stands in front of one of the "house horrors" that my sister and I, during our teenage infatuation with anything novel, considered the worst kind of kitsch: a foot-high reproduction in white marble of the Nike of Samothrace on a tall column of red marble; in this version, my mother looks at it with the same stunned expression of past happiness lost with which she had once gazed at the picture of my dead sister. This idle fantasy seemed to me to have pertinent symbolic connotations: it was as if the mutely thunderous wing-beat of the Louvre's goddess of victory epitomized all the dreams and aspirations of her youth, which now she had to give up forever.

The relocation brought her first to a camp in Upper Silesia. Being of "high-grade race," she was scheduled to become a "defense farmer in the German east," specifically in the province of Warta, as the southeast part of Poland had been renamed. (Her Polish housekeeper Valerka, who suddenly discovered her German origins but was nevertheless racially of somewhat lower grade, was sent to Nuremberg, where she died shortly thereafter. Unfortunately, nothing could be done for Cassandra, for the ethnic mishmash of her component parts was as variegated as her language; it allowed neither racial classification nor, as its consequence, relocation.) In the camp, my mother shared a tiny cubbyhole with Philip. They never spoke to each other and she left Philip for good when I succeeded in freeing her from the camp and sparing her the fate of becoming a defense farmer. But this was possible only on condition that she contribute in some other capacity to Germany's ultimate victory. In an air force office in Vienna she managed to advance to the rank of civil disbursement officer. She saw Philip once more, by sheer coincidence, at a post office. With a satisfied mien—a mingled expression of both her resentment and her guilty feeling of inadequacy—she told me that while standing in line at a stamp window, she suddenly felt that someone was staring at her; the sensation was so strong that she turned around and there was Philip, transfixed in shy veneration. I told her I hoped she had taken him in her arms, to wipe out once and for all the bitterness between them, but she vehemently shook her head. It did not matter that by then the Odaya, the bone of contention between them, was as far out of reach as the moon. He had been her enemy and he still was. She turned away from him.

Nor did she forgive her relatives for the fact that her return to the lap of the family did not lead to the permanent bliss that during her years of separation and unhappy marriage she had dreamed of as the outcome of such a reunion, however improbable it seemed. Two of her sisters were still living with her widowed mother—one also widowed, the other a spinster. They were all too dissimilar in character and similar in irascible temperament to get along for any length of time, but soon this was all obliterated by the rush of historical events. Vienna was bombed—much against the expectations of those Austrians who (after the event) considered the annexation of Austria by the Third Reich a blunder that the Western powers not only had tolerated but had even encouraged and for which Austria was therefore in no way ever to be held responsible. The office in which my mother labored for the ultimate victory was relocated to Bohemia; as a conscript employee, she had to go along. Soon backward-fleeing elements of the defeated German armies in the East swept over her. The Czechs rebelled. Her office was plundered, and she herself was almost shot. She fled to the West. A former receptionist at the Hotel Pupp in Karlsbad (now Karlovy Vary), who knew her as a young girl when she had stayed there with her parents, picked her up in the street and gave her shelter for a few days. When he and his family were also driven out, she set out on foot. During the night, she was overtaken by an American army vehicle full of black soldiers. One of them lifted her up by her backpack—"like a puppy being lifted by the skin of its back," as she later told the story. "Come on, old girl," he said, "we're all the same underdog." Thus she too, although to the Germans racially more valuable than Valerka, landed in Nuremberg—or more accurately, in the expanse of rubble that remained of that city.

It borders on the miraculous that in the chaotic period between 1945 and 1946 she managed to find out whither the war had driven me: from Silesia to Hamburg by way of Berlin and finally to the Lüneburg Heath. In the bombed-out landscapes of cratered and flattened cities, where telegraph wires hung like whips from slanting masts and rails were tangled in knots, the German postal service continued to function. On a winter day in 1946 the news reached me that she too had survived the war. We exchanged letters with reports of what we had experienced. I had married and was the father of two children; a third was on the way. Forthwith she considered this a call on her maternal duties. I hesitated to grant her free play for her pedagogic ideas and methods with my own children, but my wife welcomed some help at home. After years of separation, we faced each other again. The elapsed time had left its mark on us, but that was not what stood between us as a deep estrangement. Rather it was a drifting apart of the most basic kind.

Nothing can explain the end—and generally also the beginning—of a love affair. In our case it was indeed a love affair: her maternal love for me and my child's love for her in all their volatile passion had been much closer to an amorous relationship than to a natural growing-together of mother and child. From the very beginning, Cassandra had stood between us, Cassandra who—at a clear remove from my mother—had let me taste the animal delights of brood-warm love and had thus transposed my mother from the realm of a primeval mother to that of an intellectual experience in which her magic charm and seductiveness, her pride and her vulnerability, her obsessions and her whims had joined together to form for me the allure—and possibly also the travesty—of the quintessential feminine. I was on guard against her long before I watched out for any other women. Even in our happiest hours, when she visited me in Kronstadt, I loved her at a distance, with reservations about a possible sudden sobering, in the twilight of fundamental otherness: that never-entirely-to-be-understood being that woman represented for me. I think too that she had perceived in the love object "child," assigned to her as "mother," the man into whom the little boy—Baldur-like—would grow under her maternal nurturing, and had believed he would also embody the qualities she most hated in men. All too often her demonstrations of maternity had had the earmarks of rape.

Now, faced by a grown man who himself had raised sons, she was helpless. And I was not perceptive enough to forgive her for never having been a true mother. She took possession of our sorry household and my children with all her tough energy, now concealed by a newly acquired submissiveness. We lived in much straitened circumstances; in those days, hardship was general in Germany and we might well have ended up with hunger edema like so many others had we not received some help from abroad through one of her sisters (the socialist who had married a Jew and who, repudiated by the family, had emigrated to America, whence she helped us keep body and soul together by sending us CARE packages). Mother gave us her all. She assumed the lowliest chores, as if she had to atone for being tolerated by us and by the world. Yet her presence was not always a blessing. Her fidgety absentmindedness, her overwrought anxieties and her occasional outbursts, her sporadic forlorn musings and wool-gatherings, from which she would rouse herself as if sternly called to order, could hardly calm our already exacerbated nerves. She lived as if constantly rushed and hunted; she stinted herself on every mouthful of food, sewed children's coats from her last warm blanket, managed at the cost of indescribable abasement to get hold of black-market goods and procured ration coupons from unfathomable sources; she would hand these benefits to us with the hectic sacrificial eagerness of someone in full flight who rids himself of excess baggage to appease his pursuers. But she meant us to come along on this flight: a demonically driven flight in which guilt pushed her into self-annihilation. Her solicitude, her kindness and her self-devotion were as imperious as they were obsequiously degrading, and the angry servility that accompanied them, ever more exhibitionistic, turned into a formidable blackmailing weapon.

To protect my children from it, I told them the fable of Sindbad's rider: the old man dying of thirst on an island, asking the sailor who had been cast off on its shores to carry him to the well on his shoulders and who, once astride, took him so firmly between his iron thighs that he almost rode him to death. The allegory was not quite accurate, since it was my mother who had saddled us with her fate and who now was carried by us to her own death, yet the parable illustrated well the two-edged nature of despotic altruism.

I left the end of the tale untold: to wit, Sindbad manages to rid himself of his tormentor only by racing under the low branches of a tree, against which the head of the old man is finally smashed to death. This was a much more pertinent pictorial simile for my comportment toward her, though I could not be proud of it. The jumble of world events covered the torment of our private history only inadequately. Nor did the past offer consolation. The loss of her home and fortune pained my mother much less than the numberless small wounds inflicted to her pride in happier times. Hardly ever did an image arise from the magic formula "Do you still remember . . . ?" that wasn't marred by bitterness or corroded by irony. Only memories that were ludicrous and typical of absurd circumstances were acceptable; one feared to evoke hidden sufferings. She told us of the first peaceable occupation of the Bukovina by the Russians in 1940: the colonel who was quartered in her house showed exemplary manners. He spared the bed linen in fear "it might get dirty," and she found it each morning neatly folded next to the bed. After a few weeks, he was joined by his family: a hefty wife and an equally generously proportioned nineteen-year-old daughter. The two ladies, summer-clad in cotton shirts through which saucer-sized nipples were darkly visible, went on a shopping spree for whatever had not yet disappeared from the shops of occupied Czernowitz. They came home with strange-looking bonnets made of light netting with puffy pink paddings, held by two ribbons knotted under the chin. They turned out to be sanitary napkins, whose true purpose was unknown to the ladies.

But even in these merry reminiscences of the terminal phase of the great shoveling-under of the old world, preparing the soil for a new one, my mother's jagged edginess made itself felt. Thus she told us that one day a young man called on her who showed an astounding resemblance to my father. He introduced himself as the offspring of a little love interlude between my father and some local maiden, a pleasurable byplay during a hunting expedition, with its imprudent but foreseeable consequences. The mother had been a Ruthenian. Because he himself was married and the father of small children whom he wanted to grow up in Germany rather than Soviet Russia, he asked my mother to testify to his racial high-grade value and thus to enable him and his family to be relocated. She did so, "for the sake of the children, of course," she explained in a brittle aside. I can well imagine the icy disdain with which she comported herself on that occasion. The man and his family were indeed relocated, but she stubbornly refused to divulge where or under what name, so that I know nothing more of him and of my nephews and nieces. Nor was it of any avail when I explained to her that I felt guilty toward this half-brother: in a way, I had cheated him of primogeniture, as I had done to Cassandra's son, from whom I had stolen the mother's milk rightfully belonging to him.

Her life together with us—myself and my wife and the children—was not to last long. My marriage soon broke up. It was as if my mother forgot that I was her son and not her irresponsible husband; she began to address me by his name and blamed his escapades for the failings in our family life. She identified wholly with my wife of the time and, with a fervor she had lacked at the meetings of the feminists in Reps, lectured her on her right to emancipation from the bondage of marriage and from housewifely and maternal duties. These sermons did not fall on deaf ears. My wife emigrated to Africa and I too left Germany; the children were sent to boarding school. My mother remained alone in wretched circumstances, which I could have alleviated somewhat. I did not do so. She probably derived some consolation and a few happy moments from her love for my youngest son. In her relation with him all her lyrical capacity for love, freed of trivial obsessions, blossomed once more, and he kept as affectionate an image of her as I in the days of my childhood.

On a single memorable occasion I saw her emerge once more from the spell cast by her lifelong rancor. It must have been at some time in the early 1950s, when we lived in a village not far from Rothenburg ob der Tauber. She was waiting for us in this toy-box town at the top of a street sloping up to the city hall square, among turrets and gabled houses. Summery crowds were all about, as she stood looking for us over the heads of people around her . . . and there she appeared to me for an instant, stretching her head, as remote from the world and astounded as a mermaid about to arise from the waters, peeking through reeds into the alien world of humans to see if she could not find one among them who would free her by saying the magic word. . . .

She was wearing one of those cakelike hats, a fashion by which elderly ladies seem to demonstrate their loyalty toward erstwhile local sovereign princesses, foremost Queen Mary of England. For once her pale blue eyes under her high arched brows were not clouded by bewilderment and terror-bound panicky expectation of ever new catastrophes but instead expressed a determined distancing from the world around her: she knew she was different from the crowds; they were not of her kind. As soon as she had caught sight of us, she once more began to flicker in nervous anticipation, besieged again by claims to which she was unequal and by which she was burdened by unjust fate. Her head sagged, her movements became wooden, her speech fidgety. But for a fleeting moment she had echoed her former self: delicate and fair, in all the comeliness that had been hers before the bewitchment set in.

Finally, after another two decades, at the age of eighty-six, she found her way back to her true self. I visited her in a home near Starnberg, where she led a vegetative existence. She was as fragile and bleached-white as a stranded piece of cuttlefish. A gentle smile nested in the web of hair-thin wrinkles spun over her face. *I* felt very guilty. With a ruthlessness that I may well have inherited from her, I had kept myself remote from her; now she enfolded me in her arms as her long-lost son. I took her to a restaurant close by, on the lakeshore. She was barely able to eat a mouthful of trout. She set her fork down, looked at me and said: "Why can't I die finally? I can't eat anything anymore, I can barely crawl, can't sleep—and the worst of it: I'm getting dottier by the day!" With which she burst into the same relieving and redeeming laughter as on that day, some fifty years earlier, when we lost the beautiful ship's model in Constanţa.

A few weeks later she fell into a coma. Blue lights flashing and siren howling, an ambulance took her to the hospital's intensive care unit, where she was kept alive for another six months, connected to a multitude of tubes and pipes, even though she was barely conscious. Under the still full hair, much finer and less vital than Cassandra's—never had she shielded me protectively in its wealth, nor had I ever wished for her to do so—there no longer was any flesh on her face: the skin was stretched like crumpled paper over her head's delicate bone structure. Around the thin lips, barely parted, there still floated a forlorn smile. When I took her hand—a fragile, almost desiccated hand, with blue veins bulging under the skin—her lids twitched as if she were trying to look at me. She could no longer manage this but her smile deepened: she had recognized me. "Thank you," she whispered tonelessly, "thank you."

The Father

The windfall is so old that one can walk straight through the fallen trees: they crumble like tinder. Only the thick moss that has grown over their bark holds them together in the form of trunks. In between, primeval plants proliferate: ferns and horse willow; club moss, which takes decades to grow an inch, crawls yard-long all over the soil. From the giant pines still standing, pale gray lichen hang like the beards of old men. The eagles here are double-headed, but they are without aeries. Except for the ghostly drumming of woodpeckers near and far, a deadly silence reigns. The stealthy steps of the hunter are those of a murderer.

If I am to say which of his traits was most characteristic of him, I would say his brightly luminous
temperament. I speak of "brightness," for his mood
was not always cheerful and at times could be very
bad indeed. But even when he was in a bad mood, cross, sullen,
coldly vexed, prone to dramatize, sharply cutting or on occasion
thoughtlessly destructive, it was like a rainstorm over Naples:
over the massed clouds and their occasional discharges stretched
a sky that soon again was certain to be as immaculate in its light
blue expanse as before. When nothing untoward happened to
annoy him, he would sing in the mornings, loudly and out of tune:
a medley of arias from operas, folk songs, ditties and student
songs from his youth. His temperament was innately radiant.
Given the decisive importance this kind of physiological predisposition holds in the alchemy of getting along together, I can
understand my mother's nagging resentment of him: what she
really objected to in him, morally and psychologically, were his
high spirits. It was the resentment of the supposedly ailing against
the healthy, of the allegedly frail against the rudely robust. As he
himself used to say repeatedly, "It's all chemical anyway."

At one time or another his early-morning singing triggered the rancor of helpless vexation in all of us. After he had separated from my mother and when I had taken over her former bedroom, which was connected to his own by a bathroom—between schools I spent a happy year at home together with him—I waited each morning burrowed under the pillows, in nervous anticipation of the beginning of his unfailing ritual as he cheerfully embraced the new day. This took place with clocklike regularity, with only a half-hour's difference between winter and summer: in winter the bathroom door was flung open and his balled-up pajamas were flung at my head at half past five (five in the summer). Even though I expected it and knew how much pleasure the day would bring (woe betide the day when I might be awakened less boisterously!), I could not rid myself of a momentary and involuntary annoyance with this loud disruption.

True, it expressed his affection and his happiness in our being together, as did the rough jesting with which he treated his dogs (who idolized him for it), and he expected correspondingly high spirits in return, but I was not always equal to it. At times—for instance, during an uneasy phase of my adolescence when I would have preferred to stay in bed listening to records and dreaming of life's grand promises—the morning ceremony seemed tiresome, though I appreciated its disarming humor. I never took it crossly, but sometimes I wished for a dampening of his early-hour boisterousness without having to fear that he was in a brown mood. I am certain that he never dared to wake my mother up in this manner (she kept the connecting door of the bathroom locked, probably also for other reasons), but I can imagine that similarly hearty attestations of his affection played havoc with her nerves.

He did not begin his vocalizing when he threw his pajamas at me. The next procedure, during which I had time to overcome the initial drowsiness that follows a rude awakening, took place to the accompaniment of other noises. Faucets were opened in the bathroom; water bubbled, rushed and roared. A descant howling was heard, not unlike the wintry sound of Carpathian wolves howling at the moon; this was my father showering for ten minutes in ice-cold water.

Then he appeared, all six-foot-two of him, clad in a hooded bathrobe reaching to his feet and giving him the appearance of a militant monk, with which he rubbed himself with jittery hands—here and there, up and down, left and right, front and back, as if he had been stung by a swarm of wasps and was desperately massaging the stings. As he rubbed himself dry, his shining blue eyes checked whether perchance I had not gone back to sleep. With a shake, he threw back the hood so that his round head appeared, tanned and glossily bare. He was almost entirely bald. The sparse fringe of hair at the back of his head, he shaved off. The smooth, freshly showered and rubbed-down skin exhaled an aura of intense health and cleanliness. He was brimming with life like a Cossack by Repin.

While he proceeded with the complex ritual of his shaving, he would talk. Dreams made him voluble: he would impart droll, drastic and scurrilous excerpts from them. His dream life was as filled with fanciful imaginings and humor, as illustrative of his shrewd cleverness as his way of grasping reality when awake— again I cannot think of a better term to describe it than "bright," even though occasionally this could darken and shift to ill humor, irritability and even rage. His moods were all of a piece, never equivocal. I could not imagine him losing himself in daydreams, as my mother so often did. He experienced the given moment too wholeheartedly, though never prosaically. His lyricism was of another kind than hers, more Dionysian, to express it in Nietzsche's terms (whom, incidentally, he considered his great brother in spirit: in this he was wrong, as he generally was with respect to himself).

His dreams were a vivacious, topsy-turvy farrago, and usually most amusing. Occasional nightmares did not seem to frighten or oppress him. He spoke of them as if they were performances he had attended: they might be exciting but, after all was said and done, were merely fantasies. He was vastly intrigued by a dream in which Miss Strauss, Bunchy, appeared to him as a man, even though as our governess she had always comported herself in a most feminine manner and dressed in the dignified fashion of a turn-of-the-century matron. To find out her true sex, he—still in his dream—had thrown an apple at her lap, for, as he explained, "to catch something thrown at them, men will close their knees, so that it won't drop through their thighs, but women open their thighs so as to catch the object in their skirts."

As he told these stories, his shaving brush would whip up rich bubbles of white snow from the English soap in its wooden bowl, which he then applied, carefully and with much skill, on his cheeks, chin, throat and the space between lips and nose. All my life I regretted that with my many resemblances to him I had not also inherited his full lips. My own have taken after my maternal forebears: thin and with the tendency to become pinched, particularly with age. In a photograph taken a year before his death— he had grown a short badger-gray beard toward the end—his lips protrude as they did in those far-off days from the snowy foam of his shaving soap: carnal, sensually joyful, firm without being grim, and closed with an expression of reliable virility.

I always enjoyed watching how his expression changed as his razor scraped off the foam from the delicate spots on his upper lip and in the corners of his mouth, the dimple in his chin, and the throat above his Adam's apple. It wasn't merely a full catalogue of his mimetic abilities but a manifestation of the eloquence of the mute mouth per se—from bacchanalian amusement through mild benevolence, serenity and humility, to arrogance, derision, contempt, fury, horror, and then bitter disappointment and deep sorrow—all this magically produced in reaction to the sharpness of the blade, in lightning-quick changes that flitted by like a play of shadows.

Like everything he did, the shaving every morning was of a ritual regularity that could have been called maniacal if it had not also been so obviously playful. It always started with the selection of the blade. He had seven of these in a leather case, ordered from London in conformity with the Anglophilia of his generation, each of them engraved with the day of the week on which they were to be used: MONDAY, TUESDAY, WEDNESDAY and so on to

SUNDAY, the handle and back of which last blade was gold-plated
to distinguish it from the others. Though the choice could, therefore, hardly be arduous, he first tested the sharpness of several
blades with the tip of his thumb before removing the one scheduled for that day from the dark purple velvet of the box and
stropping it with a few quick slapping strokes. The blades were
profiled concavely from the back to their cutting edge, a mattely
mirroring, dangerously sharp steel that I was forbidden to touch
as a child. I cannot say what more vividly remains in my memory:
the mixture of the various smells of soap and leather, the delicate
fustiness of the velvet lining of the case, the biting sharpness of
the alum stone and the aromatic essences with which he rubbed
his skin afterward; or the foamy crunching sound, testifying as
much to the toughness of his stubbles as to the sharpness of the
blade with which, after first setting it delicately and then drawing
it down resolutely, he bared broad bands of suntanned, leathery,
manly skin from the snowy richness of the shaving foam.

This used-up foam, accumulating on the blade, was then
stripped off with his left index finger and proffered to the dogs
assembled around him. Shuddering with disgust, they licked it up
to the last smear. They seemed greedy for it each morning and
would fight each other for the privilege of getting the biggest balls
of soap from the master's stubble. He laughed heartily when the
dogs shook in revulsion, and he laughed even more when they
nevertheless scrambled for the suds. He would have laughed still
more if one of them in greed and anger, forgetting his slavish
adoration of his master, had attacked him—and he probably
would not then have hesitated calmly to cut the dog's throat with
the blade. His temperament was as bright as the sky over Naples,
but just as that sky always showed some threads of smoke from
Vesuvius to remind one of other, more primeval subterranean
forces, there were reasons to believe that in him too something
deep down lay in readiness over which he himself had no control.
And this threatening plume of smoke was perceptible even in the
usually unperturbed serenity of his matutinal hours.

Meanwhile I managed to disengage myself from the comfort of
my lair and also repaired to the bathroom. While I opened the

faucets of the tub and drowsily tested the temperature of my bath, I would be struck by the blue flash from his eyes in the concave shaving mirror. Only a single eye would appear in the circle of the mirror, as he brought the various parts of his face close to the magic concavity to ensure that not the slightest hirsute remains had escaped the blade; there was no doubt that this monstrously enlarged eye searched only for singular hairs and did not apprehend me at all. Yet to me the eye appeared as if it belonged to a resident of Brobdingnag, ironically observing his dwarflike toy through a hole in the little box in which Gulliver was held prisoner.

My father would begin to sing as he turned to the plethora of his other toys. After he had washed the remaining foam from his face with a large sponge and rubbed his skin with shaving lotion, the well-being of his body drove him to other activities beneficial to the state of his soul. Of these there were many and various, beginning with pistol-shooting practice (after which one could be certain that no one in the house was still asleep), and proceeding, by way of floriculture, watercoloring, the filling of his shotgun cartridges, etching and photographic work in his darkroom, to the mixing of poisons and the training of young dogs. And in none of this was there a system or regularity. One activity superseded the other or was simply interrupted and postponed to the next day, while others were begun or resumed. He did not lack for time. It was six-thirty in the morning and he was several hours ahead of people who started their day at nine or ten o'clock. His singing filled the house until noon.

This house changed when my mother moved into town. The garden went to seed but, in exchange, gained in romantic appeal. The so-called reception rooms, which had seen so few receptions, turned into storage rooms for hunting trophies and related paraphernalia. My mother had had a loathing for walls decorated with stag antlers and stuffed grouse. Now antlers, horns, pelts of stags, hunting knives, pheasant tails, shooting sticks, cartridge boxes, dog leashes, bird snares, spring-traps and cleaning utensils for rifles were stacked high between and on top of the furniture. Our old nursery rooms were now the realm of his own games. On easels stood canvases and aquarelle papers on which he painted rather mediocre wildlife scenes and occasionally produced quite attractive architectural studies. His lack of self-criticism surprised me until I understood that he was interested much more in the process of painting than in its result. He stretched his canvases himself and mounted the Japanese papers with masterly skill on the drawing board; I admired, even envied, his knack in sharpening his pencils. No doubt he would have liked to grind his own colors. He was anything but a hobbyist, but he cherished craftsmanlike thoroughness and the excellence of select materials. In his search for the best in everything he was uncompromising: just as his shotguns had to come from Purdey and his custom-made rifles from Mauser, he bought his brushes, colors and papers from the most expensive suppliers in London and Paris; this fastidious insistence had been the despair of my mother. In addition, he bought everything in stock quantities, as if he feared that in so remote a corner of the world as the Bukovina he might be cut off at any moment from his sources of supply.

There were towers of boxes with mealy-greasy pastel crayons from which a whiff of the eighteenth century seemed to emanate; different oil brushes bundled in dozens, the bristles attached neatly and very firmly by metal clamps to elongated, top-flattened handles; other bundles of watercolor brushes made of marten hair, generously heart-shaped at their bases and tapering to thread-thin points, tied with red-lacquered silk yarn and attached so painstakingly to quill holders as to suggest the expert hand of a Chinese master. In between, on top of and next to piles of all kinds of hand-laid papers rested the small windowlike frames, meticulously lined in thin green felt, in which his photographic plates were exposed to light to make prints. He was a passionate photographer, and during our childhood he subjected us to all too many trying sittings. But for these I found myself amply compensated by the cavernous mystical experience of the darkroom, where, bathed in the blood-red shimmering obscurity, the yellowish coating of the glass plates slowly began to darken in the shallow rectangular pan rocked gently by Father's skillful hands, releasing both acidic and basic fumes, magically to reveal, in the gradually separating depths of lighter and denser mist grays, the emerging pictures.

There was a great deal of medieval craftsmanship in the instrumentarium of his manifold hobbies. The sunlight that had once fallen on our dolls and toys was now reflected richly in the copper plates used in his (unfortunately rather amateurish) etchings, and all about were strewn—as heretofore had been our building blocks or my tin soldiers—his bottles of chemicals, his printing rolls, his scrapers and his palette knives. With the difference that all this paraphernalia of his playful enthusiasms was invested with the solemn aura of art utensils, just as his hunting weapons and implements were witness to adult occupations that were to be taken even more seriously. The very abundance of all this equipment, bought in quantities of dozens and lots, made it awe-inspiring. It was as if the bohemian atmosphere of the artist's studio were transposed to a higher level by the very costliness of the materials, each of which had the select character of a bibelot. Furniture, on the other hand, was expendable unless its immediate usefulness was obvious, though he loved the clublike comfort of deep leather armchairs. With maniacal care he watered and cultivated his plants in the many-shaped planters, species that seldom blossomed but were all the more luxuriant in their verdancy: asparagus ferns spilled out from their stands and crept along the floor; cacti achieved monstrous sizes.

He attended to his matutinal activities unclothed, covered merely by a bath towel girding his loins, a liberty he indulged in after my mother left. Once, when his faithful friend and professional colleague Paul H., who came to fetch him each morning, impatiently demanded at around ten o'clock: "Finally, would you go and get dressed?" he sheepishly donned his pith helmet, which had hung unworn since the days when he had gone to Egypt to visit my mother.

When finally—after many an interruption—he was dressed, there followed the great ceremony of his departure for the archiepiscopal residence at the other end of town, where his office was located. As architect and art historian, he had been reassigned from the former Austrian civil service to the so-called Religious

Fund—which administered the estates belonging to the Orthodox Church—with the special task of looking over the monasteries of the Bukovina.

It was never revealed to me in what exactly his duties
at the office consisted. No doubt some desk-job activities, though
it remained unfathomable how and when he accomplished these.
His desk was littered with photographs, drawings, periodicals,
watercolors, catalogues from weapon dealers and safari outfit-
ters, but never any documents. No one could have been more
unsuited to be a functionary. Yet it would seem that he attended
to this part of his daily labors with his usual assiduity. He was
highly respected in the spiritual hierarchy of the church-estates
administration, in which he held the rank of a councillor of the
consistory. Yet he certainly was not liked, but rather feared, for
his sharp tongue and total lack of respect for any form of authority, especially that claimed by the representatives of God on
earth. Unabashedly he called them "frocked vultures" and never
hesitated to denounce publicly even the most hushed-up scandals
in their state-within-a-state. Somehow he disarmed opponents by
his rigid sense of duty, developed under the old Austrian monarchy. His daily trip to the archiepiscopal residence was a demon-
strative act.

All of us had to accompany him on these expeditions in a
solemn procession: Paul, his colleague; my sister and I; and all the
dogs—though the dogs were sent home with a magisterially
sweeping gesture once we reached the edge of town. The image of
their happily wagging tails sagging sorrowfully between their
hind legs as they trotted homeward at this mute but commanding
gesture will stay with me to the end of my days; nothing illustrates
more tellingly how our own moods dampened whenever my
father was ill-tempered, packed up his things and disappeared
from our lives for weeks or even months.

Officially, these disappearances were announced by the sentence: "I have to go on assignment!" This left no doubt as to the
importance of the undertaking, since it sanctified it as a fulfill-

ment of professional duties. The "assignment" meant inspection trips to the historic monasteries of the Bukovina and on the upper Moldau, the structural condition and maintenance of which it was his task to supervise. Why he had to take along his rifles and shotguns was an open secret. The Religious Fund owned enormous tracts of forest. My father, who was on equally good terms with the abbots and the local forestry administrators, was granted free shoots in hundreds of thousands of acres of largely virgin Carpathian forest.

When I had grown up enough to have at least a rough idea of hunting, knew how to handle rifles and dogs in a sensible way and only seldom made mistakes in the peculiar esoteric idiom of venery, I was allowed to accompany him on his work at the monasteries. In those days, this meant laborious trips by railway, automobile or horse carriage, or at times by narrow-gauge forestry rail lines that penetrated deep into the remote fastness of the timberlands. Even today, those monisteries on the Moldau (in that section of the Bukovina still remaining in Romania and now a part of Moldavia) are placid islands in the barbaric hustle and bustle of our civilization. In the wind-swept, rustling spaciousness of those forests spanned by majestic skies, green clearings open up with the cloistered churches standing in the center, blazing in color and surrounded by protective walls. Not only the interior but the exterior walls of six of these are decorated with magnificent frescoes in the Byzantine style. I envied my father's knowledge, which allowed him effortlessly to interpret the pictography of heavenly and hellish scenes, the symbolism of the images of martyrs or of the cloisters' founders, and to decipher the Cyrillic inscriptions in Old Church Slavonic as easily as if he were reading his morning newspaper. Suddenly this ironic and lighthearted man in hunting clothes, always so ready to jest and frolic, showed the dignified gravity of the scholar. Or rather, it was not that he showed it (though he liked to show off his other skills, such as—alas!—his dilettante daubings) but that *it* showed itself, without any help on his part. The deep seriousness of his professional routine had the modest matter-of-factness of the former Austrian imperial functionary. It wasn't the profession of his choice. He had wanted to study chemistry instead.

I often thought that his all-consuming passion for hunting was in reality an escape to and a shelter from the reminder of a truer and unrealized vocation. This seemed plausible when I observed the passivity with which he let venery overrun his entire existence untrammeled. One had the impression that, fundamentally, he had no thoughts other than those related to hunting, that he hardly spoke of anything else, and that it determined all his moods. Without any doubt, his decision to forsake a more rewarding career in the civil service in favor of remaining in the Bukovina and entering the service of the Romanian Orthodox Church had been influenced by the outstanding hunting possibilities of that region. Venery, taking full possession of his many-faceted being, pervaded all his other interests and hobbies. Ever more frequently, the scenes he would draw and paint were of wildlife, though he lacked talent for drawing; his mathematical knowledge served only his understanding of ballistics, and his chemical skills were used only in the mixing of various gunpowders. He was untiring in his correspondence with renowned hunters and writers on hunting, with zoologists and ornithologists, as well as with botanists on questions of game feeding. He wrote articles on game for specialized journals like *Wild und Hund* (Game and Hound), *Der deutsche Jäger* (The German Hunter) and *Chasse et pêche* (Hunting and Fishing) in Luxembourg, and he hardly wore anything but hunting clothes. By nature cyclical and determined by seasonal changes, and by tradition severely ritualized in form, hunting became for him a cult to which he dedicated himself with an almost religious fervor. One was led to think that at some point he realized that the diversity of his talents would lead to a frittering away unless they were made to serve one overriding creative impulse, so he decided to bundle them all together in a single passionate avocation. A gesture of defiance stood at the very origin of his fixation — indeed, obstinate defiance was the determining trait in his character.

This defiance runs like a red thread through what little I know of his childhood, adolescence and young manhood (and how little we know generally of those who have helped make us what we are!). One of my aunts, his younger, undauntingly cheerful and courageous sister, Bettina, told me something typical from their shared youth: she and he, together with his other sister, Sophie, were enrolled in a dancing school in Graz, where my grandparents lived before the turn of the century. The two girls were very beautiful and spoiled by their mother. For the dancing lessons, which were held in winter, the girls were given pretty overcoats trimmed with mink, while he, as the son for whom such luxury would be in poor taste, was measured for something of sober military cut. He hated his coat so much that in protest he behaved badly during the dancing lessons, so badly that he was sent home. He never again danced a single step and all his life avoided balls and other functions involving dancing. That his bride would indulge in the lifelong illusion that her fate had been decided on the dance floor he would have considered a very poor joke of destiny indeed, had he ever learned of it.

His obstinacy destroyed his relationship with his mother. He responded to her strict commands and punishments with an intractability that drove her to even more draconian pedagogic measures. She also thwarted his chemical studies. Because of her he sought a professional field in the vast expanse of the Austro-Hungarian monarchy that on the one hand would not be too close to the Ministry of the Interior, where his father labored, and on the other was as far removed as possible from her vicinity. When she died, he was in far-off Bosnia. He shed no tears for her, nor did he ever mention her—not so much as a single word—to me or my sister, though he liked telling us about his father.

Of my paternal great-great-grandfather I own a miniature and of his son, my great-grandfather, a daguerreotype, but of my grandfather I have only a single photographic portrait, which I cut out of a magazine from the turn of the century, where it appeared on the occasion of the opening of a building he had designed. In the correctness of his frock coat he shows an almost fraternal resemblance with my maternal grandfather; although lacking the latter's short-trimmed beard and overbearing self-importance, he shares the same manly solemnity, stiffened by ascot and starched shirt as if by armor, typical of the period and of Western Europe's last empires, both Victorian and Habsburg. The amused shrewdness in the corners of his eyes—a roguish hint?—is barely cloaked by the discipline of the functionary; he managed to climb the hierarchic ladder from government architect, by way of privy councillor and department head, all the way to ministerial councillor.

My grandfather hoped for a similar or even more glittering career for his son, but my father's rebellious disposition ran counter to such hopes. Some of his youthful pranks (painting a moustache on himself with silver nitrate, which took months to wash off) seem to express the fashion of the time rather than individual singularity: the turn of the century has a whole literature testifying to the likes of it. More serious were the conflicts that developed between father and son in my father's last years as a student.

In accordance with his rank and position, my grandfather was unconditionally loyal to Emperor Francis Joseph I. This was not in contradiction to the Italian origins of the family, which he proudly acknowledged, but rather was strengthened by these ultramontane traditions. The Rezzori name derives from a fief in Sicily which, until the Bourbons, had belonged to the Holy Roman Empire of German Nations. Thus, Rezzoris had always been loyal subjects of the Habsburg monarchy. After an offspring of the family by the name of Ambrogio, as ambitious as he was poor, migrated to Vienna in 1750 by way of Lombardy (an Austrian possession at the time), the Austrianization of the family proceeded with all due speed: Ambrogio's son still was called Giovanni Battista, but his son bore the name Johann Nepomuk. And Johann Nepomuk's son was none other than my grandfather Wilhelm. Though he liked being called Guglielmo and spent every moment he could spare from his official duties on the Adriatic, he was a Habsburg subject through and through. Quite in contrast to my father, Hugo, who was swept along by the *Sturm und Drang* zest of the Greater Germany movement.

This was a secondhand Storm and Stress, fomented by the murkiest impulses of the time. When in later years my father, having become at least as conservative in spirit as his progenitor, ranted against the calamitous consequences of the French Revolution, he overlooked the fact that one freakish revolutionary offshoot was surely the Napoleonic Wars, which in turn helped to produce the disastrous German nationalism to which he had fallen prey so blindly in his youth (including its raging anti-Semitism). The strange reciprocity between spirituality and daimon inherent in any enthusiasm—enthusiasm that often deteriorates into fanaticism and corrupts the original purity of great ideas (and, inversely, filters pure intentions and aspirations from what is foul, placing them in the service of the devil)—seems to emerge quite regularly with each new generation. And nothing seems more difficult for the young than to elude the currents of their time. My grandfather's cast-iron monarchical loyalty had no argument strong enough to muster against the collective folly of youth; on the contrary, it served only to inflame his son's pigheaded stubbornness.

This led to unpleasant scenes. That he was sent from the family dinner table because, with an irony anticipating that of Musil's, he asserted in the presence of guests that the Emperor Francis Joseph I was certainly not the model for all of Austro-Hungary's full-bearded janitors but, rather, that it was he, first servant of the state, who assiduously emulated the janitors, this is to be counted among the more harmless conflicts. Much worse was that he adhered to the Break with Rome movement and left the Catholic Church. A final rupture became unavoidable when he participated in the Badeni riots. Count Badeni, minister of the Interior at that time, provoked the German nationalists by favoring the Czechs in a school reform. The students took to the streets, my father was arrested and, as an ardent admirer of Georg von Schönerer, challenged a high police official to a duel in which shots were exchanged. As a result, he was stripped of his newly acquired commission as an officer in the reserves, which meant the end of the many hopes his father had entertained for his future.

He hesitated at the university between chemistry and mathematics but finally decided in favor of structural and civil engineering. What determined his choice was not so much that conforming with the career notions his father still held for him was more promising than the uncertain future of a so-called free profession: rather, he was swayed mainly by the chance to get as far away as possible from his mother, as well as from the bureaucratic environment, which struck him as stuffy and confining. The Austrian monarchy in those days stretched all the way to the southeastern corners of Europe: a colonial empire whose colonies happened to be located contiguously on the same continent. And there was room in it to realize adventurous pioneer aspirations. He joined a railway construction project in the recently acquired province of Herzegovina, which at the time seemed as remote from civilization as Karl May's wildernesses of Kurdistan. When he had earned his first spurs in that service and after some grass had grown over his rebellious aberrations, my grandfather used some pull. Together with a new chief provincial administrator, my father was assigned to the Bukovina: the position was a sinecure.

He played excellent tennis, which led to his introduction to my mother and to their subsequent engagement. She was what is called a good catch—and not only as a tennis partner. So everything now seemed to follow a track toward orderly, normal circumstances. However, long before the First World War eradicated an era of European history and disrupted the old order, it became apparent that this no longer young gentleman hardly fitted the unsettled conditions of the times. He was an anachronism, though in an entirely different way from my mother: she had been molded entirely by an obsolete past, but he belonged to a type whose time had not yet come; to a high degree, he was the "artistic human" Nietzsche anticipated—his nonconformism, his rebellion against the bourgeois social framework, his manifold talents and minitalents, his urge for independence. But he saw himself rather as a representative of the world of the Baroque who had landed in the wrong century.

.   .   .

He attended to his hunting with scientific thoroughness and at the same time with an almost cultic observance of its
traditions, all the age-old lore that invests the hunt with solemn
poetry. He intended to train me in the medieval rigor of venery's
three disciplinary phases: "houndsgroom" to "small-game apprentice" to "stag maturity"; unfortunately, as in all his other
pedagogic endeavors, he had only moderate success. Nevertheless, our relationship changed fundamentally as soon as I was
able to handle a gun. As a child, I had feared rather than loved
him. When he punished in anger, he wasn't choosy as to the
means he used: the closest dog whip came in handy. He seemed
much fonder of my sister than of me, but she belonged to the
female category of the species and as such was the opposite of
everything manly that was connected to hunting. That the divine
protectress of the hunt in antiquity was a goddess, Diana (or, as
he preferred to call her in humanistic pedantry, Artemis), was not
a contradiction. He was fond of expatiating on this subject:
Artemis was not truly a woman but a virago—a male spirit in a
female body, beyond all sexuality, in a higher kind of virginity. A
mortal was among her retinue of nymphs: Atalanta, forsaken
child of King Oinoïs of Arcadia, a great hunter who had wanted a
son and rejected his daughter. Abandoned Atalanta was nursed
and nurtured by a she-bear and accepted by the goddess in her
cortege of hunting companions. When she became nubile, she
was compelled to leave and return to the world of mortals, cast
out from divine purity back into the gloom of the sexual. It wasn't
as if my father disdained this domain of human nature; he
experienced the carnal with full-blooded vitality. But he chose to
believe his own daughter immune to its enticements. He would
have wished her to be a virginal nymph like Atalanta who, upon
her homecoming, had become the perfect hunting companion for
her father. Because my sister was nothing of the sort—she showed
no disposition at all for the hunt—he sought the ideal hunting
buddy in me, one to whom he would pass on all he knew and
loved.

From that moment on, I was no longer a child to him (he hated
children). Even though I was still a boy, he considered me a small

man and as such possessor of an honor that was not to be
violated; he no longer punished me corporeally — the disgrace of a
blow could be expiated only in blood, and he expected me to
appreciate this. He castigated any carelessness in the handling of
arms and the slightest misuse of hunting terms. I was not yet a
dozen years old when I was no longer forgiven for errors when I
confused antlers with attire or hornings; rutting with mating;
singles with brushes; or when speaking of fowl, of fangs or
clutches (in the case of birds of prey), of webs (of swimmer birds)
or, exceptionally, of simple feet (in the case of the Tetraonidae:
capercaillie, woodcock and hazel hen). In comparison to this
rigidly esoteric terminology, Cassandra's linguistic patchwork
was moronic babble, and I wisely took good care not to let any of
her distortions enter my speech with my father.

In anything concerning hunting, he was of unrelenting sternness. In the forest, playful jocularity was replaced by watchful-
ness in all senses, more concentrated than any enjoined discipline, and resulting in the most stringent control. Nor would he
tolerate negligence in attire; even on the hottest summer days an
open shirt-collar was taboo. The slightest complaint about heat,
cold, hunger, thirst or weariness drew harsh reprimand. Thanks
to him, I learned to sleep on the bare ground as in a feather bed,
even when soaked by rain or, in spring during the shooting of the
capercaillie and in late autumn after the stag season, when I
awoke on occasion covered by snow. When I went with my
mother in August to the Carinthian lakes, I was embarrassed to
show my bare legs while bathing, because they were covered with
stings and scabby with scratches from the swarms of mosquitoes
during the buck-shooting season in late May. I had to watch
greedy insects gorging themselves in my blood without being
allowed to chase them off (one has to remain absolutely still when
sitting in wait for game), and ever since, a mosquito bite has been
of no concern to me. In winter, upon returning home from long
treks in the forest, my feet would swell up the moment I took off
my shoes so that they wouldn't even fit into slippers. But when
once my father caught me asleep on a clattering rack wagon, on
which a peasant had given me a lift partway home, I got such a

dressing down that my ears rang: this, after all, was hardly proper form for a huntsman.

His softer side showed when he thought of rewarding me. Like any boy who grows up with air rifles and BB guns as soon as he can hold them, I shot with murderous accuracy. If you showed me a fly on a wall and asked me to nail it in its place with a shot, I would not consider this a great feat. When I was allowed to go with my father shooting ducks, quails or hares, he let me sometimes try a shot with his gun. Of course, I was much too excited to be able to hit anything with his large and heavy gun, and he understood this soon enough. Among the guns at home, there was one I admired ardently. Long before, it had been his gift to my mother, who, however, never went hunting with him; it stood, new and never used, in the gun cabinet—a French gun of the Second Empire from Lebrun in Paris, Lefaucheux .24 caliber, for cartridges with pin ignition. Even then it was a rarity; today it would be a museum piece. Its light weight and elegant design, the beautifully hand-wrought hammers and the damascened barrels were sheer delight. I was overjoyed when one day my father placed it in my hands and took me along to the fields. It was then that the long-dreamed-of miracle happened: I shot a hare, dead center; it rolled in exemplary fashion and lay like a stone; our dog retrieved it in fine order. My father went to the next oak, broke off a twig and presented it to me as my reward. Ordinarily, such a twig is given only for the shooting of nobler game, such as capercaillies, bucks or stags: a pine or oak twig is dipped symbolically in the blood of the bullet hole, the maw and the vent of the felled piece and presented to the huntsman, who then sticks it into his hatband as the day's trophy. For small game one is not given such a trophy except as a special courtesy for the first piece shot by a young hunter. I was delighted, astounded. "It isn't just your first hare," said my father, "but the first piece of game you shot with your own gun."

The days I spent hunting with my father are among the truly happy days of my life—and there haven't been that many. I remember images and episodes of incomparable splendor, brimming with life, in which the beauty of the Carpathian landscape contributed as much as the colorful population. I was allowed to go with my father on his visits to the monasteries, in the surrounds of which we would then hunt together. I preserve in my memory a whole sequence of images—but they are of which of these jewels: Putna, Dragomirna, Suceviţa, Voroneţ . . . ? We are guests of the abbot; with paternal kindliness the prior shows me fifteenth-century illuminated manuscripts in bindings of chased silver; sunlight falls through the high windows, in broad stripes alive with dancing motes of dust, into the semidarkness of the library, and outside, jays are heard quarreling in the pines; my longing thoughts wander to the glories of the autumnal forest beyond the church walls blazing in picture-book colors. I am proud of my father, whose talk with the abbot gives proof of his profound and esoteric knowledge. With envy and sorrow I realize that I shall never get so far in any branch of science. Later we are joined by a half-crazed monk who seems to know more about game than the gamekeeper whom the forestry administration has assigned as our escort. We enter the forest. The monk, in his black cassock and his stovepipe hat on shaggy hair, knows that he is not quite right in the head, but he is a genius at tailoring priestly attires and vestments and is sent all over, to archimandrites and metropolitans, to clothe the princes of the Church. He chatters on as we walk, much to the annoyance of my father, who prefers to observe silence in the woods. Suddenly the monk stops in his tracks as if nailed to the spot: in the fork of the branches of a rust-red beech tree a golden shimmer appears, only to vanish in an instant. For a split second we are granted the sight of one of the forest's most elusive dwellers: a lynx in the wild is very rare. An enigmatic simpleton's smile plays around the monk's mouth. Within minutes, he lures a buck into our sights by tweeting on a leaf of grass spanned between his thumbs. Then he resumes his chatter: he spends most of his time in the woods when he doesn't happen to be busy making a new robe for one of the high priests. I ask him whether he doesn't have a sister: he might be Cassandra's brother.

The hunting rights that went with Father's (professionally legitimate) assignments extended all over the Bukovina and deep into Moldavia; my father took them as his self-evident due and privilege. This gave me a feeling of unrestricted freedom: wherever we went, we were honored guests. But I was at home truly only in that part of the Bukovina which he had deliberately selected, with thorough knowledge of the local topography, as his very own, right in the heart of the Bukovinan Carpathians, between such world-remote hamlets as Cîrlibaba and Rusmoldavita, twenty miles west of the Bargău Pass. Long before I was born, my father built there for himself a hunting lodge made of wood that over the years turned silky gray. It stood in a clearing that sloped down to the swift flow of an ice-cold mountain brook. In the deep water-holes downstream from its innumerable cascades, the trout hung perfectly still; only the gentle fanning of their gills betrayed that they were alive. Otters fashioned their slide chutes in embankments overhung by dense bushes. With the exception of two or three huts of some Huzules who grazed their sheep on the mountain slopes, no human habitation was within miles. The village of Cîrlibaba was an hour away on horseback. The woods all around had hardly ever been touched by human hand and only rarely were visited by some stray shepherd or by a Huzule poacher. To spot and scout stags, we sometimes lived for weeks in the open.

One might have believed that in these circumstances my father would be just as happy as I. Yet a shadow of melancholy often darkened the grave serenity of his comportment while hunting. He saw that such idyllically primeval conditions would soon be over. One day he told me: "Remember this day. It will soon be impossible to spot within the span of a few hours a pair of ravens, two imperial eagles, a golden eagle and a peregrine falcon." He was right. Nor was I ever again granted the pleasure of luring hazel hens all the way to my feet, though we frequently did this right behind the lodge whenever we fancied them for our cooking; or of lying in an old cutting, looking up to the starlit sky through the flying sparks of a short-lived campfire, while the bellows of stags could be heard echoing back from the surrounding hills. On such a night beside a campfire—I was not quite seventeen, and proud as a peacock because I had spotted the herd with the bull stag that had been more elusive in the grease than any other, far and wide — as we sat in silence and listened in the night, I suddenly felt my father's hand pressing something into my own. It was his seal ring, which four generations had worn before him.

A similar recognition came my way only once again, many years later, and not from him. I was with friends in Transylvania in order to study the rugs that the Turks, on the occasion of their generally bloodless capture of the localities, had presented to the peace-loving town elders — rugs now kept in the fortress churches of the small market towns; you can see the dedicatory inscriptions on their so-called appendages (the unknotted endpieces of the underlying fabric). It was spring, at the time of the cherry blossoms. We had stopped at a little town with miniature gabled houses, and all around the snowy globes of cherry trees crowded up the slopes of the hill on the crest of which stood the fortified church. The surrounding fields shone with newly sprouting green, and pale foliage shimmered on the black-and-white-flecked birches. The baroque convolutions of a huge white cloud stood motionless in a sky of immaculate blue. We sat on the market square in an old pub — we should have been wearing wigs and buckled shoes in such a place — and drank the sweet heavy wine of the region; our mood became cheerful and animated, as the innkeeper proudly brought us ever more select vintages from his cellar. In a corner of the room sat an old Romanian *cioban* — a mountain shepherd — who watched our doings with a benign smile. He wore traditional garb — the garb of the old Dacians as it can be seen on the Trajan Column in Rome: a roughly woven linen shirt over close-fitting cotton trousers, girded by a red sash; a sleeveless sheepskin jacket, heavily embroidered in many colors; and high-laced buskins. On his hair, falling to his shoulders in straggly silver-gray strands, towered the *cioban*'s high black lambskin bonnet. His stubbly face shone with guileless sympathy. We invited him to join us for a glass. He accepted. Upon hearing that we had come from Bucharest, the capital, he nodded in acknowledgment, but then pointed at me and said, "But you, you're from the woods. I can tell. You're dressed like someone from the city, but that doesn't deceive me. You grew up in the woods." We all laughed and my friends said they had always known I had come straight down from the trees. But from him, the recognition had been like a patent of nobility. I bowed, grateful and proud, and thought that my father would have been pleased to hear it.

I know — I always knew, intuitively — what the woods meant to my father. He who seeks solitude is a solitary. And he was a solitary to the point of melancholia. Only his defiant contrariness, the innate rebellion in his nature, the stubborn persistence in any decisions or judgments once formulated forbade him to yield to spleen and, at the same time, lent him his air of eternal boyishness. Yet they mutually generated each other: defiance was born of melancholia and melancholia of defiance. At times it seemed incomprehensible that someone of such clear-headed intelligence could be so set in absurd prejudices and outlandish fixed ideas. His view of the world was that of a medieval woodcut. Humanity was divided into those to be taken at full value (huntsmen) and those he called perioecians: the multitude who lived marginally, a motley agglomeration from which he sometimes would pick the odd, queer specimen worthy of passing interest — apothecaries, for instance, because they knew how to mix poisons. He respected conventional painters such as Rudolf von Alt or the portraitist Ferdinand von Raissky and of course painters of animals (all presumed to be hunters) such as Ernst von Dombrowski, in addition to Rubens (because of all that alluring female flesh). He detested music, notwithstanding his zestful morning vocalizing — with the exception of Richard Wagner, ideologue of the Greater Germany movement. All this was proof of a disarming mediocrity in matters of taste. But his lack of cultural sophistication was compensated by a decisiveness in choice that was the mark of both his intelligence and his obsessions. Anything connected with the military was distasteful to him ever since he had lost his commission as reserve lieutenant. Though he rose to the rank of cavalry captain in the

First World War, anything to do with soldiering was repugnant to him. Socially unacceptable were all those in trade, and totally despicable was anyone dealing in money.

This judgmental hierarchy — which, incidentally, did not assist him in his own handling of money — produced some deplorable effects. Before I was old enough to serve as his hunting apprentice and companion, he took a liking to a young man who, although the son of a former captain in the imperial medical corps — that is, an academic renegade who had deserted into the military — at least answered to the Germanic name Ingolf and, more important still, distinguished himself by a feverish passion for hunting. For a time he was my father's favorite and accompanied him on all his shoots; he was, to my intense resentment, presented with the gift of some rifles and was praised to the skies. However, the young man also had to think of his future and therefore entered the service of a bank. From then on, my father no longer knew him and barely reciprocated his greeting when they met.

While such attitudes were already close to mental derangement, my father's anti-Semitism was outright pathological. This aberration even crept into the articles he wrote for hunting magazines. What the chosen people can possibly have to do with the observation that longbills tend to skim along forest lanes and drift toward smoke remains totally unfathomable, but he managed to find the association — as, for instance, that no lure is of any use if one happens to encounter a Jew in the morning before the hunt, or that Jews nowadays even have the impudence to participate in snipe shoots. Such idiotic derogations were eagerly printed in German periodicals of the 1930s, though this did not mean that my father was a friend of National Socialism. Much as the nationalist element in the Greater Germany concept appealed to him, he was repelled by its socialist component, on sociological rather than ideological grounds. Together with Lord Russell he shared the view that one had to be a very great gentleman to be a good socialist. Who was not a gentleman had better keep out of politics if he did not wish to be placed under police supervision as a club-swinging anarchist. He showed me some illustrated magazines on whose title pages could be seen pictures of the new

Führer of what soon was to become the Greater German Reich. "It's all very fine and well," my father commented, "Germany rises once more. But have a look at this fellow: I wouldn't hire him as a stable boy!"

He would not even concede to the new regime its hatred of Jews, which in his eyes was a privilege reserved to him and his peers. "To be sure," he would say, "Jews are blood-suckers, but that doesn't give anyone the right to steal from them." That much worse was done to them he preferred to deny. "Admittedly, in Russia pogroms were possible—and might even happen in our day. But the Germans are a cultured nation." (After all, they produced Nietzsche and Wagner.) When the followers of the Romanian anti-Semitic leader A. C. Cuza started to beat up Jews, he closed his eyes: it happened, he said, because the Jews in the countryside exploited the peasants. His moral condemnation was directed at anything having to do with or motivated by money; and as everyone knew, money was the main concern of the Jews.

On one occasion his prejudice caused me such intense embarrassment that I began to doubt all his notions. It was prior to the great depression of 1929; I was barely fifteen years old but was considered an equal by my father, while my mother still treated me as a petted child. I saw myself somewhere in the middle of those two contrasting attitudes, each of which probably held some truth. As a boy, I played at cowboys and Indians; as a moony adolescent, I saw myself playing the role of future worldling and ladies' man. The movies provided the models for those dreams in the persons of Rudolph Valentino, Douglas Fairbanks or Lionel Barrymore, according to one's mood. The female dream goddesses were Lia de Putti, Louise Brooks and, ultimately, Greta Garbo. Out of sight of my father, I brushed brilliantine in my hair and wore white-and-brown co-respondent shoes with baggy white Oxford trousers. Among the young ladies of whom I was enamored, one was the local tennis champion. In those days, one did not yet play in bathing suits. The headband and white skirts ending above the knee featured by Suzanne Lenglen lent even to young girls a feminine allure that compelled us, their young male partners, to observe a gentlemanly comportment all the more pronounced in its punctilious correctness for being precocious.

The president of the tennis club was a Jewish banker, *the* fashionable man in town. He had known my mother's family for decades and treated me with the most engaging courtesy. That he was also a hunter goes without saying: there hardly was a sport in which he did not participate. That to my father hunting was not a sport but a sacral act was another matter. In any case, the two Nimrods had never met. It so happened that a big drive shoot was arranged on which I was allowed to accompany my father. When we arrived at the meet and got out of the car, my father froze in his tracks. Among the guests who had arrived before us was the Jewish banker. My father turned to me and said cuttingly, "I'm afraid we're in the wrong place. We were supposed to come for a shoot, not to the stock exchange." He turned on his heel and went back to the car. Before I could follow him, the banker came up to me, shook my hand most politely and said, "I trust we'll see each other soon for tennis." I bowed in agony and hurried after my father. He spoke not one word to me on the way home or for the next few days.

It need hardly be said that such eccentricities did not make him friends. But the prevailing tolerance in a region distinguished by so motley a mixture of ethnicities, where everyone accepted the others with all their peculiarities, with either a sardonic smile or an indifferent shrug, conferred a kind of fool's license on mavericks like my father. Few had much esteem for him. He made no bones about the fact that he counted Romanians (after Czechs and Poles) among the body-strippers of the corpse of the defunct Dual Monarchy. Russians, Poles and Ruthenians were mere colonial populations. He saw himself as a leftover functionary of a liquidated empire. "We have been left here as a kind of cultural fertilizer," was one of his favorite sayings. With violent abhorrence he rejected any identification with the local ethnic Germans of the Bukovina, whose black-red-and-gold Teutonic affectations, elastically adapted to Romanian conditions, seemed to him as presumptuous as the anti-Semitism of the Third Reich philistines. Aryan zealotry and hatred of Jews were not hallmarks of the aristocracy: quite the contrary; in those days they were the characteristics of the newly risen bourgeoisie. Withal, he had an inkling of the dangers inherent in such pettifogging fanaticism. "Such people always tend to exaggerate," he would say.

At that time, however, he could still count on many people approving of his peculiar ideas—though not my mother. His thoughtless excesses and oddities she would counter with the terse comment: "One's mind is well rested when one has so little in it"—one of her few ironic remarks. On the whole, she thought of him as literally insane and of his insanity as directed maliciously against her. That there were other women who found his traits amusing enraged her. She hated him too much to be jealous, but she felt ridiculed by the pleased complicity with which these other women laughed and carried on in a lightheartedly cheerful manner with him. During their life together she suspected him, probably with good reason, of extending his frequent professional assignments not merely to hunt but also to spend part of his time at various estates where he was on equally—if not more—intimate terms with the lady of the house as with his host. That he never even suggested taking my mother along was a social affront that she held as much against the innocent hosts as against him.

I don't believe that his escapades were accompanied by much passion. He was sensual but unsentimental in his relations with women. Yet those who knew him well knew that he could be unreservedly affectionate. In this too his defiant contrariness was involved. He too had experienced a youthful infatuation he had not gotten over—with a highly musical young lady by the name of Olga, who all her life kept contact with my sister and me. This unfulfilled love—which in his case surely meant a love not killed by marriage—left him disappointed, with a scornful attitude toward women.

The admixture of self-irony could be misleading. He frequently advertised his crushes with such abandon, for all the world to see, that one could hardly deem them serious even when they were. He serenaded the lady of his heart of the given moment in his early-morning vocalizings, praised her beauty and virtues at the top of his voice, showered her with flowers and the disastrous products of his painterly zeal, and was offended if she did not decorate her rooms with his capercaillies bubble-plopping their mating calls in the rosy dawn or his stags bellowing in autumn mists. Not all women were willing to become his desired playmates; when one or the other obliged him, he soon carried the game to such lengths that she was forced to break it off if she did not wish to be hopelessly compromised. I recall a significant episode from my childhood: one of my mother's sisters came from Vienna for a visit, my much beloved Aunt Paula. She, my mother, my sister escorted by her temporary English—or French?—governess and I holding on to the hand of Cassandra are taking a demure walk in the People's Park. Along one of the avenues my father approaches from the opposite direction, in the company of a lady. The exchange of salutations between the grown-ups is icy. I can't understand why and notice only that my father and the lady are dressed precisely in the same way: both are wearing traditional Austrian costume, which was beginning to be rare in the Bukovina but was nevertheless worn occasionally, especially by hunters. I am innocent enough to see in this harmony of attire—gray loden with green facings and side braidings, and stag-horn buttons—nothing more shadily significant than an entertaining masquerade, and I cheerfully crow my discovery that even their cuff links are identical: stag teeth set in gold. Without a word my mother tears us from our escorts, turns on her heel and majestically sweeps us away, followed by the crestfallen aunt, the deeply shocked governess and an incomprehending but amused Cassandra.

When my father observed greater discretion in later years, he did so mainly out of consideration for my adolescent sister. If one assumes that there really is such a thing as a "single great love in life," then my sister was his. Surely he also loved my mother in his unromantic way and would have known how to invest his feelings with greater affection if only she had met him halfway. That he was not insensitive to her charm he revealed on many occasions: with the gifts he gave her, the books he sent her even after they had separated, such as, surprisingly—in some way as a counterweight to his mating capercaillies and bellowing stags—*Sonnets to Ead* by Anton Wildgans, and also, almost as antidote, the scandalous diaries of Franziska von Reventlow. Unfortunately, he could not dampen his humorous impulses; he had overpowered her with indomitable vitality from the very beginning of their marriage, provoking ruffled resistance, then stiffness and ultimately anger. Rarely can there have been a more unhappy combination of temperaments, and when he said, "It's all chemical, anyway," he spoke a heartrending truth. They were certainly not well matched.

In the case of my sister, the chemistry was right: she was blood of his blood, though quieted by the thinner blood of our mother, and curbed as well by a clear intelligence, similar to his own but more disciplined. Her love for him was as unconditional as it was luminous. She would sometimes shake her head at him but laughed as she did so. In amusement she would follow his scurrilous train of thought, and she always knew what was meant as a joke and what was to be taken seriously. Her attitude toward his escapades was one of maternal tolerance, and whenever he went too far, she found an outlet for her irritation in the convulsive laughter that shook both of us when we spoke of the vagaries of family life.

My father no longer saw her during the last year of her life, which she spent partly in Vienna, her spirit unbroken despite the futile and tormenting efforts of the doctors to check her inexorable decay, and partly in a sanatorium near Hall in the Tyrol. She loved the Tyrolean Alps, but there was another reason for this choice. Of the separation from him, she spoke only once, when I saw her for the last time. She said: "If he were here, he would give me something to save me from this death-in-life." It was as if she and he, in perfect understanding of their psychic accord, wordlessly had agreed to spare each other the sight of their dying. He did not visit her during her last months in the Tyrol, respecting her discipline in dying, the same discipline he himself displayed at his own end. It was based on the sober conviction that dying is a strictly private matter that cannot be shared with anyone, and that the pain is only sharpened if one allows this ultimate and most revealing manifestation of one's innate archsolitude to be witnessed by the one person whose love enabled one, fleetingly, to deceive oneself as to its inescapability.

Despite my love for him, which never for an instant was diminished by the usual and allegedly unavoidable father-son conflict, I could never deceive him on this point. With the exception of the mutually shared hours of hunting pleasures, which each of us might have experienced just as well with some other congenial intimate, we left each other alone. Neither of us was given the blissful ability to communicate our emotions. True, on many occasions he gave me touching proof of his affection. We were not estranged or at a distance from each other; on the contrary, we were close — yet noncommittally so. There was never between us the same degree of intimacy as between him and my sister. Various experiences I have had with my own brood lead me to surmise that the much vaunted parent-child love is closely linked with the nurturing an infant receives between the stage of his helplessness and his first expressions of independent development. Without doubt, a father's soul is touched more deeply when he observes in the eyes of his newborn daughter how he is beginning to glow for her like a star on which, with each passing day and with growing consciousness, she bestows her smile, than when, upon meeting his almost five-year-old son for the first time, he sees how the boy stares at him as at a stranger, turns around and speedily takes refuge in the arms of his nurse. To this must also be added "chemistry." Psychologists of all schools will have to relegate many of their pet theories to the wastebasket once the cross-reactions and interplay of purely physical emanations are elucidated more fully.

It need be said, however, that my father showed me affectionate understanding even in my early childhood. I was in the habit, as soon as I was put to bed, of crawling entirely under the bed covers. Embryonally curled up in that uterine cave, I made up all kinds of stories — or more accurately, situations that were as eloquent as stories. These were surely proto-erotic: I can still feel the intimate passion with which, as I fantasized tender episodes, I would press the back of my left hand with the right hand against my cheek, as if it were a loved one asking to be caressed. Whenever the blanket was torn away by some adult wanting to find out what the devil I was doing, I was always found in that same innocent position—which should have allayed suspicion that I was masturbating in the dark. But this failed to convince my concerned mother. Cassandra was given strict orders to prevent my holing up under the covers. There was mention of strapping me down to prevent any possible movement: the transformation of a child's cot into a straitjacket. My father forbade such nonsense. Instead, he came in and sat on the edge of my bed one evening and asked me in passing what I liked to do under the covers. "Undercover games," I answered ingeniously. For instance? I said one was called "Naked and Sword." Oh, and others? Another was called "The Golden Rose," and still another "The Wreath." Quite satisfied, my father told anyone interested that my childish fantasy was animated by images of knightly symbolism of the early Middle Ages; this was no reason to think of metempsychosis, since everyone carried elements of humanity's age-old heritage in his innermost self, usually buried at the bottom of the soul and hardly noticed, let alone recognized when they fleetingly floated to the surface in dreams or visions; instruction was given not to disturb me in this storing of psychic flotsam. At that time, the theories of C. G. Jung had not yet reached Czernowitz. My mother opined that my father's follies had now come to the point that it was time to place him under guardianship.

He was less perceptive in the matter of my schooling. The constantly changing governesses—in addition to Bunchy, there were five others during the four years my sister and I were at home: two misses, one of them from Gibraltar, who my father steadfastly maintained wasn't English at all but Jewish; and three French mademoiselles, all of them, to my father's great disappointment, rather homely and each one staying only a few months—unhappy creatures who hated and feared him and his cutting sarcasms, and all of whom he dismissed with a shrug. The nursery was my mother's domain, into which he intruded only to take my sister off on long walks, during which he instructed her lovingly in botanic lore, or to provide her with books—boys' books, really: Viktor von Scheffel's *Ekkehard* and *The Cat Hidigeigei;* all of Scott, Kipling and Twain, but also Brentano, Storm and Fontane; and earlier, children's books like *Alice in Wonderland* and *Pinocchio*. He didn't bother with books for me, apart from occasionally expressing his dismay at the fact that I was so late in learning how to read and write. After my first year at the *Gymnasium* in Kronstadt, he addressed me in Latin, which he spoke fluently and colloquially, and was outraged when I couldn't answer him. "You dullard, how will you make yourself understood if you ever go to China?" he asked. "You don't speak a word of Chinese. The only way out is to talk in Latin to a Catholic priest."

He followed my schooling with utmost skepticism. As a consequence of the constant struggle between his views and my mother's, I was removed from Kronstadt and sent to the German *Gymnasium* in Czernowitz, from which I was expelled almost immediately as a result of some misdeed. For one happy year I was then instructed privately, shunted from one tutor to another; during this time I learned more than in my entire formal school education. It had long since been decided that I was to conclude my schooling in Austria, and at this juncture my father's interest in me was reawakened. The Theresian Academy in Vienna he considered too elitist, infected with affectations stickily preserved in Austrian high society, the nasally drawling snobbism reminiscent of a monarchical gentry. For the Scotch Fathers, also in Vienna, he considered me too stupid. (I believe this view was strongly endorsed by my sister.) In Kalksburg, masturbation was rampant; buggery was prevalent in the Stella Matutina in Feldkirch. Waidhofen on the Ybbs and Waidhofen on the Thaya were not quite right either. But in his assiduous correspondence with school principals, he found one who turned out to be the son of a man he admired above all others: Professor Valentinitsch, the author of the definitive work, six hundred pages long, on the partridge. Thus, I was placed finally in a kind of reform school in

Fürstenfeld, in eastern Styria. My stay there was also of short duration. When, after further years of torture, I was actually graduated and obtained my high school diploma, my father wired me a single word: "Ahi!"—an exclamation current in the Bukovina to express utter amazement.

My great passion at the time was to draw, for which I had an undeniable talent. However, he insisted that first I was to finish some academic work regardless, before devoting my time to graphics. In my various attempts to conform to this request—at the Mining Academy in Leoben, in architecture at the Technical Academy in Vienna and by short digressions into medicine and stage design—I lost those years that truly could have been fruitful for an artistic formation. And then I had to return to Romania to do military service. At that point it turned out that my Austrian high school diploma was not recognized in Romania—with good reason, in my case: I was as ignorant as a carp. So I could become an officer candidate and not have to play soldier for three years, I obtained a supplemental Romanian baccalaureate. Only then, at the age of twenty, did I finally learn something of the history of the country in which I had been born and whose citizen I was, and discover the treasures of Romanian language and literature. I did not hesitate to express my enthusiasm for all this in every way I knew, assailing my father with questions regarding the monasteries he knew so intimately. I met with a strangely cool reaction. He understood my sudden thirst for knowledge of Romania as a sign of my defection from the values of Western Europe, perhaps even as my betrayal of himself: with the newfound pride in my Phanariot forebears, I professed, in his eyes, a shift to my mother's family and thereby also to my Romanian origin. I was strictly forbidden to show myself in Romanian uniform. When I later moved to Bucharest to work there, he wrote me off completely.

But I'm jumping ahead of my story. I still shuttled between confused stays in Vienna, filled with all kinds of other activities and pastimes rather than studies, and vacations in

Czernowitz and the Carpathians that were pleasurably eventful with respect to both erotic and hunting experiences. My head was buzzing more generously with tie patterns and lecherous crushes than with useful knowledge, a fastidiously barbered, sleekly slick lounge lizard in pearl-gray chalk-striped double-breasted suits and suede shoes, blindly absorbed in the trivial doings of bars and nightclubs, in the boudoirs of demimondaines and the beds of dubious hotels. For the latter, my father showed tolerant understanding. When I then declared that I wanted to give up my studies for good, he made one last, lame attempt to persuade me to study what he himself had missed out on: chemistry. After which he gave up. It was too late to make an educated man out of me in accordance with his own standards. From then on he considered me an ignoramus, a mere consumer of illustrated periodicals, a harbinger of the barbarians who, he foresaw, would soon engulf all of Europe.

He perceived this barbaric invasion as advancing from two sides: from Bolshevik Russia as much as from an America dancing in worship around the Golden Calf. "To fashion present-day Americans from the Pilgrim Fathers, we sent them our human dregs," he was wont to say. "Jefferson's America was drowned in the flood of human riffraff flushed in from Ellis Island. With the conquest of the West by the immigrant rabble, the greed for possession has become epidemic. Any act of violence, any fraud, any whopping lie is all right as long as it serves the pursuit of money, success and power. And it infects us all." These were controversial words at a time when America was regarded as the rising star of all future hopes. My mother dismissed them with a shake of the head, as she did with all his oddities.

As for the Russians, no comment was necessary. They were the murderers of the tsar's family, butchers of the flower of their nation. The rabble of the entire world found in them not only a horrible model but a political objective, more bestial, more inimical to life and more alien to reality in its utopianism than the calamitous French Revolution. Moreover, the Russians were threateningly close. The border of Soviet Russia was only a few dozen miles to the east, on the other side of the Dniester, a stone's throw for a motorized army. Sooner or later a little excursion to a neighboring country would be made—that he foresaw with certainty. A chain of events in his personal life made it easier for him to draw his own conclusions. The first of these and the most personal affected him grievously.

My sister had finished her studies and in the course of these—true to tradition—had found the "man of her life": in her case, unfortunately, quite literally the one and only. That this might be merely a harmless school flirtation can be ruled out; the young gentleman showed honorable and serious intentions, and she no less. Nothing could be said against him. He was the scion of a prominent Austrian family who would one day inherit lands in Styria and Galicia, and he had trained—like her—for the diplomatic service. They did not plan to marry right away; after graduating from the Consular Academy, he had to obtain a law degree and spend a year at an American university; his grandmother was American, a fact my father could not carp about, since she was a southerner and, in addition, wealthy. Nevertheless he behaved as if a Lebanese white-slaver were about to kidnap his daughter, and treated the presumptive suitor accordingly when he came to pay his respects and introduce himself.

My sister was deeply wounded. She found it hard to accept that her beloved father could show so little perception, and she held it against me for a long time that, in his most childishly defiant manner, he dropped her forthwith and turned to me, by then a tolerable hunting companion. We spent an unpleasant summer, riven by dramatic tensions—partly in Jacobeni, my mother's newly acquired property that was meant to be transformed into a sanatorium, and partly at the deserted Odaya. Before it was over, the second and third events occurred that were to ease greatly my father's departure from the Bukovina.

The supreme authority of the Orthodox Church in Romania issued a decree according to which administrative officials not belonging to the church hierarchy could be retired after thirty-five years of service instead of the customary forty. My father claimed that this totally arbitrary decree had been promulgated only to get rid of him, but he was not the only person whom the

Church had taken over from the former Austrian civil service. He may not have been wholly wrong, however, in believing he was the main target of the decision to cleanse the Religious Fund of all foreign elements. Greater Romania, the product of the 1919 Treaty of Trianon, was at the peak of its vainglory and did not like to acknowledge that, together with its minorities, it had been bequeathed their cultural heritage. My father never let an opportunity pass to proclaim this loudly, and on one of these occasions he had precipitated a nasty dispute with Professor Jorga, pope of all Romanian historians, an effrontery equivalent to lèse majesté and defilement of the national flag.

Be that as it may, he could only welcome the premature termination of his service, since he could now indulge his passion for hunting without restraint. Unfortunately, there was a snag: the "frocked vultures" argued that he had been in their service for merely eleven years, namely from 1919 to 1930, and that he was entitled to a pension for that period only. Pension for the remaining twenty-four years, from 1895 to 1919, he kindly should collect from the Austrians. This was clearly contrary to the provisions set forth in the state treaty regulating the takeover of former Austrian civil servants. But even if the Romanian government had agreed to pay him for that time, it would have meant a severe curtailing of his benefits: eleven years in the service of the church and twenty-four years in that of the state did not equal a full pension for thirty-five years of service, especially if these thirty-five years were to be counted for the customary forty. My father was ready to submit his case forthwith to the courts, where undoubtedly he would have prevailed if he had had the support of similarly affected colleagues. But of these, none was ready to make a move: they were all of shorter service and his juniors in rank, and trusted in some future compromise.

While negotiations in this matter were pending, he was the victim of an additional misfortune. For years he had undertaken to collect and transfer the retirement benefits of colleagues who had been pensioned earlier and who had returned to Austria. By giving him power of attorney for these transactions, they saved themselves the time and the bother of coming back from God knows where to collect their monies. While at the bank collecting this large sum of money, the yearly remunerations of several high-ranking colleagues, he placed the entirety in a billfold next to him on the counter of the bank window and filled in the forms for the transactions; when he was finished, the billfold was gone. He had to make up the money from his own pocket. He always had lived well above his means and was heavily in the red at the bank. The bank proceeded as banks are apt to do: it granted him the credit and in return took everything he still had. The beautiful dream of living henceforth in the woods and only for hunting dissolved.

He was not the sort to lament such strokes of fate. His mood was in a minor key only when he spoke of his diminishing chances for hunting because of the "damn continuous and forever grow-ing depredation of God's nature by the ever greedier and more numerous human herd." What then remained for a huntsman but to withdraw to the depths of the woods, where they were still relatively untouched, where one's last shot and the dog's barking in sorrow for a dead master would be lost in pristine remote-ness . . . ? But he would wait a while longer before taking this step. For the time being, thanks be to God, the Carpathians were still rich enough in trees and game to make the heart of any true huntsman leap with joy at the mere thought of it. Even as he saw his dreams in the Bukovina evaporate into thin air, he began to realize their fulfillment by other means elsewhere. The virgin woods were his only true home and hunting was now his only profession. Count Mikes of Zabola, who owned immense tracts of forests in Transylvania, was looking for a manager to organize high-priced shoots for foreign hunters. My father applied for the position and was accepted.

There, in Zabola, in 1932, he received the news of the death of my sister. He, who was in no way superstitious, reported a strange occurrence in this connection. He had spent the night in the forest under the skies and had been awakened by a something that most tenderly stroked his cheek. He had not doubted for a moment that it had been a message from his dying daughter, even though he tried to explain it away by the touch of a moth: but could there be a moth in early March in mountain woods? a bat?

the wing of a wood owl? Whatever: he knew my sister had died, and went down to the village to collect the telegram with the news of her death. Countess Hanna Mikes later told me that he sat motionless on a bench in front of the castle, holding the telegram in his hands, while the tears ran down his cheeks. Then he got up and returned to the woods.

His stay in Zabola was short. He had a falling-out with the count, who wanted to sell shoots of stags that my father considered not sufficiently reconnoitered, let alone securely positioned. They separated in anger. My disputatious father immediately wrote an article, triumphantly printed in a German hunting periodical, in which he warned against misleading promotions of capital game shoots in Romania. The matter was brought before a kind of court of honor of the hunters' collectives in Romania. Its decision overwhelmingly found in favor of my father on all points, praised the manly courage with which he had uncovered a disgraceful blotch on the national honor and committed it to extirpation. He was presented with a ceremonial hunting knife, which he put away in a corner of his gun cabinet with the comment: "Those arseholes would like nothing better than to stick it in my back."

He moved to Hermannstadt (now Sibiu), in the heart of Transylvania. Never for a moment did he grieve for the house of my childhood on the outskirts of Czernowitz. From it he took with him only his guns, his painting gear and his spaniel, Trixy. Even easier to him came his leave-taking from the "Jew city" and the fake "black-red-and-gold Bukoviniensers," the "frocked vultures" and "Russnyaks and Polacks." He loved the Saxonians of Transylvania, who for eight hundred years, as he conceived it, in defiance of the wrongs inflicted on them throughout the history of Eastern Europe, wedged in between Hungarians, Romanians, Turks, Wallachians and Poles, had nevertheless managed to preserve a German heritage to his own liking: pre-Bismarck, even pre–Frederick the Great, also pre–Maria Theresa and, in fact, anti-Austrian. He capped the Wartburg pathos of his youthful *Sturm und Drang* period with this Meistersinger version of the idea of the Reich. That it wasn't so very different from the

Bukoviniensers' "phony black-red-and-gold Germanistic to-do," which he despised, need hardly be stressed. But he believed that the evidence supported his assertion that the Germanophilic attitudinizing of the Bukovina Swabians was nothing but presumptuous affectation: they deformed spoken German when they opened their mouths — in truth, it *was* an ugly dialect — and, generally, got along well with Jews.

Such wrongheadedness in an otherwise intelligent and highly educated person of superior character is less surprising when one remembers the spiritual situation of the period. In those days, the nebulous romanticism that conjured a mystic aura around the idea of a Greater German Reich was an infection spreading like an epidemic among German-speakers in Central Europe, a disease to which not even the Transylvanian Saxonians were immune, even though they were absolutely sure of their unequivocally defined identity. They were first of all Transylvanians, German in origin and language but completely independent and themselves almost aboriginal to the region: deeply rooted in a country they had inhabited for almost a thousand years, with a self-assured culture they had created themselves (and, incidentally, a culture that conferred much of value to the people between whom they lived, the Hungarians and the Romanians). They were connected to the German world of their origin, but no more emotionally tied to it than, for instance, the German Swiss. But when they forgot all this to follow the mythic call to greater national unity trumpeted in its most depraved form, that of the Third Reich, they lost everything: their country, their culture and their identity.

There was, however, quite some time left before reaching that point, though it was only half a decade — time appears short only in retrospect. My father blossomed in Transylvania. The world of the Saxonians seemed to give reliable support for all his psychic needs. Here he no longer had to play the thankless and tiresome role of the leftover colonial master. Though Romanians were Transylvania's sovereigns, in this region they comported themselves with discretion. The problems of living together and of getting along had been fought over and settled long before.

Hermannstadt, a thoroughly German city, prettily centered around its cathedral, was a world apart from Czernowitz, a "town of the steppes" and devoid of tradition. The burghers' houses were strung together along streets and perspectives of venerable dignity. The gables left over from the late German Renaissance evoked, indeed, an atmosphere reminiscent of the Meistersingers; the baroque and classical façades were of old Austrian vintage. The Saxonians themselves were a solid, upright sort of people, and their broad dialect resembled that of the Baltic with which my father felt affinities. In like manner he was fond of Hungarians; having served in a regiment of Hussars, he spoke Hungarian better than Romanian. The countryside was magnificent, large forests were close by, and the trophies of the bucks were several degrees better than elsewhere. What more could he ask for?

It never entered his mind to think of himself as impoverished. Curiously enough, his painting earned him some rather substantial pocket money, though the pictures no longer consisted exclusively of mate-calling capercaillies and bellowing stags. He produced pleasing watercolors of the churches, which he knew better than anyone else: his impressions of Voroneţ, Dragomirna, Suceviţa and all the others found buyers in friends with a taste for folkloristically accented art. In fact, a series of these paintings of monasteries, done for the Bishop of Hotin, is now shown with great pride in the Museum of Arts and Crafts in today's Chernovtsy. And he did have friends. He no longer scorned contact with the locals as he had in the Bukovina. A friend of old was the Saxonian bishop Dr. Viktor Glondys. Another was the royal Romanian hunt marshal of that time, Colonel von Spiess, a *Ganghofer* type in folksy flowing pelerine, eagle wings adorning his Lettow-Vorbeck hat, and an open Schiller collar worn with a jacket that, thanks to an abundance of stag horn and oak leaves, combined the glamour of a marshal's uniform with the woodsiness of a forestry apprentice's jacket, and that, in its modishness, might have incited the envy of Emperor William II or Hermann Göring. Colonel von Spiess had a bevy of charming daughters, with whom my father surrounded himself as with a garland of flowers. These beloved friends stood as assurance that he could feel welcome in his new surroundings.

He lived modestly in a small house with a housekeeper, Mrs. Agnete, who—as was to become apparent later—knew how to feather her own nest. There wasn't much to be had. Occasional remaining artifacts of his once expensive life-style showed his insistence on quality even in reduced circumstances. He had always lived rather abstemiously: he liked good wine but drank only moderately, and smoked each day four or five cigarettes which he rolled himself. One pocket in each of his jackets was lined in doeskin: in it he kept long-fibered blond Macedonian tobacco and some very thin cigarette paper. I never overcame my envious impatience as I watched him lower one hand into that pocket, listening almost pensively to its hidden manipulations, and come up a few moments later with a perfectly rolled ciga-rette, the paper of which he merely had to moisten with the tip of his tongue to close it before lighting up. My efforts to emulate this sleight of hand led only to a disgusting mixture of crumpled paper and tobacco crumbs that could not be brushed from the pocket seams. When I asked him how on earth he managed to accomplish it, I got as answer, with the same astonished shaking of his head that my and others' inadequacies elicited from him: "How else can you do it when you're on horseback holding the reins in one hand and have only one hand free?" It was left to me to ponder whether some Catholic priest in China might give me a more illuminating explanation in Latin. His hands, incidentally, were like rough paws, coarse and red from sunburn and frostbite, but his nails were regularly cared for by a very pretty manicurist.

Whether it was because he relished the idyllic and easygoing yet by no means narrow-minded town of Hermannstadt, or because his mellowing sunset years mitigated his harsher traits, he seemed to me more amiable and relaxed and less aggressively eccentric. His figure soon became an integral part of the town-scape of Hermannstadt, for he was set in his habits and these led him, day after day, through the same streets—he called them his "runs": easily recognized from afar by his height, his rural clothing and his old hunting hat, he walked with deliberate steps, his feet pointing slightly outward (a dandy's affectation from the turn of the century, which one can see in the caricatures of Caran d'Ache) in his mirror-polished, rakishly narrow custom-made shoes, one of the expensive relics from better days, his black-and-white cocker spaniel, Trixy, following at his heels like a shadow. That he now wore a short-trimmed ice-gray beard did not diminish the hardy freshness of his cheeks. His blue eyes flashed above cheekbones that a fine web of small red veins transformed into rubicund apples. Whenever he lifted his hat in greeting—which he always did with an ironically wide flourish—his shining head would appear like a dark ivory billiard ball. He always looked as if he had just emerged from his bath, the blood circulation still invigorated by the ice-cold shower, scrubbed dry with rough towels, and the skin freshened by sharp lotions. His fragrance was not ostentatious but unmistakably individual: a highly masculine, acidulous scent, composed of good soap, leather and fresh linen from a closet in which he also kept heron feathers, an ermine skin, a little box with medications (some of them highly poisonous) and pistols emitting a faint whiff of gun oil and gunpowder. He no longer practiced pistol shooting in the first light of dawn; his present dwelling was too confined for that. But it was now his pleasure to let a visitor select a green nut on a tree in a neighboring garden that he then would shoot off its stalk with unfailing accuracy.

It goes without saying that he was not entirely free of his old crotchets, oddities and paradoxes. Any talk with him might be diverted toward a dead end by his pedantry. All too often he would interrupt a general conversation to leave the room and return with a pile of lexica and encyclopedias, so as to ascertain a disputed word or an ambiguously defined concept, or correct a wrongly spoken name. His lack of self-criticism in the matter of his painting was disarming, but it seemed inexcusable and irksome that he also stuck to the most incomprehensible prejudices and fixed ideas. Among these were several that he himself breached in practice, especially those involving women. In his world order and following Nietzsche (and his favorite author, Péladan) in an interpretation rather more naive than philologically accurate, he classified the weaker sex as belonging to a species predestined for bondage and submission. But when actually confronting a woman, he would suddenly emerge as a compliant knight, extolling the virtues of his chosen one to the heavens. His tendency scornfully to dismiss whatever did not conform to his expectations in no way contradicted his basic inclination to faithful devotion. I was not surprised that he asked me to propose to my mother that she might return to him should the discord between her and Philip become unbearable.

She took it with a hint of a sarcastic smile around her slightly compressed lips, which at the same time drew down at the corners in bitter disdain, and there was even the beginning of a contemptuous nasal snigger, as if she understood only too well the true motive for this belated contrition: past middle age, impoverished and deserted by his "other females," he would try to come back to her in repentance. Nothing could illustrate more clearly how deeply she had misunderstood him all her life. To be sure, he had not always been considerate of her, he had failed to behave well, scarcely mindful that he had married not a mature, experienced woman but a dream-besotted child, rigidly educated according to prevalent doctrines that she then followed meekly as a lamb, in both thought and deed. In all their life together, she had never understood that he too thirsted to be redeemed. And though he would have liked nothing better than to show her this, he would have done so with deplorable awkwardness. His lovable traits—his limpid lightheartedness and playfulness—drummed down on her as something frightening. Everything about him was a size too large for her, too impetuous. Significant for this was the moral indignation with which she complained, even decades later, that he had not understood her loathing of his physical advances. (She did not speak of this often, but at one time or another everyone she considered an intimate—an ally—learned of it.) She spoke with the tight-lipped restraint she considered appropriate to so delicate a subject, summed up in the verdict: "In a word, a man of uncontrolled animal instincts." Had she not had to witness how her husband, his amorous approaches rebuffed by her, disappeared for hours into the darkroom with one of her cousins, whom allegedly he instructed in the art of photography? She shared the opinion of him that presumably she was accepted in Czernowitz: cold, arrogant, vain and mad, but mostly mad — an opinion that probably is held all over concerning those who tend to react to stupidity, provincialism and philistine narrowness of mind with acts of jocular rebellion à la Till Eulenspiegel.

He lost none of his bright nature. Of his dead daughter he spoke without a trace of sentimentality and with a loving cheerfulness, as if she were still alive and he were merely reporting an engaging example of her graceful charm. Once he did this quite extensively. He had come back to the Bukovina on the matter of his unlawfully premature retirement from the Religious Fund. The dispute between my mother and Philip concerning the Odaya finally had resulted in my usurping the property, so that now I considered myself the proprietor of this forsaken piece of no-man's-land. I found it amusing to invite my father to *my* shooting grounds for a change, though I didn't have much to offer: a few ducks and hares in the wetlands of the Prut. But I knew that he would be pleased to see again the house in which my sister had been born and in which she had spent her first four years more under his own loving care than that of her repeatedly absent mother. We both were aware of my sister's ambivalence about the Odaya, oscillating between mute and bitter resentment of the essentially Eastern, only marginally European nature of the Bukovina and, on the other hand, her love, repressed into a mythic past, for the land of her childhood: the grove of firs, beeches, birches and willow trees that lay behind the manor house like an oasis in the desolate landscape. A small pond and two or three benches on its winding paths, laid out God knows when, gave it the appearance of a park, even though this pretty stand of trees soon diminished into bordering scrub, lost in the wide spaces of maize fields and the Prut River marshes. Jays, magpies, rollers and songbirds took refuge in the crowns of those trees, and from their mystery-laden dusk could be heard the crepuscular hooting of wood owls and the ringing song of nightingales; woodpeckers, their wings stretched or retracted, flitted to an fro in whirring flights and accompanied their rising or descending loops with the corresponding scales of their laughter. Hedgehogs rustled in the leafage under the brushes; frogs croaked in the reed banks around the pond, in which an old rowboat with a seat made of curlicued cast iron lay rotting. My sister, conscious of my mother's complicated feelings about the Odaya, balked at spending time there; she preferred to dream of the lost past while reading the fairy tales of Brentano and Fouquet's *Undine*. But for a child who had been taken in hand by a loving father, to whom every chirping bird and every scurrying mouse, each crocus blossom sprouting from the spring-moist soil, and each hazelnut breaking free from the heart-shaped leaves of its stem had been shown, explained and given, a child who then had had abruptly to leave all this munificent glory—the place was bound to remain in the soul as a lifelong and lovingly preserved dreamland.

On a blue-golden autumn day in the year 1937 I strolled with my father through those river marshes. We had shot a few ducks; my father, to his joy, also a late longbill. The dogs were working diligently with their tails straight up in the air when a hare abruptly jumped from the undergrowth and crossed my sight. I fired a shot after it—it was one of those shots whose success has something of the divinely ordained: the hare rolled over perfectly and lay stock-still, dead already when the next dog reached him for its recovery . . . and in an instant of illumination I knew: this is a final point, the full stop at the end of an era. Never again would there be for us a repetition of such a day in this country.

I took the hare from the dog, looked at my father and knew that he felt the same. He gave me a brief nod, we stopped our hunt and went home. My father continued to show signs of unrest. He declined the dinner I had ordered prepared for us and insisted on being brought back to town. During the drive, he spoke of my sister. Among the anecdotes that showed her in the ideal transfiguration into which his loving memory transposed her, the one that amused him the most was the following: It was shortly before the onset of her disease; she had started working for the International Danube River Control Commission in Galatz, whence she sent him the following telegram: "Important discovery: Teskovina [a rough Romanian brandy] with soda almost as good as whiskey!" She could have given him no better proof that she was his true daughter. But for the first time he said this as of someone dead. It was the end of an epoch. Indeed, it was the last time we were to see each other.

With the year 1938, political events began to overturn each other in frantic succession. In Vienna I experienced the annexation of Austria by what now had become the Greater German Third Reich, and was surprised when my father commented on it in rather restrained terms in a letter. Wasn't this the final realization of his youthful political dreams? A German hunting companion who spent those March days in Hermannstadt told me of a rather strange occurrence: everyone of consequence had assembled around the radio in the house of Colonel von Spiess to listen to the news from Vienna. After the triumphal announcement of the consummation of the Ostmark's "homecoming" to the Reich, the German national anthem was intoned — as is well known, the megalomaniac text by Hofmann von Fallersleben, "Germany, Germany Above All," that was phonily adapted to Haydn's melody for the Austrian anthem "God Save Our Emperor." At the first of these notes, now no longer played in solemnly imperial cadences but blared in marching rhythms, my father made a rejecting gesture and shortly thereafter stood up to take his leave, nervously impatient. He went home. There was no need for an explanation in the house of a former Austrian imperial colonel.

Soon there was hardly any need to explain away my father's growing skepticism of the Third Reich by his all too well-known affinity for paradox. The invasion of Czechoslovakia occasioned a letter in which he expounded for my benefit on the catastrophic consequences that always ensued whenever the storms of history engulfed Bohemia. It may well be that his unconscious association with Sadowa had incensed his Old Austrian feelings against the obvious Prussianization of the Greater Germany idea, about which he commented in his letters in increasingly testy tones.

Father always considered Prussians as not Germans at all but, rather, Wends and thus Slavs, an unpleasantly assertive minority in the German-speaking world. "Prussia," he used to say, "is a typical upstart nation: one of the colonies of the Reich that seceded from the mother country and managed to rise to prominence. Similar developments caused the downfall of the Roman Empire. Frederick II of Prussia dealt the death blow to the Holy Roman Empire of Germanic Nations, whose imperial crown legitimately had been worn for six hundred years by Habsburgs. Later Hohenzollerns, foremost William II, extended the damage to catastrophic proportions. A former colony preserves the spirit in which it was founded and administered. The Prussian concept of the state, according to which each citizen is primarily a soldier, should never have impinged on the old dominions of the Reich. But it isn't merely the calamitous Wilhelminian militarism that is Prussia's legacy . . . " and so on.

Whether he considered later developments with an equally consistent perpiscacity and saw in the Third Reich of Hitler (whom he termed a "vagrant housepainter") the ultimate debasement of a Prussian pseudo-spirit and thereby the true betrayal of his much beloved concept of a Greater Germany is a moot point. He could not express this in letters; even then, any mail reaching the ever larger realm of Greater Germany from abroad was filtered through a censorship that never would have permitted such heresies to go unpunished. Still, I had many reasons to assume that he was greatly pained by what he saw as a profanation of once pure and stimulating ideas, which were then further perverted by misuse. His quixotic disposition prompted him to translate these convictions into action. When the Transylvanian Saxonians became infected by Third Reich delusions, their leader, a Mr. Roth, managed to extort from the Romanian government, under pressure from the German authorities, the privilege of issuing special passports to German-speaking ethnics in Romania. My father declined such a passport with an expression of thanks. He declared that he was a citizen of the Kingdom of Romania and intended to remain loyal to this allegiance. Unfortunately, the Romanians too no longer had much comprehension for such an attitude. As a result, he remained without a passport. But he had no intention of leaving the country.

The year was 1939 and war had broken out. Russia's initially peaceful occupation of Bessarabia and the northern Bukovina took place in 1940. The state treaty that made this possible neither surprised nor deceived my father. "Remain where you are," he wrote to me in Vienna. "One has to go into cover." He too remained where he was. He still hunted occasionally and cultivated a special friendship with a Princess Sayn-Wittgenstein, born a Nabokova—member of a family with whom I was linked by many independently formed friendships. And then his health began to fail. The irony of fate ordained that the illness that felled him was the one of which my mother imagined herself to be the victim: a kidney ailment. In his case, its origin was clear. While visiting friends, he had contracted scarlet fever from their children. That he survived at all at his age bordered on the miraculous. Without waiting for his complete recovery, he then had jumped into an icy river in the dead of winter to recover a piece of game—he wanted to spare his dog. In September 1943 he took to bed with uremia. It was his wish that I not be informed. Dying is the most private of matters. When he realized he was going blind, he resorted to one of the "strong remedies" from his medicine box in the linen closet.

His friend Bishop Glondys had visited him on the preceding day. To his question whether, after all, there was a message for me, my father replied: "Yes. Please tell him I'm sorry to be dying in a year in which the wine in Transylvania promises to be so outstanding."

The Sister

A child's paintings on some sheets of paper: large, wondrously dark-shaded flowers, stemless and floating in space as in the world of the blind. Next to it an owl with reading glasses on its round eyes — a sort of student joke, and also a finely chiseled, very pointed stiletto. All this framed by a branchwork of mistletoe twigs in the Art Nouveau style and inscribed with a name, forming an ex libris. The name sounds neo-Romantic, as from a knight's tale of the turn of the century: Ilse.

Now that I write this down, she has been dead for fifty-six years and not one of those years has gone by without her being close to me in an almost corporeal way—not in the abstract sense of a lovingly preserving memory, but in a well-nigh physical presence, often anything but welcome. Whatever I do or fail to do, whatever happens to me, she stands constantly in front of me, next to me, behind me, observing; at times I even call her to make sure she's there. For fifty-six years—a whole life span—there has not been for me a single happy or unhappy moment, neither success nor failure, no significant or even halfway noteworthy occurrence on which she might not have commented. She is mute but she is there. My life is a wordless dialogue with her, to which she remains unmoved: I monologize in front of her. In the sequence of images in which I experience myself in life, she is included in every situation, as the watermark in the paper bearing a picture: she has the face of a twenty-year-old, clear eyes watching me with an amused air, one brow raised skeptically, full lips, inherited from her father, ironically angled at the corners. The watchful expression is constant; it is always there.

I would not know where to look in me for the key traumatic experience that generated this obsession, nor do I know how I could find it. With psychoanalytical methods? I don't quite believe in them. In the 1930s in Vienna, when I still could have consulted the great Sigmund Freud himself, I came across a copy of his case history of the "Wolfman." I could not imagine how the distraction of this unfortunate man, scion of an assiduously suicidal family, widower after the suicide of his wife as well, a former millionaire whom the Russian Revolution had driven into exile without a cent, saddled with a hysterical and ailing mother who refused to die, himself afflicted with an exemplary checklist of neuroses—I could not imagine how the derangement of this poor devil could be traced to nothing more than that, as an infant, he had accidentally witnessed his parents engaged in *coitus a tergo*. Even today I find myself unable to deny my skepticism about such allegedly scientific assumptions, especially when I'm supposed also to believe that the discovery itself would induce the healing process (which, incidentally, was not the case with the Wolfman).

Nevertheless, deference to the spirit of the times prompted me to push my investigations in that direction—most inadequately, no doubt, since I undertook them on my own, using only the rather crude means at my disposal. With a fine-toothed comb I went through our jointly experienced infancy, as well as through the adolescent years during which I was separated from my sister, all the way to her death at twenty-two—I was eighteen at the time. All I could have come up with on the notorious oilcloth-covered analytical couch was an expression of gratitude to my parents for having arranged—although not millionaires (not Russians either)—for our nursery to be far enough removed from the scene of their (fairly infrequent) sexual activities, to spare us early traumas. Even if this had not been the case, I would have observed such a happening with the same clinical interest with which, instructed by Cassandra, I witnessed similar activities between dogs, cats, rabbits and other animals; the experience left no lifelong repercussions in my psyche. I should add, though, that the nonsexual tensions between our parents and their uninhibited explosions in front of us triggered a fairly complete anthology of neuroses. My efforts to deal with these on my own, without professional rummaging in my unconscious, greatly enriched my life. Insofar as my sister is concerned, however, it may well be that they contributed to her early death.

That she was endowed with a special quality I've heard from all sides and so persuasively that it finally could not be doubted. Nor was this the transfiguration of someone prematurely taken by death, but quite simply something that resisted definition. No one could say precisely what it was that distinguished her, for it could not be illustrated by a specific out-of-the-ordinary quality. She was intelligent, she had my father's cheery temperament, she liked to laugh and had a sense of humor, and she was mature beyond her years. That was all—and yet it was not that alone. She was astonishingly precocious. For her eighteenth birthday, I, fourteen years old, thought of a very sumptuous present: a writing case of green morocco leather, each sheet of stationery engraved with a fist-size monogram. She never used it for her correspondence but kept it reverently; I still have the case to this day. After her death I discovered that on some of the pages she had recorded diarylike notes: lists of books she wanted to read, character sketches of persons she knew, accounts of her pocket money and, strangely enough, a short essay on jealousy. Some twenty years later I showed all this to a friend who understood something of graphology. He was amazed. "Unbelievable that this should be the writing of an eighteen- or nineteen- or even twenty-year-old. It is the fully formed writing of a mature person. A forty-year-old woman with a great deal of experience in life could have written this."

Amateurs of palmistry (and why not, since we are talking of arcane sciences?) may be interested in the fact that her palms showed no other lines than those of the heart and life, the second not notably short. Whether this allows for a conclusion about her exceptional nature I leave undecided. In any case, everyone seems to have noticed her unusual individuality. A sober and worldly old lady, aunt of the young gentleman whom my sister intended to marry, told me: "She would arrive, a young girl of excellent manners, pretty but not of conspicuous beauty, very graceful and well groomed without being ostentatiously elegant, with carefully selected shoes, hats, gloves and other accessories, nothing extravagant, completely natural in her comportment—and yet the attention of everyone present would concentrate on her, without her having done anything to attract it; even old people like myself fell immediately under her spell."

This is how I remember her too—or, I should say, this is the image which for fifty-six years has been imprinted, transparent though indelible like a watermark, on my experience. Naturally, I can also conjure up any number of other images of her, depending on where I stop the filmstrip of my life's record, freely reeling it forward and back to a moment in time when she had not yet turned into a ghost: for instance, to a day in early childhood, it must have been during our refugee period in Austria; I cannot yet climb alone and unaided over a picket fence in our garden, although it is not much higher than the currant bushes bordering it; she stands behind in a meadow plucking flowers, a long-legged girl with the somewhat awkward grace of a foal, typical of a seven-year-old, in a short flowered dirndl dress with a little apron and a big bow in her hair; she watches my ineffectual efforts to join her in the freedom of the meadow and maliciously sticks out her tongue at me.

Another snapshot: She is ten or eleven, I am seven, and we are standing at the nursery window in Czernowitz. I like to hide in that recess; it is the starting point of many of my emotion-filled flights of fancy, with a view over the tree crowns of the People's Park out to the poplar-lined arterial road leading into unknowable remoteness. My sister has planted herself in front of me, looks at the sky and commands: "Turn, sun! And you, moon, stand still!" It is a senseless rigmarole, as I well know, and I also know that she does not have the power to order celestial bodies, but her presumption is all the more vexing, so that I tremble with anger without being able to throw myself at her, as I would like to, because my father is standing next to us, relishing my helpless rage. It is one of the games with which he makes her happy at my expense. I cannot hate him because he is my father. I must not hate her, for she is my sister. I am helpless.

And again: I am awkward with knots and cannot tie my shoelaces by myself. She stands in front of a mirror, deftly undoes the bow in her hair and reties it into a perfect knot with playful ease and speed; then she throws me a mocking glance through the mirror and bounds away.

Frustrating episodes, without doubt. They can be classified together with the humiliation of having to inherit, during the war years and immediately thereafter, when children's clothing was scarce, my sister's underwear, the lace panties slit behind instead of in front; later, when Mother fancied to put us on parade in identical attire, I had to submit to being clad in the same short, light-colored paletots with velvet collars, the legs in gaiters buttoned above the knees, and on our pageboy haircuts — my hair too was cut like a girl's, which in Czernowitz was unusual for boys at the time — the much hated Christopher Robin hats, secured with thin rubber bands, a favorite article of attire for a mother who could not comprehend a boy's soul. I cannot describe the despair with which I tried time and again to bend down one side of the brim so as to transform it into a safari hat or something resembling Buffalo Bill's cowboy hat, only to feel the finger of a governess, with a light nudge, making the stiff brim snap back. My sister would observe this maliciously, and she wore the costume with all the more ostentatious satisfaction since it made her look boyish, while I felt like a little girl in it.

One last small vignette: We stand in the bathroom and are both naked. My sister looks at the thing hanging between my legs and screws up her face in disgust.

Not so fast, my dear psychologists! Let us not jump to conclusions; there were also moments of sibling harmony that offset all antagonisms. Still in Austria around 1917, we had visited acquaintances in a neighboring locality and, back home, were raving about their wonderfully warm toilet. No one quite understands what we are talking about. But our hosts of the day eventually show themselves to be peeved and fail to send their own children on a return visit, as had been promised. They finally disclose our outrage: we had defecated into their fireless cooking box. (Cooking boxes were cubelike felt-lined appliances, used in wartime to save heating material, to finish the cooking and keep food warm. We had seen a *chaise perchée* that looked more or less the same in our grandparents' house in Vienna and had misinterpreted the purpose of this contraption.)

And then again in the Bukovina, after 1919: we have disappeared for a worrisome long time, the whole house is searched until we finally reappear from somewhere, talking confused nonsense, laughing without reason, finally sinking to our knees in front of the nursery stove, tearfully begging God that He may prevent it from falling to pieces, which would cause us to freeze to death in winter. We are put to bed, our temperature is taken but we have no fever. We forthwith fall into a deep sleep from which we regain consciousness only on the following day. This time we speak with delight of some delicious fruit compote which we found in Father's study and consumed almost to the last. It was Father's rum pot, in which, each year, he marinated ripened fruit, berries and green nuts.

The list can be continued. But what is decisive is the fact that in all these episodes from our early time together, even in those in which I stood helpless against her delight in mocking me, I felt my sister to be a part of myself as self-evidently as my arms or my legs. There was as yet nothing that separated us. She did not take advantage of the superiority, conferred upon her by her greater age, as perfidiously as she did later on. She occasionally played tricks on me, which prompted me to complain to Cassandra or to my mother that she was bullying or "ragging" me, but this remained within the boundaries of the perfectly normal; matters were no more tumultuous between us than they usually are between siblings. In vain do I look for occurrences that would correspond to the relations between brother and sister as described by Krafft-Ebing. *Patient Baron F. corporem superiorem partim nudavit et puellas trans pectus suum et collum et osradere*

inbit et poscit, ut transgredientes summa caleibus permerent.
Nothing of that sort. She never tormented me physically. If ever
she should have felt envy for my tiny penis, she was able to repress
it with ease. I suspect that somehow and at some time she had had
occasion to observe the difference between boys and girls and to
be annoyed by it even before my own appearance in her life. In
any case, I cannot remember with the best of intentions an
instance when she would have tried to eliminate that difference
with a knife or a pair of scissors.

Yet one thing is certain: I was not welcome to her. I had to be a
thorn in her flesh. For four years she lived alone in the radiance of
her father's love, unmolested by her mother's shifting emotional
outbursts and in the stable world of the splendor and (deceptive)
self-assurance of imperial Austria. Then one day I appeared on
the scene—and forthwith the splendor faded away: her father
vanished from life, the house that was hers alone, the garden that
was her realm, the toys, the animals, the beings who looked after
her suddenly came under a terrible threat; she had to leave them
from one moment to the next, she went through a terrifying flight
and entered surroundings that were both confined and anguish-
ing, under the exclusive domination of a panicky, nervous mother
who had eyes only for me, the newborn, who devoted all her care
to me and who pushed her aside impatiently, reprimanding and
punishing her both erratically and excessively. She was bound to
associate all of this with my existence. In a word, she held me
responsible for the First World War, and this she made me feel
throughout her short life—although so subtly that the accusation
may seem absurd.

Only after we returned to the Bukovina at the end of the
war did her finely spun, spiderweb-like acts of malice become
obvious. Circumstances may have fostered vindictiveness in her,
if merely because of the festering boredom resulting from the
restriction of our freedom. We lived in a state of suspension that
excluded us from the world at large. House and garden, at the
edge of town in a "villa district," were adjacent to maize fields
and pastures (in those days, cities were not yet girded by mangy
belts of messy construction sites, small industries, auto repair

shops and storage sheds; behind the last houses, open land lay directly before one's eyes), but it was not a landscape in which we were allowed to roam freely. We were enclosed in our garden as in a cage, cordoned off as much from the town as from the fields, which did not belong to us and in our mother's eyes were dangerously wild. We lived as on an island enclosed by the garden's iron picket fence; beyond was the uncertain and alien world in which adventurous souls might find their way about, but certainly not we, who lacked experience.

Our social life was of like insularity. We considered ourselves members of a class of masters, although we were no longer masters of anything, taken over by another class to which we deemed ourselves superior but which, in fact, treated us as second-rate citizens because of the odium attached to an ethnic minority. We felt excluded, but on the other hand, our isolation made us feel out of the ordinary and even that we belonged to a chosen elite. The myth of lost wealth rankled in us but also made us arrogant. All our efforts were directed at not being deemed déclassé. Nothing was entirely unambiguous. Nothing was what it really was with any degree of certitude. Everything was bathed in a dubious twilight. In every way our existence was tinged with irreality—and if this irreality also possessed a highly poetic element, this was due to the queerness of our situation. Our parents were odd and off center, each in his or her own peculiar way, each in his or her own wrongheadedness, the cause and origin of which could be found in their quixotic reaction to an out-of-joint world. Their obsessions—our mother's anxiety-whipped, guilt-ridden sense of duty and our father's blindly passionate escape into his mania for hunting—were specific responses to circumstances that in no way fitted their upbringing, their existential concepts and expectations, even less their dispositions. We lived in the Bukovina—more radically than would have been the case elsewhere—as the flotsam of the European class struggle, which is what the two great wars really were. Our childhood was spent among slightly mad and dislocated personalities in a period that also was mad and dislocated and filled with unrest. And where unrest leads to grief and grief gives rise to lament, poetry blossoms.

Among the theories I developed concerning the possible causes of my sister's premature death, there is one according to which the gradual loss or, more accurately, the renunciation of the poetic content in her life contributed to a psychosomatic preparation for death. I do not speak of the ordinary loss of childhood's poetic quality, nor of the profanation that set in with the growing realization of the dwindling quality of life in our time, its loss of individuality. It is hard to describe this without being reproached for myth formation and nostalgic idealization of the past; essentially, one can't quantify the degree by which the quality of life not only of the privileged but also of the disadvantaged has been cheapened and debased in our century. The tangible expression of this—depredation of nature, hybrid growth and chaos of cities, drowning of the world in junk, lack of orientation in Man—has been pointed out, and yet it does not address the substance and core of the loss. In 1919, when we returned to the Bukovina after our refugee years in Italy and Austria, we were terrified by the specter of Bolshevism looming right at our doorstep. What had taken place a few dozen miles from us on the other side of the Dniester River since the revolution of 1917 sounded bad enough to conjure a horrifying transformation of reality. If any of this ever was to reach us, it meant the end. Not only could we expect to be mistreated, plundered, pillaged and finally shot; we feared more the gray subsistence that would be our lot if we were allowed to survive: the immense pauper's asylum into which so animated and varicolored a world as that of tsarist Russia had been transformed and which our own world would irrevocably turn into. Had I fallen asleep at that moment of history to reawaken now—a modern Rip Van Winkle—I would have to consider our worst fears of those days childish in comparison to the present actuality, which is grayer, more dreary, more anxiety-filled and more hopeless than we could have imagined. Withal, I would have to admit that the changes in the world only kept pace with the changes in me. Not because I might have been compelled to adapt myself but, quite the contrary, because I, as a true child of my time, carry in me, together with all my contemporaries, the quality of our time. We who live today are a species of human beings different from the one we were a mere fifty years ago; but even then we carried in us the seed of what we have become today. This truism can hardly be thought through too much.

Yet this is not quite what I mean by the loss of the poetical, or rather its renunciation, which led to my sister's death. I have to be more explicit. There are times when I spend idle moments speculating on how far one can elude the impact of worldwide changes occurring in the spirit of the time—and what price is exacted for even trying to do so. Occasionally I encounter people who, seemingly unaffected, survive from a former world and populate the present in odd incarnations, like dinosaurs; when I look a bit closer, they seem somehow hollowed out—all of them without any doubt personalities, that is to say, utterly and completely *personae:* masks shaped in a period-given stereotypical form. The growth of a shell around the time-resisting personality has eaten away the individual within. What remained, irrespective of the personal qualities, is a more or less anachronistic period document. I often wonder whether this was not the case with my father toward the end of his days. His apparently sovereign stand above the times seemed less a declared anachronism because he had donned the timeless mask of the huntsman. It did not cover the individuality but rather served to emphasize it. The mask was acquired by obstinate monomania, and he paid the price with alienation into loneliness.

The opposite seems the case with my mother: a typical example of a failed attempt at adaptation. The angry piety with which she endeavored all her life to "go with the times," first in slavish observance of Victorian rules and regulations, and then in an uncritical acceptance of the shallowest modernizing reform trends and emancipation efforts, always along well-trodden paths, always only halfheartedly and yet with total self-abnegation—all this led her into an unrelievedly prosaic existence, an ever closer adherence to prevalent commonplaces and current platitudes, an ever more confining entanglement in the allegedly necessary and supposedly beneficial, and ultimately in the merely material. By the end of her life, she had erased, denied and canceled out all traces of her beginnings, so that finally nothing remained of her that could recall the era of her girlhood, neither a cogent content nor a recognizable outer shell, neither she herself nor a living document of her time.

Of my sister I know that she died early because she could not take her time into the present. It was not the brutal breakup of the idyll of her infancy that destroyed her capacity for the poetical and, together with it, her will to live. Quite the contrary: the Odaya's house and garden, which she had had to leave in such a headlong rush at the outbreak of the First World War, in her inner self she turned into the myth of an incomparably lofty existence, truly her due, her secret distinction. Until our parents' separation, her girlhood was spent being reprimanded by her mother and spoiled by an all too often absent father, and in the conceit of being a princess in rags. Only when a further decline in our circumstances forced her to realize what a fairy-tale delusion she had been living did she reconcile herself to the prosaics of reality. And this broke her. Even more heroic than my mother—and unfortunately also more clear-sighted and disillusioned—she too tried to adapt herself, but none of the realities that offered themselves to her could make up for what she had lost.

One can preserve the treasured moments of the past as one would a hidden jewel; or one can be dragged down by them as by a convict's ball and chain. For sensitive natures, these alternatives are very close. If there is any resemblance between my sister and myself, it is little else than our shared innate knowledge of the essence and value of renunciation. Our spiritual development proceeded along entirely different lines. Hers was fed by books; mine thrived on dreams. She was educated more or less systematically by halfway qualified governesses; I struggled in vain to catch up, never content with what I was assigned, which seemed like crumbs fallen from the table of the rich (encouraged in this by my sister, who spitefully denigrated what little I learned as inferior dross). All the more avidly I took refuge in Cassandra's fairy tales, peasant anecdotes and picaresque stories. My big sister bore herself with the self-assurance of a privileged birth; I was the late-born offspring of an unglamorous, restless and plebeian era. I envied her for being our father's favorite; she despised the blind infatuation my mother showed me, suffered maternal injustices with mute pride and devalued her mother's preference in my own eyes. She was a graceful girl, when I was a small oaf; she was a precociously exemplary young lady while I still was a lout. Only in a single matter did we feel an identical, close affinity: in the perceptive handling of unavoidable losses. We knew the fabric that fed the poetics of our life; we knew the value of those myths into which lost realities are transformed. But my sister lacked the strength to hold on to them all the way through.

One example: When I was sent to school in Kronstadt, feeling as orphaned as only a homesick nine-year-old can feel, I was granted the blessing of the friendship of an eighteen-year-old. Here too I must warn against any assumption of sexual connotations: nothing could have seemed more absurd, ridiculous and insulting to either my protector friend or me. It never even entered our minds. What happened between us was nothing more than that he treated me, quite naturally and without the slightest condescension, as someone on the same footing. We chatted in the recesses between classes in the schoolyard; we walked home together; once I went with him into town when he bought a new pair of gym shoes; once we went to the movies and together doubled over at a Fatty Arbuckle film; another time he took me to his boxing practice and once to a philosophy lecture of which I didn't understand a word. If all this was quite natural, in no way extraordinary, I nevertheless awaited our encounters with a trepidation I rarely felt later on when expecting to meet some lady-love. He was just about to take his final exams and spoke with me of subjects he felt weak in, explaining the difficulties involved as if he were speaking to a comrade facing the same problems. No one else saw anything out of the ordinary in our companionship. When I was with him, I felt nothing of the gap that in the rigidly hierarchic world of adolescence usually separates a little squirt from someone about to enter the university. My mother came to visit me in Kronstadt; I raved about my new friend and she invited him together with me for dinner at her hotel. He behaved in exemplary fashion and left her with the best possible impression. The school year drew to a close; he passed his final exams and I returned home for vacation (more accurately, I took up my shuttling between the houses of my parents, by now separated). A few weeks later I received a postcard from him: Best regards, he was about to continue his studies in Paris, this would be his address there . . . My mother urged me to write without delay. "Never!" I exclaimed, "I never want to see him again." My mother was outraged by this incomprehensible mulishness. But my sister understood and said, "He is right." At thirteen she knew as well as I with my nine years that to preserve something valuable, one has to know how to renounce it in good time. I only wish she had stuck to her guns.

I also understood why, after our return to the Bukovina, she balked at visiting the Odaya. The old manor house on the Prut vouchsafed for her the imagined survival of those years she had spent there as a fairy-tale princess. There were times when she even pretended to be sick to avoid going; later, she simply refused—and in this found the support of her father, who also seemed to have an inkling of why she behaved this way. Anyway, it was not as if other people were wildly enthusiastic. Nothing impelled our mother to go to a place that held nothing but painful memories for her. To reach it, moreover, was complicated, since there was no rail connection, and the roads were impassable by car in winter and even more so after the melting of the snows in the muddy season, while in summer one choked in dust; by horse carriage, the fifty miles were a trip of at least two days with no accommodations for spending the night. Once at the Odaya there was no distraction, the landscape hardly invited one on walks, the park had grown wild, the farm was run sloppily and brought in

hardly anything; there were quarrels with the manager and muti-
nous threats on the part of the field hands whose wages he stole.
When my parents lived together, my father would go for some
shooting in the Prut wetlands, and sometimes he took me along. I
looked forward to these rare occasions with the same trepidation
with which I anticipated my meetings with my friend in
Kronstadt. I loved the Odaya. What drew me there was the secret
concealed in the period when my sister already had been born
while I had not yet arrived.

That after our return to the Bukovina she no longer spoke of
that period made it all the more impenetrable — and all the more
alluring. Earlier, in our refugee days in Austria, when I had
grown up enough for my sister to be able to make fun of me, she
never tired of teasing me by vaunting the legendary glamour of
those early days. No day passed without her itemizing the number
of dolls she had had, how many horses had stood in the stables
and what a great show was put on whenever our grandparents
came to visit. Against this, not even Cassandra could offer protection: she too had not yet been "of that world." But all these
boastings ceased as soon as we returned to the Bukovina and
moved not to the Odaya but to the house outside Czernowitz. My
sister's refusal to visit the Odaya, her silences and her frequently
abrupt and noncommittal answers whenever I asked for details
about life there made me envious: I saw that her reticence concealed something she begrudged me. I did all I could to eavesdrop
on her secretive myth.

Whenever I went with my father to the Odaya, I searched in
every corner for a clue to the magic world I fancied she kept for
herself. My imagination was powerless to reproduce that past. I
closeted myself in the dusty rooms, where curtains and uphol-
stery fabrics were moldering away and pale reeds and straw
flowers, as ghostly as if they had been plucked from an ossuary,
proliferated from tastelessly opulent Chinese vases. I tried to
imagine my sister in her animated games, surrounded by grandparents and youthful aunts; I stared as if hypnotized at the
crumbling oil portraits of heavily moustachioed men in beaver
caps and laced-up velvet jackets, of women with towering

powdered hairdos, of spruced-up children—all of them supposedly our forebears. I listened to the heavy silence which, when
not interrupted by the noisy quarreling of jackdaws in the trees or
the rattling of a wagon on the far-off road, would grow to
terrifying proportions . . . until I had to escape out into the
glaring daylight. The yard was bare; manure heaps lay untidily
about; the few head of cattle were out in the fields; the two old
horses whom I loved slowly drew the carriage, on which my
father sat with his guns and his dogs, over the tracks of the
marshes; nothing could be seen of the farmhands and stable
maids. I fled into the garden behind the house, where cabbage
rotted on the stem in poorly kept patches. This was timeless,
rural, everyday reality, nothing else. And nothing of all that
yielded anything that brought me closer to my sister's secret.

Nor did I find her in the so-called park, growing into un-
checked wilderness behind the strip of vegetable garden. Only the
rotting rowboat in the pond—and of this merely the convoluted
wrought-iron backrest—spoke of those dimly apprehended days
. . . but this it did with such force that each time I stood before it,
it struck me as with a blow. And yet it was indescribable. I
trembled with impatience at the notion that a simple object could
be charged like a Leyden flask with the very essence of an era—
and that, after it had discharged itself on me with a shock, I
should find myself unable to clothe the suddenly recognized
unknown in words, unable to express what so intensely had
affected me, what sphere of mysteriously innate or inherited
knowledge had been touched and perturbed, this something
known from all times and yet forever lost.

With our parents' separation, so much that was new and
strange intruded in our existence that earlier experience seemed
to have been removed into a background so far away as to border
almost on the legendary. While I, homesick in the animated toy-
box world of Kronstadt, was dreamily looking for a key to
myself, my sister in Vienna seemed to face the changed circumstances with a fresh vigor that was as sober as it was confident. We
did not see each other for more than a year—and that was a year
in which I grew into a darkly mulish adolescent, while she was

transformed into a rapidly maturing young lady. I realized this the instant I was about to clasp her in my arms in the stormy joy of seeing her again; she restrained me with composure as she told me firmly, "We'd better dispense with this from now on." She had become untouchable.

This was not merely a reprimand that, disconcertingly, reminded me of the sexual difference between us, in the social as well as the purely physical sense. After all, it may indeed have stood for the cut with which she wished to eliminate my little boy's penis, a cut now performed, appropriately enough, with the weapon of the taboo. She thereby destroyed at the same time the wellhead from which springs boyhood's most beautiful taboos. She made me realize that the great farewell had begun from the world of dreams in which helpless maidens are saved by chivalrous protectors.

Among the episodic events that hitherto had united us as siblings, one stands out in my memory: It is the summer of 1919 and the Romanians have only shortly before occupied the region around Czernowitz. My sister and I are on a stroll through the People's Park under the supervision of some bored governess and Cassandra. A boy, slightly older than I, son of a Romanian colonel who recently had come to live not far from us, is also walking in the park, accompanied by a soldier who probably is the colonel's orderly. Suddenly the boy approaches my sister and, with a swift gesture, loosens the black-red-and-gold bow in her hair, throws it on the ground, spits and tramples on it with his boots. He starts to turn away with the contemptuous exclamation "Dirty Germans!" I throw myself at him. My mother had given me a toy saber—secretly, for my father hated anything connected with the military—a pitiful stand-in for the dangerously genuine saber that Cassandra's feckless Hussar had brandished, but one of my most passionately treasured possessions; this saber I now fiercely swack over the boy's head. Blood runs over his forehead; the soldier tries to attack me but is warded off by the governess; after confused pushing and pulling, the fray breaks up in great excitement, each goes his own way, with the boy screaming bloody murder and the handkerchief on his head

getting redder by the minute. Needless to elaborate on the severity of my punishment. I am reminded forcefully that my rash
action could result in the undoing of our entire family, if the
Romanian colonel is of a vengeful disposition. My toy saber
disappears, never to be seen again, which distresses me most of
all. But I am proud of myself, for I showed myself worthy of my
future role as a grown-up: a knight, entrusted with protecting the
frail and vulnerable weaker sex.

My sister now suddenly repudiated all this. She dissociated
herself from me; she had no need of me; she stood more secure
alone and on her own feet. Henceforth we were brother and sister
in name only, though in our world names stood for a whole
program. As "the older sister of a teenage boy" she was granted
authority over me that exceeded the actual age difference; my
behavior, however, supported such prejudicial assessment. Her
educational progress advanced smoothly and successfully; the
model child grew into a model student; her cheeky precociousness dissolved into reserved, forthright, appropriate comportment; she managed to gain a firm foothold in the adult world.
Meanwhile I showed myself obstreperous and intractable, in a
word, puerile. I had to change schools (just as at home my
mother's perennial nervous dissatisfaction led to the constant
changing of servants). In so doing, a miracle happened and I
caught up with my sister by two years, but this was hardly
noticed by the family. Nor did it attract special attention when
she chose a curriculum that I—not being allowed to attend the
Academy of Fine Arts, my first choice—had selected for myself:
the Consular Academy in Vienna. This already had been an early
fancy of mine, for its original name, Academy of Oriental Languages, had appealed to me; I saw myself as dragoman of the
Sublime Porte at the court of the Peacock Emperor, or on the trail
of Stanley and Livingstone at the sources of the White Nile. But
these romantic notions were squelched by the sober reflection
that as a member of a minority I had little chance to advance in
the Romanian diplomatic service. My sister, however, could submit a clear-cut plan for her future: she aspired to become a
secretary with an international commission, if at all possible the

League of Nations in Geneva. There is no doubt that she would have reached this objective had she not been stricken by that pernicious disease. She had already taken the first step: as the best graduate of her class by far, she got a job with the International Danube River Control Commission in Galatz.

While she was still in Vienna, I played hooky from a catchall institute for school dropouts. I skipped so many classes that I had to allege illness: appendicitis pains are symptoms easy to simulate, and these I reproduced so convincingly that the institute thought it necessary to advise my family. Our parents were in faraway Romania and the nearest available relative was my sister. She seemed so self-assured that no one dared doubt her competence in making the right decisions. She didn't even consult me before issuing her verdict: "I give you until tomorrow morning to think it over. If then you are still sick, you will be operated on." I would rather have had both my legs amputated than admit to her that I had been malingering. The next morning I was in the hospital and was soon caught up in the wheels of the medical process. A few hours later, I awoke from anesthesia, feeling terrible. The doctor declared that my appendix had been chronically inflamed and had been removed just in time, and though this assuaged my conscience and even gave me a certain creepy satisfaction, it also laid the foundation of my lifelong skepticism about the infallibility of medical science. Nor was my sister greatly impressed by this vindication, which was as unexpected as it was miraculous. With the terse observation that I would be bedridden for the next few days and would have no use for my pocket money, she took it from the bed table where it had been lying among the thermometer, the pill cup, my wristwatch and the bed pan, and pocketed it.

She met the "man of her life" at the Consular Academy. Tall and gangly, delicate of limb, with dark straight hair, expressive brown eyes enlarged by horn-rimmed glasses, a sensitive youthful mouth that was scarcely rendered more resolute or manly by the short-cropped moustache favored by Austrian aristocrats, he was far removed from the type I had imagined as my sister's suitor. Even though I credited her with enough taste not to lose her heart to some Rudolph Valentino–Douglas Fairbanks combination I nevertheless had expected her to choose someone as superior to her as I thought she was to me. But this well-brought-up adolescent struck me as merely a somewhat older schoolmate of mine, and I couldn't understand why she considered him more than that—indeed, as a man in her life. At first, he seemed just that: a colleague as ambitious and serious, as diligent and conscientious as she.

I did not see her often in those days. When we didn't meet on holidays at Grandmother's house on Wickenburg Street, I would find her in a small coffee shop near the Salesian church, always with her chosen one—they were cramming for their exams. I felt like an intruder, and after exchanging a few laconic trifles, I would leave them to themselves and to their work.

Only the luncheons on Sundays and holidays at Grandmother's house brought us together in the old mutual understanding, punctuated by malicious winks. We loved my mother's relatives, though with reservations: my sister's unquestioning partiality for her father had automatically ranged us on his side, and we bore his name with a clearly distancing pride which, in their eyes, made us liable to the same criticism that they always leveled at him. My mother's siblings were not so much older than we that we could accept their authority over us without demur, yet they sometimes arrogated this authority to themselves, though less so over my sister. But in doing so they failed to take into account the acute perceptiveness with which young people discern foibles, scurrilous traits and idiosyncrasies, absurd situations and comical attributes displayed by those who presume to be their educators. Our Viennese relatives now provided more than ample fuel for our uninhibited paroxysms of laughter, the explosions of mirth which were our way of resolving nervous tensions. Aunt Paula's hopeless singing lessons, which had been going on for decades and resulted only in a monstrous development of her bosom, from which mighty breastwork her voice emerged with ever reedier thinness; the brainless fanaticism of Aunt Martha, who had dedicated herself to the cause of the radical left; the spiritualism, worn with a supernaturally knowing smile, of Hermine, in whose presence furniture actually creaked, chandeliers tinkled and the family's cocker spaniel would bark angrily into the empty corners of rooms; Helene's hackneyed folk-artsy hobbies; and last but not least the awesome stupidity of our insufferably handsome Uncle Rudolf—all this sweetened our duty in attending Grandmother's communal table. The smallest incident, charged with the accumulated comical effects of countless precedents, would trigger our mirth. Then we separated without the slightest sentimental feelings, I to return, after an afternoon of aimless roaming through a city empty of crowds, to the bleak severity of my institute, and she presumably to the little coffeehouse near the Salesian church, where her beloved Fritz awaited her over tomes of constitutional law, the trade balances of small and large nations, or comparative analyses of the diplomatic methods of Talleyrand and Metternich.

I was lonely in those last years of the 1920s and the early 1930s. My radical avoidance of scholastic discipline placed me apart from my schoolmates. I had no friend—even less a girl—with whom I could achieve a measure of contentment and self-satisfaction in a coffeehouse or wherever, in the shared pursuit of my current life tasks. I roamed the streets not merely on Sunday afternoons. These were still years of promise, after all, not only the promise of my own future, which still some day might spread butterflylike into varicolored fulfillment, but the promise of a fairer future for all mankind. Despite the threats that hung over the world, people lived with faith in the future, whether in a chiliastic or apocalyptic spirit, in a critical or fatalistically hopeful mood. Sharp-eyed pessimism and starry-eyed optimism went hand in hand—but both were looking ahead. One foresaw the horrors of a second world war in the near future—the first one had ended only a decade earlier—and could depict them vividly, but at the same time one expected the ultimate deliverance of the children of Adam from the curse of labor through the benefits of technology and the establishment of an earthly paradise thanks to socialism. A whole peacock's fan of glowing ideologies new and old, hundreds of reform proposals, from novel footwear for the prevention of flat feet to mystically ecstatic meditations supposed to raise the quality of life—all promised a new and better world and a grander life for everyone. Utopian dreamers designed cities such as Metropolis for a future in which the submerged masses would be freed from the yoke of proletarian slavery. One shed prejudices and one's clothes and, naked, engaged in calisthenics on mountain meadows. The uncle of one of my schoolmates in Kronstadt, son of a dentist by the name of Oberth, experimented with rocket vehicles and planned a trip to the moon, like the one that Jules Verne had anticipated half a century earlier. I was sixteen going on seventeen, and all of this filled me with a nameless anguish. But I did not live it; it was I who was being lived *by* it.

And I also was lived by the anguish of sexuality. This is not the place to confess when and how I lost my so-called innocence—I lost the innocence spiritually long before losing it in the disappointing physical act. To keep this innocence for any time, I would have had not to be raised in Czernowitz; it may well be that the cynical—or more accurately, incorruptible—sense of reality which is one of the boons derived from such East European schools of life, made my approach to the subject "man and woman" even more prosaic than it would have been, given my natural disposition. Nor did it require my father's sharp aphorisms, barely lightened by humor, on related themes. From Cassandra's earthy closeness to nature, through Mother's shifting, flickering professions of tenderness alternating with explosions of rage and cruel punishments, all the way to my sister's icy distancing from me, my childhood held nothing that would have promoted a gushing romanticism. Nevertheless, and as a docile son of the West, I did whatever possible—though perhaps not my best—to conform to the accepted norms. Love was a myth to which everyone clung all the more intensely the more reason there was to render it suspect. The reality was as the pop song lyrics had it: "Alas, love is but a fairy tale. . . ." Whoever has offered me the apple of knowledge, I have chewed on it contentedly in the gratified realization that the lost paradise was nothing but a cloud-cuckoo-land peopled by mischievous goblins.

Apart from the time I spent in the festering atmosphere of my spartan schools, with their hard benches and besmirched bed sheets, I lived as a teenager surrounded by women, in an ambience of women's dresses and perfumes and toiletries, to which my father's guns, dog collars and spring-traps provided only a somewhat inadequate counterweight. My fantasies were feverish. I was spared—thank God!—such early traumatic experiences as those of the Wolfman, while my anguish at not knowing how Cassandra and her cavalryman managed to "crap on the ground together" without leaving any visible traces lay buried deep in the past. But the needs of the flesh remained unassuaged, after the Fall just as much as before it. And it wasn't flesh alone that tempted and troubled, attracted or repelled; behind that lay something mysterious that required, through enactment, deciphering. This has nothing to do with love. While my sister was cramming with her Fritz for her brilliant final exam in the little coffeehouse near the Salesian church, I roamed through Vienna seeking to get to the bottom of the mystery of the flesh. Certain experiences should have taught me that this search would be in vain. One of those occurred much earlier.

I was very fond of my grandmother. Not because she might have shown me much grandmotherly affection but—on the contrary—because she was less rhetorical, more sober and at the same time more frivolous than the other members of my maternal family, from its idolized head, my despotic grandfather, to his caricature, the youngest offspring—foolish, handsome, conceited Uncle Rudolf, whose nose had been bitten off by my father's dog. My grandparents' five daughters, all of them cantankerous, with cast-iron convictions and outlandish notions, formed a self-righteous and irascible clan that would not acknowledge anything that did not conform to the narrowest traditional concepts or currently accepted platitudes. Grandmother came from an airier environment; foreign blood had made hers flow more freely. Small and dainty, with exceptionally fine-chiseled features and beautiful hair, she had been all her life the object of rapturous admiration; as a consequence, she had little concern for the fate of her fellow human beings and all the more interest in her own.

She had every reason to be satisfied with it. Except for the drastic curtailment of her means toward the end of her life, a curtailment that she took as total impoverishment, she could look back on an opulently well-provided existence. She had fulfilled all of her life's duties in exemplary fashion; she had been an uncondi-tionally devoted wife (concerned mainly with questions of proper appearance), mistress of a large household, the by no means exhausted bearer of eight children (two of whom died in infancy), and an adequate mother who appeared to her children as a model of evenly distributed maternal love and rigorously applied ped-agogic supervision. Apart from that, her head was filled with little but fashion and, later on, solitaire. There survived some-thing of the eighteenth century in her. I loved the canny cleverness with which, with no pretension and much deftness, she knew how to conceal her unabashed frivolity behind the façade of Perfect Family Mother. Her unsentimental comments, which in comparison with the rest of the family's self-righteousness let in some fresh air, were balm to my heart. Her little vanities de-lighted me as much as her well-hidden petty barbs. I am certain that it was with some satisfaction that she declared she had handled her own life better than her eldest daughter had, even though at times she would add pointed remarks to the chorus of voices lamenting my mother's hard lot, for which my father was unanimously blamed. Only much later did I realize how many of her character traits my sister inherited.

My insight into the insidious ambiguity of her character was, as is usually the case, less the result of years of observation, of carefully collected and reviewed impressions, than the rich reve-lation of a single moment. Once — it must have been the year after our parents' separation and my own separation from my sister — I burst into my grandmother's dressing room in her house in

Vienna without being announced. And there she stood in her underwear like an erotic vignette of the past century, her waist tightly cinched by a corset, puffy underpants tied under the knees with pink silk ribbons and, below their lace edging, elegantly shaped legs in black stockings and high-heeled strap shoes. She turned toward me in surprise but without the slightest embarrassment, her hair carefully coiffed, a full-bodied iron-gray hair which, held in a transparent bonnet, appeared as if still blond in the light slanting in through the angled louvers of the Venetian blinds. All kinds of morning noises reached us through the open windows: the melodious calls of street hawkers, the hoofbeats of fiacre horses and the rumblings of motorcars (in those days individually discernible), the jingling of streetcar bells and other signals of awakening urban bustle. Together, all this had an electrifying effect upon me. I had come from the rural Bukovina to the capital with high-strung expectations. Babylon's pulchritude lay spread before me in all its wickedness and I was eager to savor it. So there I stood all the more perplexed; surely I was not mistaken when I thought I detected in my grandmother's sharp question whether I had not learned to knock before entering a room a coquettish undertone that was already addressed to the future man in the grandson. The glance between us—I a malicious imp of barely ten, and she a sixty-year-old as frivolous as a drawing by Félicien Rops—was unmistakably one of shameless mutual recognition. Only too clearly did I see before me an inveterate seductress, ready to be seduced, and even the twin taboos of incest and the difference in age failed to inhibit her from acknowledging this: it struck me as equally comical and disturbing. Years after, a similar incident with Bunchy convinced me that the flesh never entirely renounces its domination nor completely reveals its secrets—but of that later, in its own place.

This was but a small pebble in the mosaic of my erotic enlightenment that provided, as in a Klimt painting, the background for the drama (tragedy? comedy? penny-dreadful?) of my actual sexual experiences, which threw me into disarray and alienated me forever from my sister. With the cool gesture with which she had distanced herself from me after our first separation, she placed herself in an enclave of untouchability, not merely for me but for the world at large. I was unable to imagine her in any erotic constellation whatever; she remained the personification of an asexual ladylike entity, a romantic ideal bereft of true reality. In the years that were to be the last of her life, the impression of irreality, even implausibility, in my own existence — and perhaps in that of all of us — led me to harbor extravagant notions. Among these was an almost magical obsession with matters sartorial — though I shared this aberration with many others; it was, one might say, a collective neurosis of the era. But hand in hand with this went a general propensity toward a make-believe attitude in the whole life-style, as if anything might happen merely for the sake of appearance. While I thus impersonated the ideal of the dandy, my sister presented herself — in all the youthful radiance of the promise of her life, perky, spirited, intelligent, ambitious and purposeful — a splendid specimen of a girl, in comparison with which my immature foppishness was bound to seem all the more fatuous.

Only one little episode in all that time reminds me that we were chips off the same block. Once, after a Sunday lunch at Grandmother's house (and the inevitable laughing fit), my sister invited me to a movie. Still in our naughty mood, we sat in the dark and giggled about the screen ongoings, making iconoclastic remarks, among them that a particularly silly scene could have happened only in Czernowitz. The voice of a gentleman next to us said, "So you are the offspring of my old friend Rezzori?" He said it could not have been otherwise: nobody else in Czernowitz would make such irreverent remarks in such good German.

Thus we came to the summer of 1930. My sister was graduated with flying colors from the Consular Academy, well versed in political and economic sciences and constitutional law, with a diploma as an interpreter in English, French and Italian; she was closely followed in achievement by her classmate Fritz, whom she now intended to show off to our parents in the Bukovina as her future husband. I have reported earlier on the unhappy outcome of that meeting with my father. My mother showed herself of greater understanding. All of us proceeded to Jacobeni, the site of my mother's putative sanatorium, to enjoy the benefits of the piney scents and the sulphur mud baths. No clients had arrived as yet. In the hope that they might, a medical director and partner in the enterprise, Dr. Z., together with his wife, and an estate manager, Mr. von L., a decrepit gentleman who was almost blind, and blessed, moreover, with a scrofulous son who was supposed to serve as bookkeeper (both soon left the venture, presumably without ever having been paid), meanwhile took up residence and lived on credit. We—my sister, Fritz and I—were lodged in a peasant house, which Mother had fixed up and furnished on the model of that folkloric gingerbread cottage where she had spent the interim period before her second marriage. I still can see my sister standing in front of it, amidst the luxuriant greenery of mountain meadows, her arms full of cornflowers, birdgrass and daisies, happily smiling up at Fritz; he wears a gentle, solemn and somewhat owlish look and is clad in leather shorts and white half-stockings, foolhardily exposing his spindly aristocratic legs to the potential bites of vipers, which happened to be plentiful in the region. Together they are—as the saying goes—but one soul and mind. I am totally left out.

That, shortly before, my school in Vienna had granted me a diploma, I owed solely to my inspired idea of declaring that I would study at the Mining Academy in Leoben, in Styria. This venerable institution, housed in a building that my grandfather had designed, was about to be closed for lack of students, so that even such scholastically deficient pupils as myself were encouraged to matriculate there. To demonstrate how serious I was, I decided to undergo some practical training in mining. I didn't have to look far for such an opportunity, as Jacobeni is (or rather, was, since Comrade Ceaşescu has since seen to it that Romania is cleansed of most minorities) a settlement of German miners from the Zips region. Not far from it, an ancient manganese-ore mine was still in operation, and it did not prove difficult to place me there as a volunteer.

In this heartland of the Bukovinian Carpathians I was destined to feel my Germanic sympathies reach their apogee. The woods I crossed each morning, climbing to the mine entrance long before sunrise, epitomized the dark coniferous forests described by Stifter, with morning winds rushing through the fir trees under turquoise skies breaking in sharp suddenness from the darkness of the night; it was Caspar David Friedrich's spruce forest, its mad lighting clouded in white fog, its stillness pregnant with the purling of hidden sources and the silence gently scanned by the falling of dew. The blood drops of wild strawberries shimmered among the rich greenery of their earth-hugging leaves, the moldy and mushroom-scented thickets half concealing an entrance to the gruesome stronghold of Siegfried's dragon; at any moment the scaly monster might emerge, snorting fire, clawed fangs raised in awesome threat, exposing its yellow-ringed belly as it writhed over mounds of whitened bones and staring death's-heads, of fallen knights' swords and broken lances, of the treacherously murdered eremite's cowl and cross.

I believe I now know what prompted me so eerily to Germanize that arch-Romanian forest in the Carpathians where I felt more at home than anywhere else in the world: it was the carefully barbered, smooth-haired adolescent in Styrian summer garb, down in the valley, who sought to abduct my sister and take her with him back to his country, our own parents' land of origin, home to the mythical, mystic fairy-tale Holy Roman Empire of German Nations (or the sorry shambles of its remains); and it was the careless lightheartedness with which my sister bade farewell to our own Romanian homeland (which she probably had already repudiated when she lost the house of her childhood) to become once again the daughter of the Occidental world toward which our father had always steered us. I had to admit I was jealous. Not merely of the gently arrogant wearer of horn-rimmed glasses and leather shorts, under the codpiece of which garment successive generations already lay in wait, who would bear another name and would split my sister forever from our clan. I was also jealous of the advance she had once again gained over me: the legitimacy of an Austrian affiliation to which I too aspired, even though I knew my true roots were right here in this

country which, notwithstanding its variegated historical for-
tunes and constantly changing national flags, official languages
and custom tariffs, had imprinted on the medley of races that
lived on its soil an unmistakable, undeniable stamp. Despite
which it pleased the rulers of that country at the time to consider
me an alien interloper, while for my Austrian schoolmates I was
but a Balkanic gypsy from the remotest southeastern backwoods.
The untainted Germanness extolled by Hauff and Schnorr von
Carolsfeld was denied me forever.

I strove down to the Mothers. When I descended into the mine
pit, it was as if I penetrated deep into the womb of the earth that
had borne me. Cassandra's nourishing maternal milk aside, only
one-eighth of my blood had its origin in this earth. And yet it was
my own soil, and the bond with it was stronger than the Wagnerian sounds that my father had implanted in me, stronger than
the All-German aggressiveness with which every schoolchild was
inoculated by the politically assiduous German Scholastic Association, stronger too than the German Romantics' seductive
world of fairy tales and legends, which were no match for the
mystic appeal of Cassandra's earthy sagas. The mine in which I
lent a hand here and there was old and dilapidated, a labyrinth of
shafts and drifts, where manganese ore was still being mined in
only a few adits. Most of the old faces were decayed and had been
abandoned. Here too I roamed and ventured to descend to dangerous depths, into precipitous shafts and tunnels that long ago
had become insecure through random pillaging. My miner's
lamp darted spookily over a subterranean forest of posts and
cappers sunk centuries before, barely able to withstand the mass
of ceiling weighing on them, over walls hung with old men's
beards of arctically bleached lichen, glittering with moisture
dripping from above, apocalyptically snowy and pointing down-
ward to fathomless abysses as in a delirious vision of Edgar Allan
Poe. The smell of the rock intermingled with that of the carbide
fueling my lamp, a clammy smell of mineral ore pervaded by the
sinterings from sulphurous veins in the rock. These could have
been the antechambers of King Laurin's ruby-shimmering empire of dwarfs or the bottom of the dream lake, the Mummel

Lake, to which Simplicius Simplicissimus descended. In my innermost self I felt the arch-German poetics, the deep mythical truth that all of this encompassed. Yet it was also my direct and immediate existence into which I penetrated here, my true homeland, irrespective of the language and the emotional world, the circle of myths and legends and fairy tales I had been raised in. I felt so closely linked to this earth that I thought of my sister, now happily ready to desert all of this, as a renegade, even worse, as a traitor.

For she too was a daughter of our mother—even though she seemed so exclusively her father's daughter that no one would have thought of counting her with the distaff side of the family. Among us blue-eyed family members, she was distinguished by the greenness of her iris—a lightish green which, strangely enough, was also to be found in all her dogs (all of whom too, except Troll, her childhood playmate, died young). Irish eyes, it was said, from my mother's side; or Turkish bird-of-prey eyes from the Phanariots who had come to Romania from the Sublime Porte, though it was also maintained that in that green the dark eyes of my father's Italian ancestors mingled with the blue Irish ones. Who can say what Normans or Spanish Goths in remote times, in far-off Sicily, haunted the coloring of the autochthons' eyes? In any case, the olive smoothness of my sister's skin seemed to have had its origins there, though it was of almost translucent delicacy and without the leathery full-bloodedness of the Mediterraneans. Anyhow, the resemblance of her character to our maternal grandmother, her cool sobriety and—someone finally had the courage to call it by its true name—selfishness I noticed only after her death.

In a word, she was much more of the stamp of my mother's family than I and therefore had her roots in the East as much as I. Nevertheless, she now strove "homeward"—or more accurately, she willingly let herself be repatriated to the truly Germanic world. Not merely willingly but with a sigh of relief, as of one being liberated. I know that my emotions then were bred of wild imaginings—or perhaps inversely: my speculations were the monstrous offspring of tumultuous and highly ambivalent emotions. But today it seems to me that it was no mere chance that just at the onset of the calamitous Third Reich, the union of my sister—herself of old Austrian origin—with a legitimate Austrian suitor triggered my search for our genotypical heritages, their links in blood and soil, and their relations to mystic ideas of a unified nation. We did not live our own lives. Our lives were being lived by our period.

Thus the summer of 1931 went by. Fritz went home to Styria and from there to the United States to complete his law studies. It was accepted that thereafter he would marry my sister. Meanwhile, she had gotten her job as secretary for the Danube Commission and had moved to Galatz. I enrolled at the Mining Academy in Leoben. My father was holed up in the woods. It was paradoxical: he who always had preached to us about the "return to the West" and our affiliations with Germany's cultural world, he who never tired of deploring his exile to the Bukovina and the thanklessness of serving as "cultural fertilizer in the Balkans," now balked violently and resentfully at his daughter's projected repatriation to Austria and attributed absurd motivations to it so as to hide his jealousy. The break between him and my sister was accomplished. It would have been irreparable had she not become fatally ill.

I revert stubbornly to the psychosomatic origins of her illness (even if, in truth, these are presumed by no one but myself): what happened after those summer days in Jacobeni was so grotesque as to border on the farcical—and more than once served as an occasion for one of our convulsive explosions of laughter; but the point is that it destroyed once and for all the fragile texture remaining of what we still then called our family. I am speaking of the so-called sanatorium in Jacobeni, which had its origin in one of our mother's unfortunate bursts of entrepreneurial activity. It began with a friendship between our father and a certain Dr. Z., a physician who had his practice in Cîrlibaba, a dump of a place in the deepest Carpathian woods; he was the only doctor for hundreds of miles around. The Huzules—a Ruthenian-speaking tribe said to be the direct descendants of the Dacians, since whose times they barely had been touched by the hand of progress—hesitated for years before entrusting to him their bone fractures, wolf bites, the eelworm nests in their lungs and their syphilis-eroded noses, instead resorting to their own herb-brewing witches; but ultimately they came to him, since he was covered by the state health insurance plan, and they did not have to pay him anything besides occasional voluntary contributions in the form of cheese, wild berries, or trout and grouse hens from their poachings.

Cîrlibaba was an enchanted place. It might have been created by Chagall or by a stage designer for a spaghetti western: in a green mountain hollow stood a handful of wooden huts and a minuscule timbered church roofed with wood shingles, a sawmill and three wood-framed Jewish stores in which could be bought whatever was needed in these remote backwoods—whips, axes, saws, hemp ropes, leather goods, multicolored kerchiefs, cart shafts and salt herring. The center of the hamlet was not the church but the log-framed *kerchma,* the village pub, where the men of the hamlet and, occasionally, some shepherds who had climbed down from their mountain slopes would get drunk. The wondrously luminous mountain air was saturated with the scent of freshly felled wood. A hundred feet below, in the valley, the ice-cold, lime-green waters of the Bistriţa River, rushing over white rocks, were dammed up by a wooden weir which, once enough logs had accumulated, was opened up to let the then wildly raging torrent carry the timber to the lowlands. Legs that from time to time were squashed by the playfully jumping and rolling logs were treated by Dr. Z.

He was a man of glittering abilities, small and wiry, full of beans yet somewhat abstracted, brightly alert though appearing mentally absent, highly intelligent and surprisingly well-read and informed about everything. Together with his wife, Wanda, he lived a few hundred feet from the hamlet in a spacious wooden house, a haven for a multitude of much loved and spoiled pets: hens, geese, dogs, cats, a couple of otters in the garden pool, sheep and cows and some Huzule ponies, tame as lambs. The dark forest rose behind some fat grassy meadows, where capercaillies could be heard calling in spring; the roaring of stags resounded in autumn; and wolves howled in winter, when the pines towered like giant icicles from the deep snow all around.

Yet Dr. Z. was not content with this idyllic retreat, redolent with the scents of hay and resin. Each year he closed his practice when the snows melted and, together with his wife, traveled from March to May in the capitals of the West: Vienna, Berlin, Paris and London, and home again by way of Madrid and Rome. Money was no object, for he made more than enough and had no other way of spending it. He returned covered with the pollen dust of Occidental culture and once again labored for ten months as a country doctor in Cîrlibaba. From time to time I was given a chance to nibble at this cultural honey. It was in his house that I delighted for the first time, as if hypnotized, in art magazine reproductions of the paintings of Mondrian and Modigliani, of Braque, Picasso and the Italian Futurists, and discovered, through an osmotic absorption of the style of the era, a harmonious concordance between the violence and sarcasm of Majakovsky's posters and the pioneering visions of Kupka. In the issues of *Studio* and *Gazette du bon ton,* available in my parents' houses, such things could not as yet be found.

My sister had not been in the Carpathians since her childhood—surprisingly, it seems to me in retrospect. It may be that my father considered life in the woods too rough for a girl, let alone a young lady. It may also be that he didn't want her near, when her dislike for hunting was obvious and ever present. I, on the other hand, was a frequent guest at Dr. Z.'s house. When my father went hunting, he never missed calling on him, not only because of his pleasure in the company of the doctor's attractive wife, but also because he enjoyed talking with Dr. Z. about all kinds of topics. In particular, they liked to discuss poisons, a subject stimulated by my father's early love for chemistry (and alchemy), and in which Dr. Z. showed an astonishingly thorough knowledge. This shop talk always ended with the hypothetical quest for the perfect murder by a poison that could not be detected. I remember well one of these conversations. A fire burned in the chimney, the two men sat over glasses of wine while the doctor's wife and I were busy with a large basket of huckleberries, picking out unripe ones, when the talk turned to the question of whether it was possible to detect the presence of potassium cyanide in a corpse. The closeness to our hosts lulled us into a feeling of comfortable well-being, a belief in the immutability of this well-appointed and lavishly run house and in the contented happiness of its owners. But Dr. Z. surprisingly complained of the schizophrenic nature of their life, split between Cîrlibaba and the great hotels of Europe. They had to come to a decision, he said. He wanted to change his life. But to do so he needed more money than he could make in a year and waste in three months. He had a plan, thought out in all details, as simple as it was foolproof. The valley of the Bistriţa River was rich in healthful springs, primarily sulphurous ones. He, Dr. Z.—and he alone—knew also of one that contained arsenic: it bubbled up, until now undiscovered, next to a former convalescent home for railway workers, a building going back to the days of the Austrian monarchy which had stood empty for decades and could be had for a pittance. How would it be, then, if my father were to purchase this building and place him, Dr. Z., as medical director of a sanatorium which, with the lure of sulphur and arsenic health baths, would soon attract crowds of patients, thus making both of them rich in no time at all?

My father declined forthwith. Not only had he no intention of making a fortune by means of any enterprise at all—particularly one in which the customers could be expected to be mainly Jews—but also he was much too familiar with the actual situation. Even such old and well-established spas as Vatra Dornei attracted fewer and fewer customers during the brief summer months. For rich people, these spas were not fashionable enough—the "in" set went to Biarritz or Meran; and those with more modest incomes couldn't afford Vatra Dornei. Moreover, the convalescent home referred to by Dr. Z. was a derelict rattletrap halfway between Jacobeni and Vatra Dornei, one-storied on the front side but with three stories at the back on a precipitous slope over the Bistriţa. The bathhouse was on the river, which was too shallow for bathing during the damming periods and so torrential during the logging season as to be not only a danger to life and limb but an outright playground for suicidal candidates. As far as the sulphur baths, these were available everywhere; and my father simply could not believe in the existence of arsenic spring water. He was right on all counts.

I no longer recall how the project ended up with my mother. She had known Dr. Z. for years and trusted him, especially since she heard him tell me in graphic detail about the spread of syphilis among the Huzules; it had been one of her worst fears that, because of either inadequate supervision or my father's pernicious influence, I might some day sexually assault a daughter of the region on one of our hunting expeditions. What convinced her of Dr. Z.'s qualifications to be director of a thermal spa no one could say. In any case, she took all the money she had and bought the old convalescent home. Dr. Z. became a partner in the enterprise, contributing his services and the secret of the arsenic spring, in exchange for which he gave up his medical practice in Cîrlibaba and his comfortable life. My father's urgent warnings were of no avail. Later, my mother explained to me that because these warnings had been conveyed by my sister and me, she didn't take them seriously; she had assumed that her ex-husband merely wanted to denigrate her in our eyes. No one else was consulted.

The purchase of the ramshackle convalescent home swallowed up all her available means. Philip contributed what was needed for its renovation. To make it a luxury sanatorium, it also had to be refurbished completely, and in this my mother did not stint. Over questions of interior design, she fell out with Wanda, the doctor's wife, and there were ill feelings and angry words. A year went by before the place could be opened for guests. But none came. Dr. Z., who had no income and therefore was soon left without means of support, took out a mortgage on his share in the enterprise. He also opened a new practice of his own but failed to attract patients. Another doctor, Dr. B., was as well established in Jacobeni as Dr. Z. had been in Cîrlibaba, and although Dr. Z. hatched some intrigues to supplant Dr. B. as the official health insurance physician, these failed. Winter came and with it the dead season. Once the snow melted, Dr. Z. could bear Jacobeni no longer. He left with his wife for Paris. He came back in May. In

June—the sanatorium had just opened, but not a single guest had arrived—my mother was arrested in Czernowitz. She was freed after a brief interrogation at police headquarters, but she had to keep herself at the disposal of the authorities. Dr. Z. had committed a murder; as his business partner, my mother was at the center of the investigation.

The facts in the alleged crime were incredible, and the investigation dragged on for years. What had happened was as follows: Dr. Z. had gone to see his medical rival and had told him, "My dear colleague, I am doing research concerning the measurement of lung capacity. Please be so good as to inhale the contents of this vial." With which he unplugged a vial and held it under the nose of Dr. B., who in good faith inhaled deeply. The vial contained hydrogen sulfide. Dr. B. apparently dropped dead; Dr. Z. replaced the vial in his briefcase and returned to the empty sanatorium.

But Dr. B. did not die immediately, although he had been blinded. He dragged himself to his desk and with his last remaining strength managed to scrawl on a slip of paper: "Dr. Z. has killed me." *Then* he died. His wife found him an hour later; one and a half hours later the police discovered in Dr. Z.'s consulting room all the paraphernalia necessary to prepare hydrogen sulfide. The vial was still in his briefcase.

The person who couldn't stop shaking his head over these events was my father. It seemed to him entirely implausible that a man who for years had held forth as an expert on the perfect murder by poison would choose to kill someone by such a primitive method, which any child could readily detect. It was at least equally incomprehensible that a physician with experience could be the victim of so crude an attempt at murder. "Every schoolchild knows from lab experiments that one has to run as fast and far away as possible the instant one smells rotten eggs," Father observed. "It can't have happened so simply." The investigating authorities shared this opinion. Nothing could be gotten from Dr. Z.; he remained mum and neither admitted nor denied anything. Primarily, motives were searched for, and the most likely ones were professional, that is, financial. The still virginal luxury sanatorium remained sealed by the authorities. My poor mother and innocent Philip were harassed by questions that went all the way back to elucidate the original means by which the wretched place had been acquired — which, in turn, led to punctilious and highly embarrassing fiscal examinations. (No one had ever thought of paying taxes on the Odaya.)

My sister and I heard of all this when we came back "home" — whatever that meant. She had come for a few days from Galatz and I from Leoben for summer vacation, which I was to spend hunting with my father. I fetched her from the train station and drove her to his house — we were kept away from our mother's for the time being, in order to spare us unpleasant scenes. Once we were there, I told her what had occurred; together and in tears, we sank to the floor in paroxysms of laughter. When my sister recovered, she went to the bathroom and threw up.

She returned to Galatz without having seen her father, who was away hunting. I myself stayed with him only a short while and spent the summer in Czernowitz, one of the happiest summers of my whole youth: unsupervised and carefree, playing tennis in the "Jew club," as my father called it, in love without the usual gnawing obsessiveness, unencumbered even by embarrassing arguments between my mother and Philip, which disclosed ever more and deeper discrepancies than those that were the immediate consequence of the collapse of Jacobeni. Then, in autumn — oh, the blue-golden autumn days of those years! — I returned to Leoben, still lighthearted and unencumbered, so frivolous that even today I remember that period of presumptive studies with conflicting feelings. On an evening after the usual boozing with fellow students, I somehow ended up in the kermess booth of a fortune-teller. Her gaze rigidly directed at some far-off point, as in a picture book, clad in a wrap decorated with the signs of the Zodiac, her smooth, shining black hair severely parted in the middle, she was surrounded by the complete instrumentarium of prophecy: the glass globe, tarot cards, astrological tables and, behind her on the wall, the picture of a turbaned magician with glowing eyes, surrounded by flowing rainbows. Smirking, I sat down across from her, and she took my hand, peered into its palm and said, "Soon someone who is very close to you will die." I wish I could swear by something exalted that would invest what I am about to say with the seal of gospel truth: at the very instant the seeress intoned those words, I saw my sister's green eyes before me. The next morning I got a letter from her: "I'm a little bit sick." We never had written to each other, least of all when we had a cold or an upset stomach. I knew it was she who would die.

Soon she had to give up her position in Galatz and return to Czernowitz. A small swelling of a gland behind her left ear enlarged. My mother brought her to Vienna. We saw her leave, my father and I, in the train station where so many of our arrivals and departures to and from our schools had taken place. My sister, laughing, looked down at us from the window of her compartment, and my father joked boisterously, unconcerned by the reaction of strangers and bystanders, as was his wont when he was in a jolly mood. The train started up slowly, we exchanged some final farewells, we waved good-bye, my father took off his hat and then, turning abruptly, said, "I've seen her for the last time."

In Vienna, she was treated by a Professor Sternberg. The lymphogranulomatosis, as her affliction was diagnosed, in those days was called "Sternberg's disease." But even the efforts of this preeminent authority were of no avail. She wasted away, and soon the tumescence expanded over her neck and down to her shoulder. Once she said to me, "If Father were to see me in this condition, he would help me." I knew what she meant.

To my mother, she showed great tenderness. She saw how much the poor thing suffered for her. At times, when my mother was sharp with me because of her, our eyes would meet and we couldn't suppress a smile. Once I caught her unawares as she was observing her mother's glance sliding off, as happened so often, from the here and now into an indeterminate remoteness. Once again our eyes met, and I understood something unfathomably deep: her expression was hard; she had always feared and hated the threat of slipping away into this indefinite vagueness. Had she realized that this was why she had renounced the poetry of her childhood myth at the Odaya? She gave me a brief nod: it was an admonition.

We became true siblings once more. I left Leoben and stayed in Vienna, where she lay bedridden in our grandmother's house. I became friends with her kind and gentle Fritz; our close friendship was to last for many years past her death and until his own. Fairly soon it was clear that there was no hope for her. Because she loved the mountains, she was brought to a sanatorium near Hall in the Tyrol, in beautiful surroundings. It bore the somewhat creepy name of Gnadenwald, "Mercywoods"—an occasion for more of our macabre jokes. She herself had no illusions about her condition. Although her suffering reached almost biblical proportions, she lost none of her courage or her readiness to laugh at absurdity. When I visited her for the last time, she drew me close and whispered, "I must tell you something that will make you laugh. I myself can't anymore. It hurts too much." The tumescence had fused her head and shoulders; her hair had fallen out; while receiving radiation, her larynx had inadvertently been burned and now she coughed incessantly; her whole body was covered by an itching rash. What she told me was something that in times past would have united us in laughter.

My mother would not tolerate that any of the sanatorium's friendly, well-trained personnel took over the care of her daughter. For weeks my sister could not sleep and my mother would keep vigil with her, barely resting between periods of wakefulness. Finally her exhausted child fell asleep, and my mother, almost blinded by fatigue, was about to retire and find some rest herself. But as she stood up, she noticed with horror that a spider was lowering itself on its thread from the ceiling precisely over my sleeping sister's head. Spiders always had been an abomination for her; there was nothing she found more loathsome. And now here, floating above the face of her deathly sick child, this creature appeared to her as the embodiment of all the evil that had befallen her. Mindless, on blind impulse, she took off her slipper and squashed the spider to the wall with it—with the obvious result that my sister woke up in shock and could not sleep again for weeks.

My sister feasted on my laughing to tears. She whispered that she'd like nothing better than to follow suit—for wasn't it one of the funniest, most characteristic episodes, typical of her mother's always misguided good intentions?

A few weeks later we buried her in the cemetery of Hall in the Tyrol.

Bunchy

In a cameo set as a brooch, a melancholy
faun, sitting under an olive tree, blows on his
panpipe; above him are seen the three richly
flowing feather panaches of the crest of the
Prince of Wales, together with the device Ich
dien. The brooch lies in a velvet jewelry box in
the lid of which, tipped open, the warrant of
arrest for Landru, mass murderer of women,
has been pasted. There are ice-flowers on the
windows, and some newspapers in cane frames
are lying on the marble tabletop of a Viennese
coffeehouse. The lady in the back, behind the
cash box, wears her short-cropped hair brushed
down over her brow and is clad in a wasp-
waisted dress; as with "The Lady Without a
Lower Half" in a circus sideshow, only her
upper trunk can be seen. She holds a

magnifying glass in her hand which she
discreetly hides whenever someone looks at her.

Bunchy came from Stettin, in Pomerania, and stressed this in her typically cheerful, self-assured way, yet at the same time with the ironic pride with which one might speak of one's chance origin in an exotic place, such as perhaps an island in the West Indies. She had spent her life in many places but not in Stettin; possibly on some West Indian island and a number of years in America. But that she had been born in Pomerania she seemed to consider a special mark that guaranteed a native rural robustness and soundness in body and mind, qualities that Bismarckian Germanness liked to claim as its own. All her life she dressed in the fashion of that period: an imposing figure in the dark, severely waisted, ankle-length dress of the so-called lady companion, with a narrow lace collar closed by an unostentatious pin or brooch. Outdoors she was never seen without gloves of smooth black leather, but she wore no hat during the summer months, so that her hair, snow-white when I knew her, swept upward at the temples, stood up on both sides of the curved brow and dipped in the middle, "like the flame of a gas burner," as my sister said. Her large face with the short nose and the gruff though often laughing mouth also had something Bismarckian about it, a determination and firmness of character that lent the slanted eyebrows both intelligence and superiority.

She had come to the house of my grandparents in Bohemia, and later to Czernowitz, to serve as the governess of my mother and her siblings, and then, after a decade devoted elsewhere to other pupils, to my sister and me—for all too short a time. She died, almost ninety, in the 1950s in Vienna, closely tied until the end of her days to all three generations of the family—closer, indeed, to each of us than we were to each other.

The only one who kept a reserved distance from her was my father. He also was the only one who addressed her not as Bunchy but as Miss Strauss (*Strauss* meaning in German "bunch of flowers") and spoke of her as Miss Lina Strauss, suggesting thereby that he could not deny her his respect. She had a solid education and was widely read, had worldly manners, and knew how to keep her place with dignified decency and firmness. He may also have felt that she appreciated his own signal qualities better than others who were misled by his manias and spleens. Whenever he exchanged words with her, it was in observance of a respectful ceremonial, a careful distancing, as in the salute exchanged between two swordsmen. He did not feel the need to show her any additional courtesy. He would ascertain that my sister's fund of knowledge had gained astoundingly thanks to Bunchy's instruction, acknowledged that even I was giving signs of domestication under the influence of the "new" governess, before leaving "on assignment."

This coolness on his part was understandable. Bunchy had come to our house at a difficult time, a time of "brewing crisis," as my sister and I recognized later, under abnormal conditions that never reverted to normality after Bunchy left. A crisis was brewing not only in our parents' marriage but in everything touching our home life together. My mother was less and less able to cope with the willful girl my sister was becoming. At the same time, I slid out from her and Cassandra's supervision and developed into what my mother found an intolerably rowdy boy; I was far from the affectionate, curly-headed sweetie pie she would have liked to cuddle, as in a painting by Romney or Vigée-Lebrun—if not Raphael. Her increasing isolation and alienation depressed her. Family finances were precarious: her dowry was gone; what had remained of her parents' fortune evaporated in the inflation. Her husband's salary, in her opinion, stood in no relation to his costly hobbies. Moreover, our political situation was rife with ambiguity. Only now, in the early 1920s, did we realize that as former imperial Austrians we had lost not only the war but also our national identity. We trembled at the stormy awakenings of major-power aspirations and conceit on the part of Romania's new sovereigns. Taught to be submissive to any form of authority, my mother was terrorized even by the mere appearance of a policeman. Her nervousness pervaded the entire house.

We had had a confusing series of mademoiselles and misses coming and going, women who became rebellious and distraught because of our insubordination, and then even more so because of my mother's wavering interference in their pedagogy. For all of this, she held her incompetent husband in some way responsible.

Bunchy arrived as a result of my mother's desperate call for help to her family in Vienna. My father could hardly have assumed that her own dearly beloved governess, deeply attached to her family, would be impartial in relation to him. More likely, he could presume that she had been sent to back his wife in every possible way and to draw his children away from him and into the bosom of the maternal family. Yet until my mother abducted us to Vienna, Bunchy never gave my father any grounds for suspicion that she was playing a role in the family intrigues. Her attitude was perfectly fair, discreetly insistent on meting out justice on all sides in questions of conflict and never lowering herself to a cringing neutrality. Although much too tactful to remind my mother that she had once been *her* governess and as such might allow herself the odd reprimand or correction, she did not refrain from voicing disapproval when it counted. She soon gained unquestioned authority throughout the house, and she exercised it in a way that impressed my father and calmed my mother's flickering moods. But my father could not easily give up a prejudice once formed, and he expressed it by sometimes letting fall that Strauss was really a Jewish name.

Had he had an inkling that she had injected us with the "ferment of disintegration," whose origins he, as a faithful pupil of Houston Stewart Chamberlain, attributed to the Jewish spirit, he would have prided himself on his intuitive powers. But her Pomeranian uprightness was not, as he claimed, a typically Jewish camouflage: after 1938 she had no trouble documenting her untainted Aryan lineage. In any case, my sister and I continued to maintain close relations with her after she returned to Vienna, where she resumed giving private lessons in English, French, Italian and art history to innumerable pupils, many of whom became our friends, and all of whom happened to be Jews. Faithful to Bunchy's corrupting influence, these friends continued her mission of liberating us from the narrow-minded provincialism into which we might otherwise have sunk.

To my shame I did not realize this right away. I was proud to be the son of a huntsman and did not wish for anything more keenly than to indulge my father's passion wholeheartedly myself; I admired him and loved all his whims and incongruities, even forgiving him his almost pathological anti-Semitism—but fortunately I never took him quite seriously. It had always been hard for my sister and me—less so for her than me—to take anything related to our family life seriously, for presumably we had an alerted instinct as a result of some intellectual self-preservation, since otherwise we might not have sanely survived the absurdities. Many eventful years had to pass before we became conscious that some of these aberrations could indeed hardly be taken seriously enough. At first we made fun of anything and everything, especially whatever was painful. Laughter was our means of keeping operable the mechanism of the compact between matters that in fact were incompatible. We never accepted our mother without a *reservatio mentalis,* but we never doubted either that thanks to her we had been granted the very best that a good birth and a sound education could produce. Likewise, we might shake our heads and roll our eyes at our father, even censure him for his harebrained follies, and yet be convinced of

his ultimate infallibility. Our reservations did not alter our faith
in the deeply grounded legitimacy of our world. Because we were
wont to convert the eccentricities into family legend and finally
regarded them as a kind of distinction, we got into the habit of
considering (and accepting) neurotic behavior, narrowness of
mind, and wrongheadedness as a mark of class superiority. It was
at this point that Bunchy's influence had a beneficially compen-
sating effect.

Much later, when the truth had dawned on me about many
things that I had once considered self-evident but that were, on
the contrary, incomprehensible, I wondered how, in a world that
suffered day in and day out the most cataclysmic changes, we
could have remained stuck for so long in our narrow, blindered
complacency—not only our conceits regarding our social position, our assessment of our fellow beings and ourselves, but the
overall situation of the world around us. Czernowitz, for us, was
the center of the universe and our home was its very core. It was
but natural that as growing children we existed in a state of
cultural pupation, from which we freed ourselves only gradually,
through increasing our knowledge and deepening our insights,
shedding layer after layer of childhood's dream condition and the
stereotypes that indiscernibly were part of it, the wrappings that
had protected us. And it goes without saying that this process was
not a gentle, gradual one, let alone painless or unopposed; it
happened rather by sudden jolts and shoves, in insidious evolu-
tions which we perceived only long after they had taken effect.

When we had come to know Bunchy, it astounded us that our
mother had been reared by her. Obviously she had assimilated all
the rules of proper comportment, the knowledge of languages
and art history befitting a "daughter from a good house," but she
had failed to acquire any of Bunchy's sense of humor or her sound
common sense (which she shared with our father, although neither he nor she would have liked to acknowledge this), nor the
openness to the world, the lack of prejudice and the intellectual
independence of this exceptional woman, not to speak of the
generous respect Bunchy showed for other people's peculiarities.
Nor could much of this be detected in our aunts, who also had

been Bunchy's pupils; what little there was, was buried under moronic class prejudices or, worse, collective ideas and opinions. We concluded that one could teach and learn only so long as teacher and pupil shared more or less the same physiological disposition — "chemical concordance," as our father called it. Slowly it dawned on us that the oddities in our household were in some way effectively the marks of a social class, one belonging to a dying and largely already superannuated caste, and that the only remaining salvation consisted in renouncing all of it. That this did not happen violently and destructively, as was the case with later generations, we owed to Bunchy's perceptive and considerate guidance.

She never indicated with a single word, an inadvertent gesture, a glance or even a twitch of the eye that she might be disappointed with what had become of her former pupil. She treated my mother with the same even-handed, loving and tolerant care she must have shown to her when she was a young girl, her attitude now heightened by the polite respect granted to the mistress of the house. A more civil tone entered our home, where hitherto emotions had been expressed in fairly unbridled fashion. Even Cassandra straightened up with a pride that had been awarded her at long last and that no longer could be denied her by some miss from Smyrna or some vaguely whorish mademoiselle from Marseilles. Bunchy's dignity stood watch over our own; withal, we were freer in our manners, we laughed more frequently and less maliciously, and we took whatever still pained us — such as my mother's regrettable and frequent accesses of temper and manic vagaries — in a spirit of greater tolerance. When a certain pettiness of outlook degenerated into stubborn narrow-mindedness, Bunchy's determined intervention drew our attention to basic discrepancies between the conception of life held by normal civilized people and that held by us. We then made haste to follow her implicit injunctions.

When she came to us from Vienna in the summer of 1921, I was so confused by her apparition that I had to be fetched

with almost brute force from Cassandra's room, where I had
taken refuge, to be presented to her. We had heard of her for as
long as we could remember; she was spoken of within the family
as a temporarily absent relative, all the more dear because of her
absence; she appeared in most accounts of my mother's youth,
that mythic time, even more remote and splendiferous than the
period in which I was not yet and my sister already was "of this
world." I would have considered her as a pure fairy-tale figure
had we not received from her regular congratulatory postcards,
usually reproductions of paintings by old masters, especially
those of the Tuscan school (it was said that she had lived for years
in Florence), on the occasion of our birthdays, Christmas and
Easter; the golden background of those Annunciations lined the
place in my psyche where her name was embedded. She had been
a living presence in my inner being long before there was any talk
of her joining us, and when one fine day this was announced as
imminent, it seemed a barely believable miracle, almost a profanation. This witness to the lost glory of our house, a glory in
which I had not been allowed to share, this guardian of the
irrevocable, whose existence in this world reached back into the
secrets of time even further than my sister did, was now to face
me in person; she was to become flesh and blood. She had been a
participant in the reality that no longer was real but was perhaps
only an assertion by those who had lived before me, a reality
that was documented solely in a few surviving artifacts and
graspable in these only in some moments, in shadowy singular
aspects—as in the wrought-iron backrest of that rowboat rotting
in the pond at the Odaya. . . . It was she I was to face and to whom
I now was to introduce myself, as so often in the past years and
with growing rebelliousness I had done with the misses and
mademoiselles flashing by like transient comets. Cassandra
washed my hands, brushed my hair and nudged me through the
door of the study into the drawing room. There, majestically
towering next to Mother, stood the mythic figure of Mother's
family, Miss Lina Strauss, arrived that very moment. My sister
already stood confidently close to her and looked expectantly at
me—in malicious amusement, so it seemed.

It was a bright summer day and, to my pleasant surprise, Miss Strauss was wearing, not as I had expected, a severely black turn-of-the-century dress, like a child murderess in a wax cabinet, but a white traveling dress; the skirt reached to her ankles, and the short jacket, old-fashioned in cut, was buttoned all the way to the neck. It seemed a garment fitting the resplendent wearer and the radiance filling the room. "So there he is," she said, as if greeting someone she had known forever, and stretched out to me both her black-gloved hands, one of which I grasped and kissed, as I had been taught was the polite thing to do when being introduced to a lady—though at that instant I realized it was hardly proper to be kissing the hand of a governess, particularly one in a black glove. It would never have occurred to me to do this with Miss Knowles or Mademoiselle Derain (she actually had the painter's name). Involuntarily I glanced at my sister, but the imposing figure in white had interposed herself between us. Miss Strauss knelt down to me, took me in her arms and kissed me, saying, "He is too polite. We shall settle between ourselves to whom he is to show such courtesy and where this is a bit too much." When she stood up, she kept my hand in hers, placed the other on my sister's shoulder and said, "Now show me where I shall be staying. I have to recover from my journey. I've been traveling almost two days." I saw that my mother had been watching this encounter as an engaging spectacle in which her well-bred children showed themselves to best advantage—and in a better light, certainly, than at those costumed affairs she had been arranging for us. We were finally behaving with the grace and poise she expected of us, as in a genre Biedermeier painting, and she basked in the moment. Maternal satisfaction—all too infrequent—brought her a rare instant of true relaxation, and it triggered a mood wholly different from the nervously imperious harshness we were used to. This was a foretaste of Bunchy's blissful influence on the atmosphere of the household.

I watched eagerly to see whether her imposing appearance would also induce my father to kiss her hand. Quite apart from the fact that it was pretty hard to get my father to kiss anyone's hand, excepting that of his beloved of the moment, he and Miss

Strauss already knew each other. After having greeted her with a formal "Good day," he contented himself with a dry comment: "Well, this one hasn't gotten any younger either."

She was then—in the summer of 1921—probably about sixty, though we were never able to ascertain her exact age; in any case, she was older than my father, who had been born in 1876. She had come to our then eight-year-old mother in 1898 and stayed with her until shortly before her marriage in 1909. So she would have met my father as bridegroom, wearing his woolen ski cap, in the midsummer of 1908. Magical dates! They troubled me because they were preludes to my sister's birth—that is, preludes to that special world experience which was her handicap over me. Now, before me stood the Keeper of the Great Seal of this treasure, and I began to watch jealously to see whether my sister, on the strength of her advance in time over me, would try to establish a secret and deeper intimacy with Bunchy, our new and in so many ways meaningful housemate. . . . But then something miraculous happened: a few weeks later Bunchy went alone with me to the Odaya.

First, however, I have to recount how she gained my confidence. In contrast to children today, we were not spoiled with a surfeit of toys. Christmas and birthday gifts from my mother were always selected with great empathy and were joyfully received, but they were anything but lavish. The legendary ship's model that foundered in Constanţa belonged to a later period, when we no longer had a true home and my mother tried to compensate for the distance that separated her from me, at school in Kronstadt and desperate with homesickness. As long as the family lived together, we children had contented ourselves with a few stuffed animals from our infancy—and of course, our live pets: dogs, rabbits for a while, two or three broken-winged birds found in the garden, a magpie, a starlet, a robin—until our mother somehow got it into her head that they carried meningitis and tuberculosis. My sister's dolls moldered at the Odaya; she didn't want to see them ever again. My "German Brother" was in rags; shortly after the Romanian soldier had thrown him in the gutter, his belly split and a sad mixture of straw and sawdust dribbled out, leaving a slackly empty uniform—the felt it was made of suddenly seemed horribly shabby—crowned by the stupid blond head without its rookie's cap. My ball with the multicolored circus pictures I had lost to the treacherous seducer from beyond our garden gate. Of my toy saber I had been relieved, after wounding a child of one of our country's new masters with it, a deed that might have drawn on us down their vindictiveness unto the seventh generation; as to the handful of lead soldiers I had, Cassandra usually kept them hidden in a box, so as not to arouse the wrath of my father (though the real reason for secreting the soldiers was probably that they wore the uniform of Austrian dragoons and as such would be deeply distasteful to any Romanian). Miss Knowles, arriving and vanishing in our lives like a meteor, had introduced us to some indoor games, to be played at a table in sedentary gentility—such as tiddlywinks, which soon bored us after we almost split each other's heads open over it. Even worse were games like merle or ludo; neither of us was what our bucktoothed Miss called, in her jolly British way, "a good loser." I ardently wished for a miniature railway set and never got one, though the Christmas and birthday presents with which Mother bribed us became more opulent with the passage of years. From a remote and shadowy time (near Trieste? in Lower Austria?) I also seem to remember a cardboard with holes into which many-colored glass balls could be inserted to form a variety of patterns; all my life certain ornaments, some luminous advertisements and, more recently, photographs recomposed in computerized images have reawakened with almost electrifying intensity the early optical impression made on me by this toy. Any object that we could consider personal property held intense power for a while, a feeling heightened by fear of losing such a beloved object—which probably contributed, in fact, to our frequent losses; our often wounded susceptibility helped to develop a resigned, loose relationship with property. (It may well be that later this was also expressed in matters of the heart.)

The most beautiful present I ever received in my childhood I received from Bunchy. She brought it with her from Vienna, and she took it out of a large cardboard box—the first one she opened after we took her to her room and her luggage was set down. "It belonged to your Uncle Rudolf," she said as she carefully unwrapped two small wooden boxes from their layers of tissue paper; one was larger and lighter, the other one smaller and heavier. My anticipatory pleasure was so great that I didn't even care what gift my sister was getting—and now I've forgotten what it was. Urged on by the unfamiliar white lady in her white traveling suit—still too overwhelming a presence to be called Bunchy—I carefully opened first one, then the other of the little boxes. The lid of the lighter one was opened and closed by screws that, with a gentle pressure, would squeeze down on some three dozen parallel slots as on a writing block. The heavier box had two compartments, one of which contained a small hand roller and several bottles of variously colored ink, the other one filled to the top with tiny, square-cut pieces of lead. Taking one of these in my hand, I found it showed on one of its surfaces, cut in relief, the letter *F;* a second one showed a lowercase *a.* They were the letters of a complete miniature printing press, adapted to my own diminutive size. Our new governess's black-gloved fingers took the two pieces from me, placed them in one of the slots, selected some more letters from the compartment, rejected some and chose others until she composed, letter by letter, the words "Family Rezzori." Only then did Bunchy take off her gloves, as after a task well done. "This little printing press comes from America," she explained. "I shall tell you later how I got it. I gave it to your Uncle Rudolf." She added offhandedly, "He hasn't played with it very often." (Miss Knowles would have said: "We are not surprised.") I looked at the line of type and said, "But if I now put a paper on it and draw it off, our name will appear in mirror writing." Bunchy stopped short, thought for a moment, took another piece from the box and scrutinized it closely. "You are quite right," she said. "The type has been wrongly cast. That's probably the reason why your Uncle Rudolf didn't much like this printing box. You're a clever little boy to have noticed this so quickly."

This remark was more than ample compensation for the disappointment that I would never be able to compose anything on the miraculous printing box that could be read properly and as it should, from left to right. Bunchy's praise, expressed in front of my sister, was a triumph that initiated the slow recovery of my badly damaged self-reliance. From that moment on, I loved the lady in white and never called her anything but Bunchy. She reciprocated this love. She became a powerful helper during my entire adolescence, as Cassandra had been during my childhood.

It is evidence of the permanence of the impression Bunchy left with me that she remains even more vivid in my aural memory than in my visual one—this in accordance with the former's multidimensional impact in depth, which invests the sudden sounding of a long-forgotten musical motif with the power to bring forth the very essence of an entire period, and in a richer, emotionally more lasting way than any visually remembered object. There are some sounds that have moved my soul for a lifetime—and I don't mean great music or cathedral bells but rather the intimate aural experiences of my sentimental biography. (I could make a long list of acoustic banalities that, precisely because they are commonplace, epitomize the components of that biography, for instance: the wintry sounds of sleigh bells, or the crack of gunshots coming from behind yellow birch leaves on a crystal-clear autumn day; the warbling of a merl on a city side street, or the moon-sick forlorn baying of a dog and the rattling, dying away in the distance, of a peasant cart making its way over a dirt road under a starlit sky somewhere in Eastern Europe; the rhythmic creaking of saddles, accompanied by the wetly metallic sounds of horses munching on their bits during a ride with someone, or on some empty Sunday afternoon, the repeatedly interrupted and then resumed tinkling of a child's piano practice in a neighboring house, while the wind carries puffs of sound from the crowd roaring in some far-off soccer stadium. . . .) Among such aural milestones, the evocation of Bunchy's dark-colored voice and her guttural, good-humored laugh, reminiscent of pigeons cooing, brings her back to me with all the fullness of her kind understanding and wise presence—and reminds me of the proud moments when she would appreciate one of my character traits, traits that before had elicited only Cassandra's crude peasant cackle or the family's sharp rebukes.

Bunchy discovered and promoted my talent for observation and humorous description, and opened the eyes of others to it. Whether this was of unqualified benefit to me, I cannot be sure; among my shortcomings—albeit more readily pardonable than many—is my predilection for amusing others with comical exaggerations tending to the paradoxical and absurd (though not always obtaining the desired effect). But in any case, Bunchy's encouragement was a balm in those difficult days of my final severance from the sheltering warmth of childhood, the age in which awakening consciousness urges one forward helter-skelter into life, however alarmed by clear-sighted foreboding and oppressed by puberty. With her acute sense for balanced measure, Bunchy did not encourage me in the monkeyshines I was wont to indulge in when not under her direct supervision. She limited herself—and me—to a cautious appreciation of the grotesque in life. This was achieved by nothing more than a rapid, almost clandestine glance exchanged between us whenever the situation threatened to tip over into the absurd, which in our household was not exactly a rarity. Her glance was swift and covert only in the first meeting of eyes, after which it resumed its steadiness, its studied indifference, as if the reciprocity of our silent concordance had been the result of mere chance. Thus it revealed nothing to the outside, least of all its intimacy. It was a glance denoting not complicity but, rather, acknowledgment of similar perceptions by two minds on the same wavelength.

Our congeniality began with Bunchy's requesting me to translate for her the German-Romanian-Ukrainian-Yiddish linguistic salad I had inherited from Cassandra. More than willingly, I exaggerated its humorous aspects. For her, I opened up the treasure trove of anecdotes that had accumulated around my exotic nurse over the years. I gloated over the mirth this incited in Bunchy and relished even more that she did not follow the earlier examples of Miss Knowles and Mademoiselle Derain in treating "the savage one" with even more condescension and contempt but, quite the contrary, showed her a heightened affection and consideration. Surely Cassandra clung to her like a neglected dog that finally finds its master, and Bunchy took her under her personal wing. I believe Cassandra owed to Bunchy her instruction in many of the household skills she later displayed to such advantage in running my father's home. As for me, I attached myself to Bunchy even more passionately, if possible, than I had to Cassandra, and I have felt all my life that I too owe what little virtues I may possess to Miss Lina Strauss. Among these I include my lifelong striving to overcome a fatal indifference, an innate indolence of soul. For the benefit of others and for myself, I have always pretended to feelings that in truth I experience only tepidly, if at all. The only wholehearted feeling I knew during my childhood and before Bunchy's appearance was hatred.

For it would have been anything but natural if I had not hated my sister. She knew how to keep my irascibility red-hot with the same mastery with which she knew how to throw the hourglass cone of her diabolo, catching it effortlessly on the string stretched between the sticks held in her skillful hands. For that, at times I hated her with an almost religious frenzy. I came close to murdering her when she made fun of me because she had somehow found out that I was enamored of a lady whose picture I had cut out from one of my mother's fashion magazines; or when, knowing that we were still dressed in identical outfits, she intentionally chose to wear a frock that she knew would torment me because of its girlishness; or when, behind my back, she changed a sentence I had composed laboriously in mirror-writing type, so that it would be full of sense-distorting words and ludicrous orthographic errors when, unsuspecting, I thought of proudly showing my product to others. (No one, incidentally, hit upon the possibility that my type box was meant to serve for the making of matrices from which the actual type fonts would be pulled. Probably Uncle Rudolf had somehow lost these. I continued undaunted to print my mirror writing, assiduously and passionately, and resented any interference in my hobby, which I concentrated on all the more intensely and ferociously.) Just as, earlier, Cassandra had known how to exacerbate the feud between us for possession of the chamber pots until it became absurd, tipping it over into the realm of play and blunting its sharpness, so Bunchy proceeded along the same strategic lines: she expanded the textual changes made by my sister into new and hilarious sentences and distorted the orthographic blunders into amusing monstrosities, then suggested that we recompose this nonsense into readable palindromes, unaffected by the reverse mirror writing. And before we knew it, my sister and I were sitting amicably side by side over the type box.

I was an affable child and, later, a notoriously good-natured young man. Once I overheard my mother saying to someone who had praised my patience, "He is not patient. He has a cold heart." She was right. There were few emotions, however stormy their inception, that did not quickly perish in the cool climate of my inner self. Once I came close to admitting this to Bunchy. It was at the start of the winter of 1937–1938, long after she had left us; my sister had been dead for five years and childhood lay far behind in a mythical past. After some eventful years in Bucharest, I had returned to Vienna. Bunchy lived and taught there, a cult figure to her many pupils. We had not seen each other since my sister's death but were as close with each other as ever before; I felt no reluctance in telling her of the sordid quarrel that by then had erupted between my mother and Philip over the Odaya. I also told her about my last day hunting there with my father, and how I had felt that that lucky, almost random last shot of a hare marked the end of a phase in my life. "Maybe this was not the case for you alone," said Bunchy.

At the moment, I didn't attach as much significance to her remark as I would only a few months later, in March 1938, but I was intent on speaking of the past. The magical sentence "Do you still remember when . . ." was uttered in an ironic, melancholy mood, as we noted the various blind spots that prevented us from gaining a fuller and clearer view of what had once been present and was now the past. "Do you still remember," I said to the old lady in black (in the fifteen years that had gone by with spooky swiftness since her blissful presence in our house, and during those last precarious years of peace between the two cataclysmic world wars, I never saw her again in a white summer dress, so that the image I kept of her in the Bukovina unconsciously was imprinted on my psyche as the impression of a sunnier world basking under an immaculate blue sky, in strong contrast to the actual pains and tribulations that this period had held for me. Bunchy in the earlier days was a festive and youthful figure, even though she was already of advanced years. The stately matron I faced in the early winter of 1937–1938—she was living in a room crammed with furniture and memorabilia in the house of one of her benefactors in Vienna—belonged to the stormy, confusingly unsettled era of my growing up, but in her widowlike black two-piece suit, of a cut that was even more outmoded now than it had been earlier in the Bukovina, with her ramrod-straight posture and her snow-white hair over the high Ibsenesque brow, she conjured for me a Victorian epoch reaching back even further into the past than the turn of the century—now she had to be well over seventy; her mind was as alert and sharp as ever and she still had her ready laughter of earlier times), "do you still remember," I said to her, "when we went to the Odaya for the first time? We were alone. Father took us and immediately left; he was going to fetch us the next day. You took me around the property and showed me everything and explained it all in detail—how it had been in my grandparents' time, how my mother and aunts and uncle had joined you there in the summer as your pupils, how my parents had been exiled there—as Mother thought of it: Father always away on assignments, Mother most of the time in Egypt or Switzerland, and my sister sole mistress of the house with her retinue of nurses and servants, a child mostly left to her own resources, growing up almost as if bewitched, happy, rich in poetic life, yet only a mere child, family offspring no different from myself. . . . That, for me, was deliverance from the trauma of not-being when my sister was already of this world. It's hard to explain why and how, but it somehow took away the bitterness of my envy of her. At a single stroke I saw that the wondrous four years that were my sister's advantage over me did not belong to her alone. There had been others too, and then they had been joined by me, a latecomer, yet one of them. I—how shall

I say it?—had entered the flow of time. The world I had not been allowed to experience belonged to the same world in which I took breath. The Odaya was no longer a dead memorial to my sister. I had only to blow away the dust from the furnishings for the room to fill with life once again and for the specters lying in wait to be chased away. That mysterious part of my sister's life, which she so jealously guarded, henceforth also belonged to me."

"Yes," said Bunchy, "it had become history and was no longer myth."

"But wasn't that precisely what my sister died of?" I asked.

"No," said Bunchy, "though it might well be that renouncing her own myth ate away at some of her life force. But she had to do it. It is dangerous to venture too far into the mythic realm."

"Anything is dangerous that you don't dedicate yourself to unconditionally. I maintain that someone who falls from a rock face can fly so long as he abandons himself completely to the falling."

"Yes," said Bunchy, "until he hits the earth."

"What I always liked about Pomerania is its matter-of-factness."

"You're right in this too. But let's talk about the Odaya."

"Do you still remember how I told you that once I had been there with Mother and had a memorable falling-out with her? . . . It was one of our truly intimate hours, we walked arm in arm, holding each other close, mother and child in heartfelt union, like that other time—was it earlier? was it later?—in Constanţa, when my beautiful model ship foundered so swiftly and both of us just laughed and went on to eat ice cream, like a couple in love to whom nothing can matter. . . . That time at the Odaya, our harmony was even more intimate, if that is possible; we stole away from all the others; not even Cassandra stood between us. And I collected all my courage and asked her whether I could have a pony of my own; it would be so easy to keep at the Odaya, and even if I could come out only once a week or month, it would still be my very own pony. She shook her head angrily—you know well how she turns to stone once she's caught in her panicky fear. Of course I immediately understood. She feared to let me go riding: I would fall off and break my neck, the pony would trample me or dash off with me, never to be seen again—God knows what else she imagined. . . . So I said that of course I wouldn't ride alone, and only near the house, in the yard or park or whatever we called it. Maybe I wouldn't even ride at all, but just drive the little cart Uncle Rudolf used for his pony, which was in the carriage house. She became quite gruff and said, 'No, it's out of the question, and that's that.' I was so angry that I ran off to the orchard, where she wasn't likely to look for me. I hated her as much for her obstinate refusal as for the disruption of the happiness, for her lack of understanding and her manic anxiety. I hated her for having soured our happy time together at the Odaya and for all those other moments when she envenomed our lives by her foolish aberrations, for every pill of Formamint stuffed into our apprehensive mouths. Do you still remember those delicious Calvil apples, with their paper-thin skins, from the Odaya orchard? They were just about the only thing we got out of the farm—that and our Christmas carp and your artichokes; but even those had to be washed in permanganate before we were allowed to eat them. Well, when I ran away from Mother, so full of hatred for her, a whole basket of those apples stood under a tree, and just as I was about to take one out for myself, a giant of a man jumped down from its branches—a kind of cross between Rasputin and Tolstoy, in heavy boots and a Russian-type smock and scraggly hair down to his shoulders and a beard reaching all the way to his belly. He cursed and bellowed at me with the voice of a bear. . . . He was one of those Lipovanians who came and bought up the fruit harvests in the Bukovina. I hadn't noticed him up there in the tree and had no idea that we had sold our fruit. Now he'd descended from heaven and was loudly scolding me—I was not only terrified and mortified for being thought a thief, but crushed to imagine that this was meant to be a heavenly punishment for my hatred of Mother. Do you still remember, Bunchy? I told you about it when we were alone at the Odaya, and then you asked me what I really believed in."

"And?" asked Bunchy. "What was your answer?"

"What could I answer at that time? What can I answer even

today? What do I believe in? In everything and nothing. Today—
maybe with a bit more awareness—less than everything, more
than nothing. You know what our religious education was like.
You always called us the happy pagan heirs of Christendom.
Cassandra never missed the chance to drag me into Orthodox
churches, and I supposed it was there that I felt most comfortable
in the lap of God, enclosed in that mystic twilight, with the
worm-eaten wood, polished dark brown by much handling, and
the crumbling gold and ancient red of the icons: a firmament of
long-faced saints with the glittering disks of their halos crowning
their carefully combed heads; lulled to sleep by clouds of incense
and the honeyed scent of beeswax candles, gently cradled by the
fluctuating voices of bass, baritone and tenor priests with their
beards, their greasy robes and their stovepipe hats. But the most
sensually intense faith—if I may put it like that?—I indulged in
was the Catholic devotions honoring the Virgin Mary in May, for
that was my mother's childhood faith. Not much remains of it
now except a breviary bound in red velvet, which she probably
opened for the last time at her wedding and never looked at again,
and a similarly unused rosary. Of the Ten Commandments she
probably retains only the fifth, though even there she excepts
Father. Remember her indignation over his antipapal slogans
from the Break with Rome movement, which he had adhered to
during his Storm and Stress period? Yet when all is said and done,
I'm more than willing to let myself be wrapped in the heavenly
deep blue of the mantle of our Blessed Virgin with her starry
crown, and I've always tried to identify myself with the infant in
her arms (though the discrepancy in age always bothered me:
either the sweet child seemed too small and precocious or he
already wore a beard and lay dead in his mother's lap). . . .
Polyphonic bells also aroused emotions encouraging me to sur-
render to the nameless; the gold in the saints' halos, glittered as
brightly in churches of the Sacred Heart, where guardian angels
stood ready to spread open their swan's wings to guide and
protect me on the narrow path over the abyss. Long before all this
petrified into the spectacular splendor of Gothic and Baroque
cathedrals, which nowadays only evoke art-historical awe in me,

it invested my soul with a basic emotional tone that set me off to advantage, mainly over Jews, I thought, although I couldn't say exactly how. Later on, in Kronstadt, I sang in the Protestant church choir, most gloriously in the *St. Matthew Passion:* See Him! Whom? The bridegroom see. See Him! How? A lamb is He. O sacred head sore wounded, defiled and put to scorn. O kingly head surrounded with mocking crown of thorn. And soon after that, Nietzsche's observations on a God who weeps . . . But we weren't that far yet, that autumn, how many years ago?—fifteen, sixteen?—it was before our parents separated and before you left us, before I was sent to Kronstadt to the house of the subsequent bishop of Transylvania: impressive man of God, neo-Platonist, with a finely developed Adam's apple and a preacher's baritone. . . . A rigid world in the shadow of the Black Church: black robes closed with silver clasps like knights' cloaks, limp clerical berettas and philistine double chins squeezed in dignified probity into collar bands and ruffs . . . And also the singsong of pious Jews emanating from the prayer houses in Czernowitz, and their apostle heads with long side-locks under the fox tails of their rabbinical hats . . . All of that passed through and over me, leaving traces but no impression in depth. Never mind the hodgepodge of Plato, Hinduism, the cobbler Böhme and shamanic magic that the spiritualist circles around Aunt Hermine infiltrated in my brain the year my sister died. What impressed me in all that—probably because it's so comforting—was the doctrine of transmigration of souls. How soothing a distance it provides from one's present life! How long ago was all that? A mere five years of eternity . . . Well, I make fun of all of it, and yet surreptitiously I cross myself and pray that Our Lord may forgive my heresies; even though I do not believe in *His* existence, I send my fervent prayers to *Him* in heaven whenever there is danger of anything going wrong in my life or when I truly wish for something. This, my beloved Bunchy, is the reply to your Faustian question, which back then I couldn't give you."

"It could all have been foretold quite easily at the time," said Bunchy. "Together with all your signs of a predisposition to typical adolescent cynicism."

"I'm all the more grateful that you didn't intervene. For I now say, 'It's of no concern to me.' Probably I'm stuck in the cynicism of puberty. But it doesn't disturb me. I look at the garbage heap of religious impressions in my soul with an affectionate, tolerant smile. Everything lies peacefully side by side, higgledy-piggledy, and I don't want to think that one day I might be assaulted and enthralled by one or the other of the pieces lying there, that I might want to penetrate the theological dungheap, perhaps the arguments on the divine nature of Christ or the difference between 'is' and 'signifies'—certainly most interesting questions. . . . I suppose I lack something there, you know? Something is missing that other people have, which you really could get hold of me with, grasp and shake me, seize and move me for once. . . . But that isn't why I told you of the incident with Mother and the Lipovanian come down from heaven. We spoke of myths and I found myself thinking how you had opened my eyes about Cassandra's fairy tales. Up to then, everybody merely doubled over when I retold these in her own linguistic mishmash. That they contained something very beautiful, that their distortion through Cassandra's impish spirit held great fascination—only you saw this. Will you forgive me if I tell you that this has had a deeper religious impact than all the inanities the catechists and pastors tried to drill into me? If you ask me now what I believe in, I'm tempted to say that it's the magic of words. Do you remember that there was one word my sister and I would pronounce only with horror and for wicked purpose when nobody else was around? Even then we were so scandalized by it that whenever one of us used it, the other ran to the grown-ups and denounced it: 'He'— or she—'has pronounced The Word.' It was nothing more than a very vulgar expression we had picked up for 'mouth'—'kisser.' We knew much worse words, but this one—God knows why— seemed to us the utmost sacrilege. Well, one night when we were alone in our rooms, I heard my sister tiptoeing in the dark toward my bed. She bent over me and whispered, 'You shut your kisser once and for all.' It was like a curse in one of Cassandra's fairy tales, and though I was scared by it, I felt there was something beautiful in it, something that kept me in awe of its power."

Bunchy remained quiet a few moments. It is carved in my memory that she then unexpectedly asked, "Do you still draw much?"

"Not at all," I had to admit. "I lost out on the years when I could have been trained."

She didn't say "A pity!" as did everyone else to whom I gave the same answer to the same question. After another short pause she asked: "How old are you now?"

"Twenty-three," I replied resignedly, "almost twenty-four."

She nodded earnestly, if ironically, and said, "Well then, you can have a glass of sherry with me."

That was in November 1937, and we were speaking of a time that seemed to me very far removed in the past, as generally happens with a twenty-three-year-old remembering his child-hood—that is, much further removed than is the case for me today at seventy-five. The intervening years held their own disappointments and lost illusions, and Bunchy's question whether I still drew touched a sore spot. When she had been with us, she had supported my passion for drawing, and that too had been beneficial to my developing self-reliance. That I had talent—more important still, an insatiable passion that displaced and superseded all my other occupations—was commonly accepted; everyone thought of it as something I was born with and therefore as nothing special; no one considered that it also threw me back on myself; and no one encouraged me. It was also accepted that I was in another world whenever I had a crayon in my hand and thus was well out of the way, bothered no one and knew no other conflicts than those resulting from the discrepancy between my insufficient technical skill and the notion I had in my mind of the perceived subject. The household was not spared my temper, my accesses of crabbiness and susceptibility, my occasional outbursts of anger, but when these were occasioned by my playing with crayon and sketch pad, they were smiled at. No one seemed to understand that this avocation was part of my nature, indeed its very foundation, through which my personality and *life* could have developed. Bunchy was able to lay the first stones toward such a development, but there was no follow-up. She was the first—and only—person who understood my needs, who had helped and corrected me, and who had drawn the attention of others to my capabilities. Incomprehensibly, not even my own father, despite all his own joy in his pictorial creations, showed any interest in my talent; I suspect that it irritated him that I could create, with three or four strokes and more spontaneously, something that he could reproduce only painstakingly, with laborious concentration and careful constraint. He could not teach me anything in draftsmanship, and I lacked the inclination for watercolors or oils. I watched his own efforts with indifference, and regrettably, this was to remain the limit of our relations in the artistic realm. But under Bunchy's inspiration I blossomed. With a stroke of genius she had given me a toy with which I could experience all the bliss of self-forgetting, time-oblivious fulfillment: she taught me to adapt my little printing press (which in time lost many of its letters) into a linocut press. Secretly I copied Masereel and thus earned my first laurels.

All too soon these gathered dust. Away from home, in Kronstadt and later in Austrian boarding schools, different skills were demanded of me, which I managed to master, albeit reluctantly and with only a modicum of success. I had only enough time to draw malicious caricatures of our teachers, which amused my classmates. Soon any fun I took in this palled. Other and more banal passions supplanted what once had been truly a gift from heaven.

After our separation from Bunchy, my sister remained in constant touch with her in Vienna. Our beloved governess established herself as a private tutor but maintained close relation with my grandmother's household. I, for my part, found myself propelled out of the family orbit and lived an emotional double life. Between the heavy, vine-encrusted walls of the old rectory in the shadows of the monumental Black Church in Kronstadt, supervised and strictly disciplined by the taciturn and ascetic high apostle of health, Court Counselor Meyer, I pined away in homesickness. Even the bluest summer day was steeped in melancholy despondency. No game, no breathless romping, no adventurous discovery in the adult world (for instance, that a bordello, which we secretly spied on, operated in one of the city-wall towers) could still my longing for Cassandra's brood-warmth, redolent with the smell of peasant bread, or for the delicate scenting of my mother's wardrobe—I even missed my sister as an irrevocable loss. The countryside around Kronstadt was heavy with golden corn in the dark embrace of the forests; the town, comfortably embedded in a hollow between low hills, was smiling and friendly; but the high blueness of the sky above, where swallows tumbled, seemed lined in black by reason of the all-pervading bleakness of the Lutheran spirit; it was a firmly grounded world but I had not been born in it, and it was different from mine, different by its greater specific gravity, a higher degree of ethical hardness in comparison with which my world appeared frivolous and flimsy. It was a Protestant world of elders, edifyingly reminded of its own strength by regular and finely wrought sermons, mightily thunderous with pious chorales pacifying the soul—a world in which I felt futile, and as weightless as a pigeon feather tumbling down from the nowhere high above the church steeple, down to the cobblestones of the marketplace. I was of another faith (if any at all), one that in these parts was coolly rejected and one that I betrayed myself: each Sunday I lent my voice to the choir of young voices filling the majestic nave of the Black Church—never my own church—with the praises of God; I could not free myself of the obscure fear that in doing so I burdened myself with a sin. I was never quite free of other guilt feelings, tainted as I was by the ambiguous aura surrounding a child from a broken marriage, which in those days was rare and morally impugnable and which therefore made me precociously and somewhat disreputably up-to-date, a quality that in Kronstadt was repudiated on principle. I missed my sister as a companion in this misfortune and as living proof that ours was a special fate and that I was not alone in daring to be different. When I went home, after the torments of another school year, I forthwith was caught up once again in the inescapable grid of my mother's anxiety-obsessed injunctions and prohibitions, a net that smothered every expression of vitality and every initiative, numbed all pleasures and, like a Nessus shirt woven of manic precautions, instead of protecting us—as intended—from the wrongs and perils of life, irritated and burned our skin. I would have given anything to be allowed to stay with my father in the woods, but this my mother prevented by taking us to the Carinthian lakes and the Black Sea. The days on which it was granted me to accompany the Great White Hunter on his game stalks were numbered.

Time in Kronstadt then also became a thing of the past—leaving me with another kind of homesickness for its self-assured order, though this one gentler and more readily arranged. Bunchy was far away and had lost her reality, become once more a mythic figure. She belonged in equal measure to the painfully missed nesting warmth of home and, in some way hard to explain, to the firm, quietly confident texture of time in Kronstadt. Where did I stand in all this?

Naturally, I was not perceptive enough to realize that so-called reality encompasses too many aspects ever to be unambiguously that which it professes to be; reality was for me always changeable according to the belief of the moment, and thus dubious in its ultimate effect. Henceforth I looked outside my own existence for the essential. I read adventure stories, as was but fitting at my age. And I came upon Mark Twain. In the wondrous perils and experiences of Huckleberry Finn, I (together with millions of other dream-haunted boys) found everything I longed for, all the freedom I lacked.

I attempted to share this enthusiasm with my sister. (She was reading H. G. Wells then and when I asked her about it, rejected my curiosity with a cold, "You couldn't understand it," which led me to read *The Shape of Things to Come* behind her back; I failed to understand what it was that supposedly I could not comprehend—a frustrating experience.) As to Twain, she commented dryly: "If his own printing press had its letters cast like the ones in your press, no wonder he went bankrupt."

I didn't understand what she was talking about. She explained it to me but not without that subtle malice which took the wind out of my sails and at the same time kept me from—as she liked to term it—"putting one over on the rest of the world." The miniature printing press that Bunchy had given to Uncle Rudolf and then had passed on to me had come to her originally from Mark Twain: Bunchy had been his lady companion before she came to our mother's family—it must have been in the years between 1891 and 1897, when Twain indeed had engaged in a failed speculation with a printing operation.

The term "lady companion" allowed for implications that in my eyes gave Bunchy a new dimension. Not that Bunchy was actually Mark Twain's mistress, even though she remained his companion after his wife's death. But this chapter in her biography, regarding which she left us in the dark, held a definite romantic allure. Though it was proof of her discretion that she never spoke of it, this rankled in me: we had not become as close as I had fancied. Even my sister heard of the matter only later in Vienna from one of our aunts (the socialist one, I imagine).

The significance of the disparaging undertone that could not be missed in my sister's disclosures dawned on me only gradually. It referred by no means to Mark Twain, to whom my fifteen-year-old sister generously granted high rank as a writer, and even less did it refer to Bunchy's role, whatever its intimacy, in his life. On the contrary: what she sought to express was that these personalities and events were entirely outside my ken. In any connection with them, I was conceded a barely marginal and subaltern part, and under no circumstances was I to derive pride from the fact that I happened to own a memento of Mark Twain; it would have been worse than presumptuous for me to imagine that Bunchy thought me worthy enough to be connected, through her gift, to that part of her past. In particular, I was to keep myself strictly outside the legendary period when Bunchy had been Mr. Twain's companion in Florence. This was preeminent cultural territory, forbidden to Cassandra's nursling. That Bunchy had felt enough affection for me to give me the miniature printing press that possibly had been a model of the one that had led to Twain's financial demise meant nothing at all; being given a token, even one so meaningful in its allusions, was far from the same as having access to the Florentine part of her life, spent at the side of the author of *Huckleberry Finn*. In contrast, Bunchy, long before, had given my sister the poems Michelangelo had written to Vittoria Colonna, and had told her a great deal about Florence, and the connection was deepened additionally by her recent art-historical studies in Vienna. . . . To all of this I had no rejoinder: every word was true, and thus I was dismissed and could go to continue my little adventures with *Huckleberry Finn*.

This sobering reminder had its effect when next I met Bunchy. This was after some scholastic misadventures, ingloriously at variance with Huckleberry Finn's, and after the boarding school in Fürstenfeld, in eastern Styria. There too I had not remained long. Irrespective of the fact that as the admiring son of my father the huntsman, I was expected to show appropriate submissive-ness to the offspring of the author of the six-hundred-page defini-tive work on the partridge, I had shown myself a rebel and been expelled. Back in Vienna at the school for failed students, I caused my relatives serious worries as to whether I was not headed for outright criminality. At least that is how they behaved. In a way, I acted as if I were already wearing a convict's garb. Thus did I appear one day at Bunchy's, supposing that she too was outraged at the depth of the evilness with which I had disappointed her expectations.

Six years had gone by since we had seen each other, almost half of my own life. Bunchy — by now endowed for me with the fame of a remarkable biography, which had taken her overseas and had reached unheard-of heights, what with a circumnavigation of the world and an instructive sojourn of several years in Florence, mecca of Western cultural aspirations, now seemed even more legendary than before — and that first apparition of her belonged to the never-never land of a past that had lost credibility. So it was no longer a kindhearted lady in summery white whom I now confronted after so long a separation, but — if this were possible — an even more imposing matron in severe black. She seemed a head shorter, but I had grown by precisely that amount. I bowed, bashful and reticent.

"What's this?" she said. "Don't I get a kiss?"

I forced myself to relax and found myself all the more constrained. "Forgive me! It's been so long—I'm simply embarrassed."

"Embarrassed?" said Bunchy, lingering on the word and arching her eyebrows in disapproval. "Don't be so full of your own importance."

That was like the lash of a whip, particularly since it had been said in front of a witness—without having announced myself, I had burst in on one of her tutorials: an elegant young man with glasses and smooth black hair, quite obviously from one of Vienna's best Jewish families, was sitting on the sofa behind the round table at which Bunchy generally faced her pupils. At his back, reproductions of drawings by Michelangelo of Vittoria Colonna hung on the wall. I froze. The young man showed a smiling understanding that only worsened the situation. Of course, he knew my sister, appreciated her intelligence, her charm and wit. . . .

I avoided visiting Bunchy for several years. But in the interim, her admonition bore fruit. Whenever insecurity befell me, I would take her sharp reminder to heart—yes, even today. She helped me gain a good portion of disdain for this world.

Nor did I see much of my sister in those years. As long as we were at boarding school, we saw each other only on Sundays for lunch at Grandmother's. Later, she attended the Consular Academy and spent every free moment with her subsequent betrothed, Fritz. As for me, there followed a confusing succession of diverse studies, listlessly begun and ingloriously broken off: three semesters of mining in Leoben, two semesters of snipping away at corpses at the medical faculty in Vienna, two semesters of architectural studies at the Technical Academy, also in Vienna. Then one evening, at the house of a girl whom I was courting, I met Bunchy by sheer coincidence. No one there even had any inkling that we knew each other. The fact that I had been brought up by Bunchy considerably raised my standing in the eyes of both the wooed girl and her parents. Here too Bunchy enjoyed the love and devotion that all her former and present pupils and charges gave her, and something of this also reflected on me; my documented

antecedents so to speak ennobled me. Bunchy told of my grandparents, of my mother and her siblings, of my sister and me and
our father, of the Odaya and Cassandra; it was a tale rich in
anecdote, and everybody listened with all the more interest as
Bunchy knew how to place me in the foreground of general
attention time and again. I was allowed to pander to my
weakness—as my sister would have termed it—for dramatizing
Bunchy's story graphically. Once more Cassandra's linguistic
blossoms shone forth in all their glory and entertained an audience who knew how to appreciate them: well-educated Jews seem
to me to have a remarkable feel for language.

I took Bunchy home. In front of her door, the open wings of
which were secured by a heavy cast-iron grille, we bid each other
an affectionate good-bye. From then on I never let a free day pass
by without visiting her, taking her out or driving her into the
Vienna Woods or to the nearby hills, or going with her to the
theater or concerts. She knew, of course, of the worries my family
had about me. "Do you have any conception of what you really
want to do in life?" she asked me one day.

"You know it as well as I and everyone else. I've been saying it
forever and to anyone who wants to listen. I want to *draw,* and
nothing else."

Bunchy had no telephone in the two rooms she occupied in her
benefactor's house, and she was reluctant to use his. "Get me to
the next public phone," she ordered. Once there, she dialed a
number and explained my case to a person unknown to me. In
silence she listened and then noted down a number and an
address.

"Present yourself tomorrow morning at eight o'clock at this
address," she said to me. "It is an advertising studio. The gentleman I talked to is one of the managers of Siemens-Schuckert [a
large industrial concern]. The owner of the advertising studio is
indebted to him as a major client, so much so that he will not
hesitate to take you on as an apprentice. He is being advised of
your coming this very day. Woe to you if you disgrace me!"

I did not disgrace her. The owner of the advertising studio,
Karl Dopler, and his wife, a concert pianist, became my intimate

friends. Day in, day out, I drew and daubed for twelve self-forgetting hours; we shared our evening meals, our personal and professional joys and woes, the worries for the success of the agency, the pleasure over newly obtained orders and the hope of additional ones, as well as the disappointments over those that eluded us; we praised each other for work well done and consoled each other over work we happened to have botched. Karl Dopler was not a great artist but a solid craftsman from whom I learned a great deal and who gave me the down-to-earth encouragement that had been missing from the rapturous praises heretofore thoughtlessly heaped on my natural gifts. Dopler too appreciated my talents, which he acknowledged ungrudgingly as superior to his own, and he promoted them in every way he could. All this was a double blessing. Not only did it put an end to the awkward period of my disorientation—the dawdling away of my time in trivial pursuits, nightclub-hopping and whoring around—and give my whole life a happy foundation; at the same time it relieved my family of the nagging worry about my dubious fate, while delivering me from their aggravating supervision. However, a much more serious calamity entered all our lives: my sister took ill and, inexorably, followed the agonizing path to her death.

This death put a sudden end to my career as a commercial artist. It also nipped in the bud another potential career as stage designer. The parents of the girl in whose house I had met Bunchy were giving a party for their daughter in their villa in Döbling, a garden district of Vienna, and they entrusted me with the decorations. One of the guests, the writer Sil Vara, much celebrated in the Vienna of that time for his play *The Girlhood of a Queen,* was so impressed with my decorations that he had me design the setting for a party in his apartment. Among those at the party were Luise Rainer, with whom I forthwith fell hopelessly in love, and the most famous stage designer of those days, Professor Strnad, who was as successful at the Vienna Opera as at the Metropolitan in New York. He asked me to become one of his assistants. Bunchy was exultant. "When I saw your sister for the last time," she told me, "she talked about you. She hardly could speak anymore but said very clearly and slowly, 'I always knew he would turn out all right.'"

My mother would not be misled by such auspicious constellations. She had staged her bereavement over my sister's death so dramatically that everyone feared for her health. She could not be left alone in Czernowitz; her life with Philip had become intolerable; the quarrel over the Odaya was festering; and her sisters, who theoretically at least were its co-owners, made themselves parties to the dispute. Her almost daily letters demanded with ever greater urgency and with increasingly energetic force that I come to join her. She wrote that the thought of Christmas was driving her out of her mind; we should not be surprised if she were to do herself some harm. This time it sounded convincing. My aunts escorted me to the station in order to ascertain that I really took the train to Czernowitz. As I was taking leave of Bunchy, she gave me as a Christmas present for my mother Franz Werfel's *Barbara*. "It is not meant to comfort her," she commented, "and even if it were," she added—and for the first time I detected sharpness in her voice—"it wouldn't help her. For she belongs to those whom the hard words of the Bible are meant for: *For unto every one that hath shall be given, and he shall have abundance: but from him that hath not shall be taken away even that which he hath*. Don't worry. It's merely for Christmas. You'll be back right after." It was not merely for Christmas. It took me a full five years to get back to Vienna.

This had been in December 1932, when I was almost nineteen. At twenty, I was to do my military service, and the Romanian authorities, who suspected any member of an ethnic minority of readiness to commit subversive acts, particularly desertion by those liable to serve in the armed forces, refused to extend my passport before I had done that service. I was trapped in Czernowitz. Moreover, I was told that my Austrian high school diploma would not assure me of the status of volunteer officer candidate, who served only one year. As a drafted recruit I would have to serve a full three years; the only way to avoid that was to return to the school bench and get a Romanian diploma. What I then learned of Romanian history was a rightfully earned gift from the Odaya: I had legitimate roots in the country. But this was a gift like the one in Cassandra's fairy tale in which the beauteous king's daughter requests from the enamored shepherd, "Give me something that you fail to give me." He obeys the order by giving her a swallow that flies away as soon as he opens his hand.

Soon after my homecoming, my mother showed me an apricot tree she had planted years before, which had forked and grown into two strong trunks. Its health was close to her heart, for she had symbolically transferred it to the well-being of her two children. One of the trunks had now withered but the other one was all the stronger in its sprouting greenery. I was somewhat leery of this parable, for nothing could make me believe that I was anywhere near thriving. Bunchy wrote that Professor Strnad had unexpectedly died. The news left me cold; I had given up my ambitions and no longer drew. To learn Romanian as well and as quickly as possible, and to have as much fun as possible at the same time, I had surrounded myself with Romanians of my own age with whom I carried on, with wanton lack of inhibition as I had prior to the happy, salutary interlude at Dopler's studio, pub-crawling and chasing girls I also lost myself in pseudo-religious speculations and practices.

My family had been struck by death—not in the abstract but concretely and in shocking immediacy, and my mother saw to it that I would not repress this experience. Her mute despair continued to scream for the dead child; she would have liked nothing better than—as the phrase had it—to scratch the departed from the earth with her fingernails. I did my best to keep her company in this fruitless rattling at the irrevocable. The no-longer-being-of-this-life was for me as inconceivable as the not-yet-being-of-this-world had once been. In vain I tried to reawaken that dark terror which, in the remote days of my childhood and with Cassandra's gruff warning ("One day you too will be dead"), had made me realize the significance of death. It was a weightless knowledge, and lacked the stony heaviness with which earlier it had sunk into my heart. Soon the thought of my sister's death left my soul as empty as it did my brain; I neither felt anything nor thought of anything in this connection. Mother's attitudinizing like a latter-day Niobe irked me, and I suspected that she was casting a sidelong glance at her audience, while at the same time I was troubled that with my notorious coldness of heart I might be doing her an injustice. I accused myself of insensitivity and could never have dared admit that my sister's death had brought her closer to me than she had ever been in life—a thought that to anyone would have seemed absurdly perverse.

In those days I would look endlessly into the mirror until my face was no longer my own but some strange living organism entirely surrendered to the passage of time—a mechanical toy, the driving motor of which whirred relentlessly while I remained timeless in another dimension of my being and beyond the image in the mirror's depth. There my emotions were no longer my own, nor did I miss the heart I lacked.

While my sister was wasting away, one of my aunts, who headed a number of spiritualistic circles, had arranged several séances for her salvation in which I was allowed to participate. Although no medical help materialized from the beyond, there had been some manifestations that were astounding because of their inexplicability: voices spoke of circumstances that could not possibly be known to anyone unfamiliar with intimate details; admonitions and warnings made themselves heard concerning potentially wrong decisions that, indeed, did have calamitous consequences later on; but most of all, there were jubilant descriptions of the euphoria of all those who had shaken off the burden of earthly existence and now resided in the beyond, where, while not enjoying all the blissful delights of heaven, they were at least spared the tribulations of purgatory or, worse, of hell, finding themselves between reincarnations in an ecstatically timeless, weightless waiting condition, at the end of which stood that most longed-for of all goals, the promised nirvana.

Attempts were made to comfort my poor mother. Residual Catholic doctrines allowing that since my sister had died a virgin (as my mother proudly maintained) and therefore was more likely to reside in heaven than hell were inadequate to reassure her; she required certainty and, consequently, inquired in Vienna whether proof of her child's well-being could not be obtained from the unknown realm of the defunct; the spiritualistic circle headed by my aunt was fortunately able to fulfill her wish. Since it would have been onerous to travel from Vienna to Czernowitz with the whole staff of the circle, including its leader and mediums, the otherworldly committees that purportedly were in charge of determining how the over-there was to make contact with the here decided to empower my aunt with the required medial qualifications to establish a transcendental communication between mother and child.

My aunt arrived. She belonged to the dark and rather thickset type of my mother's sisters, my mother being one of the long-limbed, reddish daughters of my ethnically checkered grandparents. In accordance with her pyknic constitution, my aunt was robust, cheery and full of joie de vivre, so it was hard to imagine that she had such intimate relations with the departed that they selected her as their mouthpiece for communications from the realm of the shadows. Yet this was apparently the case. Since I was allowed to witness her mediatory services only from a discreet distance, I cannot tell whether it actually was my sister's voice that spoke through her or whether it was her own in substitution for those who had conversed with the deceased. I preferred to believe the latter, for when I had seen mediums fall into a trance (so as to lend the empty shell of their body to an astral spirit) it had been anything but an edifying sight; it was bound to frighten my mother, were she to see her sister fainting away unconscious, her eyes rolling upward until only the whites showed, raising herself up after tormented moanings and stammerings, foam on her lips, like a corpse emerging from a coffin, the glance now rigidly directed into nowhere and hands groping as if blinded. Whether my aunt had also been empowered with the ability to transcend into the astral zones, I am unable to say. My mother remained mum on the subject, as well as on the essential portent of the messages she received.

To hold these private séances, we drove to the woody hills outside Czernowitz, which in times past had been the scene for our childish games of hoops and diabolo. I now squatted on the edge of a blossomy green meadow, in the midst of which the two sisters sat down; I soon saw them in close embrace, the dark-haired one, her face lifted to heaven, apparently speaking in tongues, and the red-haired one helplessly sobbing her heart out on the former's shoulder. After they broke away from each other and we returned to the car, my mother's eyes, reddened by tears, reflected total emptiness; my aunt, on the other hand, showed her everyday cheery mien, as if nothing at all had happened. I had seen lovers returning in a similar way after indulging in clandestine copulation.

Soon my aunt returned to Vienna. Her presence seemed to have had a beneficial effect on my mother—she calmed down, but after her departure fell into an apathy of dull despair. I myself was as if boneless. I idled the days away and rampaged through the nights with my newfound friends, Romanian students with the typical characteristics of their species: proud and touchy, romantic and foolish, glowing with chauvinism. The tensions between my mother and Philip made staying in the house unbearable. I hardly ever saw my father; he came only rarely from Transylvania and tormented me with suggestions for studies I had no intention of undertaking. I was besotted with a girl whose mind and soul had been bleached to a pale blue cloudiness by Armenian clerics; I quarreled with her constantly about religious questions and she deeply resented my blasphemies. As a means of quelling my cynicism, I looked for some charitable mission and hit upon the crazy idea of replacing my aunt in her transcendental role with my mother: if my will to help her were only pure enough, why shouldn't I too be granted the privilege of being the messenger between her and her dead daughter, particularly since my sister was surely eager to provide solace from the beyond?

I sat in front of a mirror and stared fixedly into my eyes, intent in utmost concentration on emptying myself of my own being so as to be nothing but a vessel for another spirit. And then something truly uncanny happened: I felt an icy flow rising through my nostrils and into my brain . . . and I was suddenly terrified and too weakhearted to take the next step—whatever it was. I stood once again as an ordinary self, my heart pounding in my chest, abashed by my craven withdrawal from the threshold of an unimaginable adventure that might have cost me my life or my mind but probably would have enriched me by a new and unknown dimension. Yet I knew it had been my sister's wish that I should not go further. It would have established an intimacy much more indiscreet than the one I sought by kissing her at our encounter after our first separation. A short time later I broke away to Bucharest, and for the next few years all my passion was centered on horses.

This was how things stood when, finally, back in Vienna in the early winter of 1937–1938, I met Bunchy once more. Those were turbulent days when politics impinged on life everywhere in the world. But since hardly anyone I knew took any of this seriously and since grumbling about prevailing conditions was part of the everyday Viennese atmosphere, I did not grant the events any more scope than that which they occupied on the front pages of the dailies I didn't read, or in the hurly-burly of the rabble screaming slogans in the streets. I was repelled by all of it. Fortunately, this turbulence had its own tide, and so there were hours, especially in the evenings and during the night, when one was not molested by it. Bars and nightclubs thrived. The ranks of Bunchy's Jewish pupils and friends were swelled by emigrants from the German Reich, who told of horrible things happening there. One could only hope fervently that these would not occur also in Austria.

The new year began: 1938. I took Bunchy to the theater. After seeing Molnár's *Liliom* we were in such a fine mood on the way home that I linked arms with her in the fashion of Liliom, swinging her to and fro and singing: "Come, Louise, my love, come on my swing, there's lots of pleasure to be had, of our everlasting love we'll si-hi-hing!" and she almost collapsed with laughter. When we arrived at the door of her house, she coquettishly slipped behind the grille and drew it closed. For the sheer fun of it, I rattled the grille as if I wanted to be taken in — and to my incredulous surprise saw that she took me seriously, that this woman well over seventy actually assumed that I, her pupil of twenty-three, had the intention of bedding her. It amused me to no end, filled me with shame and, at the same time, much affection. I would have liked to tell her that I loved her all the more for this disclosure of the archfemale and all too human bondage to the flesh. So I pretended that I really wanted nothing more than to join her; she laughed until the tears ran down her cheeks, but saw to it that the grille was well closed, threw me a last kiss and then also closed the gate, winking at me through a gap, giggling madly, excited and flattered. Only then did the lock click shut.

Then came March 12, 1938, and Germany's annexation of Austria. A few days later Bunchy disappeared to parts unknown. It was said that she had moved to the house of friends in the country. Her benefactor in Vienna had been Baron Frankenstein, Austria's last ambassador to the Court of St. James's, who refused to serve Hitler and had sought political asylum in England. Bunchy was no longer safe in his house in Vienna, with all her circle of Jewish friends.

She remained in the country all through the war, and I had no contact with her until 1946. Then a long letter reached me that told of her circumstances and also contained the confession to a "failing." The manor house in which she had survived the war was now in the British zone of Austria. The owners, who would have been unable to produce proof of their unblemished Aryan origin, had escaped before the war, just in time. Bunchy represented their interests and continued to do so. With the end of the war, swarms of refugees arrived to whom she provided shelter and care. She was assisted in this by the British occupying forces, who supplied her with essentials. They had great respect for the old lady speaking fluent English, who now received testimonials of love and gratitude from all her friends and pupils around the world who had been able to save themselves (unfortunately not all of them, by any means). One day the British regional commander ordered all the inhabitants to assemble in the manor yard. In front of the intimidated assembly, he disclosed that among them an SS leader was hiding who was being sought for having committed major crimes. Of course he was using another name, but Bunchy was presumed to know who it was. If she were to refuse to identify him, all the subsidies would be canceled and the improvised refugee camp would be dissolved. She wrote to me that she had been left with no choice. The fate of too many unfortunates depended on her. Her conscience had to be relegated to a back place and she had to reveal whom she suspected of being the person sought. She didn't forgive herself for this denunciation and could not sleep.

A year later, came another letter: ". . . In the matter that has so heavily burdened my soul, I have finally found relief. It has come to me now how I should have behaved. I should not have denounced the man, but I should have appealed to his honor: Mr. So-and-so, step forth! That I now realize this does not absolve me of my failing at the time. But it reestablishes an ethical order: I have learned from it."

Another year later, I received the news of her death.

Of Bunchy too I have kept this weird instrument that technology has placed in our hands with which to conjure the dead back to life: a photograph. I cannot look at it without remembering something she told me about long ago on the occasion of our visit to the Odaya, her account of a recollection by my sister from the childhood days she spent there: It is a morning in early winter with no snow on the ground yet, but biting cold has settled in overnight and the world is choking in dense fog. A thin sun fights against the fog and slowly manages to consume it, so that it condenses as hoarfrost on everything; each branchlet of each bough of each tree and shrub, each bush, each blade of grass still standing, each thistle at the wayside wears a white fur that glitters under the sky, which meanwhile has become immaculately clear. My father fetches some skates and drives with my sister down to the river. The river is frozen stone-hard and black, since no snow has dulled the ice. It is transparent down to the bottom of the river, and one can count every pebble lying there. My sister is not much more than four years old; it is the first pair of skates she has ever worn, but guided by her father's gentle hand, she skates with him down the river, an endless trail, bordered by shores scintillating with rime, the reeds furry and the birches as if spun of glass, and above it all a sky of deepest blue, like the one that soon spread for her over the Adriatic.

I carry this picture in me forever: the big man on skates, clad in old-fashioned stylish garb, his bald head covered by a woolen ski cap, carefully holding the hand of the tiny girl. Her other hand is hidden in her little muff, and her face, pink-fresh from the bite of the cold, is framed by the fur-edged hood of her short coat. Thus they glide through the frost-sparkling world and draw into the black mirror of the ice the thin fishbone pattern of their traces, one in long and widely drawn sweeps, the other shorter and narrower. And all this flows together with the images of Cassandra and the lady in white who told me about it, even though in the picture I have preserved of her she is clad in black, magically arisen from the pool of memory like the shadowy apparitions that slowly took form on the photographic plates in the developing baths gently rocked by my father's hands.

Epilogue

Czernowitz, where I was born, was the former
capital of the former duchy of Bukovina, an east-
erly region of Carpathian forestland in the foothills
of the Tatra Mountains, in 1775 ceded by the former Ottoman Empire to the former Imperial and Royal Austro-
Hungarian realm as compensation for the latter's mediation in
the Russo-Turkish War; the Bukovina was at first allocated to the
former kingdom of Galicia, but after 1848 it became one of the
autonomous former crown lands of the House of Habsburg.

One can readily see that everything in this quick summary
(with the exception of the town of my birth, whose name, in the
course of historical evolution, underwent several changes—from
Czernowitz to Cernăuţi to the present Chernovtsy) is designated
as "former," that is to say, not in the present, not truly existing—
and this invests my birthplace with a kind of mythic aura, an
irreal quality. It's of no use to try to elucidate this mythic twilight
by means of historical analysis. That the Austro-Hungarian monarchy has not existed since 1918 is well enough known, yet in
Czernowitz-Cernăuţi, people acted as if they didn't quite believe
it. German remained the everyday language of most people,

Vienna was the closest metropolis, and no one thought of denying it the rank of capital. Even though the reality of Shakespearean kingdoms like those of Galicia and Lodomeria had become more than questionable, people spoke of them as if they still existed; today they speak of the Bukovina as if it were still a political entity even though it disappeared as such in 1940.

In the days between 1919 and 1940, the Kingdom of Romania governed the Bukovina with a sovereign self-assurance based on the claim that it had been the Romanians' archoriginal home soil, their Ur-land since the time of the Dacians—a claim that may be questioned. In Czernowitz-Cernăuţi, one did not go to the trouble to doubt it. In fact, that Romanian interlude was hardly more than a fresh costume change in a setting worthy of operetta. The uniforms of Austrian lancers were supplanted by those of Romanian Roşiori, infantry wasn't worth noticing much anyway, and the whole transformation was given no greater weight than the one accorded the changing scenery at the municipal theater between *Countess Maritza* and *The Gipsy Baron* or *The Beggar Student*. It took barely twenty years before the black-and-yellow on the border posts and the doors of the tobacco-monopoly shops was painted over with the blue-yellow-and-red of the new sovereigns and the double eagle on the steeples of public buildings was supplanted by the Romanian coat of arms. Then, in 1940, Cernăuţi became Chernovtsy and the whole Bukovina became something "former"; nominally it no longer existed, cut in two by a state treaty between the Third Reich and the Soviet Union, concluded in cavalier disregard of the legend about the Romanian Dacians. The region south of the Siret River, together with Moldavia, was allocated to the present People's Republic of Romania, while the northern part, with Chernovtsy, fell to the Soviet Republic of the Ukraine. As a result, Chernovtsy was no longer a capital, since the capital of the Ukraine is Kiev.

I used to hesitate when asked about my place of origin, and the reasons for this demurral were twofold: first, because the admission that I came from Czernowitz invariably drew the irrepressible comment, "Ah, I see . . ." This is not limited to former Austro-Hungarians, for whom the very name Czernowitz stands for a standard set of concepts: Czernowitz seems to be well-known everywhere as the setting of most Galician-Jewish jokes and as the breeding ground of an unmistakable type of individual. My hometown gained world fame as the melting pot for dozens of ethnic groups, languages, creeds, temperaments and customs, fused and refined there into a quintessential species of "Slaviennese" rapscallions. To what extent it is an advantage to be counted among them is a moot point. All my life I did what I could to make the best of it. The poet Paul Celan, who said of Czernowitz that it was a place where people and books had lived, has done better than I in this respect.

The second reason for my hesitation is again twofold: of the three score and fifteen years of my earthly existence I spent only the first ten in Czernowitz. After that I visited the place only sporadically — alas! for there was much to be learned there. The last time I had been there was in 1936, when I was twenty-two, fifty-three years ago. Over such a time span the original markings fade. But what contributed even more signally to my alienation was the increasing "erstwhileness" and irreality of my origins. It began to sound to me as if I had invented Czernowitz — and with it, myself.

The fact is that I actually *did* invent my own Czernowitz. Leaving aside my book *Maghrebinian Stories,* which I could not have written had I not been born and raised there, the city itself plays a fatidic role in three other of my books: significantly in *An Ermine in Czernopol* (published in English under the title *The Hussar*); marginally in the novel *Memoirs of an Anti-Semite*; and of course decisively in this one. I did not intend in any of these to write a travel guide to the actual Czernowitz-Cernăuţi-Chernovtsy, but rather to describe a mythical *topos.* Especially in *An Ermine in Czernopol,* the very title indicates that we are dealing with a literary transposition, the remembrance of the town of my childhood serving merely as a scaffolding on which to model a mythic site in which mythical events take place.

But we know that memory is anything but reliable. It selects at random what it wishes to store, discards what is not to its liking, underscores the emotional, sublimates and distorts. Thus I contributed both intentionally and unintentionally to the growing loss of reality for my place of origin, adding the odium of implausibility to its—and thereby also my own—already legendary reputation for shifty unreliability.

This hardly disturbs me insofar as the ethical question of truthfulness is concerned. I am a writer and as such I have not only the right but also the duty to raise the level of reality, as I see it, to the very point where it threatens to tip over into the unbelievable. But if one seeks to achieve this by drawing—as I do—on the autobiographical, paraphrasing and transforming it and inserting it into fictional and hypothetical happenings, then one runs the danger of falling into one's own trap, with the result that one no longer knows what is real and what is not. This exceeds the moral sphere and comes dangerously close to schizophrenia.

But since I am a conscientious person, I recently chanced the adventure of confronting my invented Czernopol with the factually existing Czernowitz still surviving in the present-day Chernovtsy. This was all the more daring an undertaking since I had given not only myself but my hometown as well half a century in which to develop into something entirely unforeseeable. Naturally I had to assume that the Ukrainian Chernovtsy of 1989, cleansed of its hodgepodge of Swabian Germans, Romanians, Poles, Jews, Prussians, Slovaks and Armenians, could no longer be the Czernowitz or Cernăuți that I had last visited in 1936. Likewise I had to assume as out of the question that Chernovtsy should have escaped the hybrid growth which, in the past few decades, has transformed all human settlements throughout the world into teeming excrescences—especially not this chameleon among cities, which the popular Austrian writer Karl Emil Franzos called around 1890 "a village of Huzules with pseudo-Byzantine, pseudo-Gothic and pseudo-Moorish buildings," and somewhat later "a Black Forest idyll" and ultimately "Little Vienna." I was sure that much of what I recalled would have to have been destroyed according to pseudo-American and pseudo-Russian notions about redesigning the future; it was likely that I would have to dig up large portions of my remembered past or else leave them permanently under tons of reinforced concrete. Equally, the erstwhile capital of the erstwhile Bukovina had meanwhile become a Soviet backwater, in which most probably dilapidation and squalor would be visible everywhere.

None of this was the case—at least it didn't seem so at first. I found myself back in my Czernowitz, the Romanian Cernăuţi from between the two murderous wars, as if I had never left, a Rip Van Winkle rubbing the sleep from my eyes without first realizing that it had been a sleep of a half-century. Everything stood in place around me exactly as it had been fifty-three years earlier. Nothing was missing—at least at first glance. A second glance revealed tiny changes. Everywhere trees had been planted on both sides of the streets, and their resplendent young greenery brought the city closer together and made the avenues, streets and alleys seem narrower and also more cheerful, almost spalike. It was altogether a Czernowitz to which I had to apologize for my skeptical anticipations. Nothing was dirty or messy. The houses were freshly painted in an imperial Austrian egg-yolk yellow that alternated with an imperial Russian pea green. The pavements were swept clean—the very same cobblestone pavements that once had been polished smooth by the hackneys' rubber wheels and the same stone slabs of the sidewalk over which I had toddled in my child's shoes and slid in my first dancing-lesson pumps, with their slippery soles, after some pretty girls along the promenade of Squires Street. The streets, to my boundless relief, were free of the tinny metastases of parked cars. Small amounts of traffic trickled by without bottlenecks, without stench and almost noiselessly. The silence made me aware of the lack of some dearly familiar sounds from the past: what was missing were the rough shouts of "Hoh!" with which the Jewish hackney drivers had shooed inattentive pedestrians out of the way of their horses, and the whirring twitter of swarms of sparrows that everywhere had greedily awaited the plentiful fall of damply steaming horse apples. The hackneys had disappeared, as had the streetcars (whose brakes had had a way of their own and often had caused confused tie-ups in the traffic). Now nimble trolley buses snaked along the old routes, the rails long since paved over, where in the past the faded red-white-and-red cars with narrow windows swayed on little metal wheels like toy boxes, to emerge in front of the town hall on the Ringplatz after having courageously mounted the steep gradient from the Prut River valley, then continuing across town, ringing their bells and shrieking at every curve, all the way out to the People's Park. Missing too was the bickering of jackdaws in the acacias across from the provincial administration building and around the onion towers of the Orthodox church, missing the rattle of rack carts on which the peasants from surrounding villages drove to market, missing their smell of cheap rotgut and the 'tinkling clopping' of their poorly shod scruffy Polack horses. The acacias were now trimmed in the Italian manner and the peasant carts were replaced by the kolkhozes' trucks. This made the city neater-looking but also more sterile.

I couldn't get over it. There could be no doubt that this was indeed the Cernăuți of my childhood, tangibly concrete and real—and yet it wasn't the Czernowitz whose vision I had carried in me for half a century: Czernopol, the city of the steppes, mythic site of mythic happenings. It was the quintessence of a provincially stolid, bright and well-kept township, undeniably revealing its imperial past, phenotypically a former provincial capital from the eastern reaches of the former Dual Monarchy, still faintly glinting with its erstwhile glory. Sensibly planned streets still presented the architectonically well-meaning and unpretentious façades of bourgeois residences from the middle and end of the last century (in which even the rare extravagances in style were tempered by the period's mediocrity). The neo-Gothic towers of the Catholic churches, the pseudo-Byzantine cupolas of the Orthodox ones and the pseudo-Moorish crenellations of the Armenian rose in urbane moderation above the level rooftops of the other buildings (I was to learn that only the flamboyant neo-Assyrian temple of the Jews had been razed during the German occupation), and in an equally mild manner the neo-Renaissance public buildings and pseudo-classic garrison barracks still helped the eye to enjoy an easy transition from

Gründerzeit architecture to a temperate Art Nouveau. All of this embedded in the fresh greenery of newly planted trees.

For me it was a fall into the unreal. I could no longer trust my senses. The city before me had been built stone by stone in duplication of my legendary Czernopol. But its overwhelming here-and-nowness was devoid of any soul; in some strange way, it was removed from its global time. Not that it had been arrested in its evolution, but rather that it had been backdated, as it were, beyond it. This present-day Chernovtsy was a repudiation both of the interwar Cernăuţi and of the imperial Austrian Czernowitz. In its unaltered surface permanence it had reverted to an abstract, provincially idyllic Belle Époque, a founders'-era dream of itself, but without spirit and life. It was the stage setting of a play that had never been produced, a contradiction in itself: a clean-up, spit-and-polish, lacquered and antiseptic city. Nothing could be felt of its once demonic nature. What could endow this cunning model of a provincial town, as the Chernovtsy of 1989 presented itself, with the wide-awake perceptiveness, the bright resourcefulness, the sharp powers of observation, the delight in ridiculing others and the biting wit of—well, precisely of Czernowitz? Nothing could be detected now of the restlessly vivacious, cynically bold and melancholically skeptical spirit that had distinguished the children of this town and made them known and famous throughout the world as Czernowitzers. And yet the city before me was an undeniable reality, and it was more persuasive than the myth, which was merely my own assertion.

It has been claimed that the spirit of Czernowitz was due to the unique propinquity and juxtaposition of the Bukovina's multiplicity of populations and to their furiously fermenting compression in its capital, their reciprocal insemination and abrasion, the challenging, constant need to react quickly and adapt shrewdly, a need that had been vital especially for the Czernowitz Jews. All of this seemed invalidated in the here and now of Chernovtsy. The motley ethnic variegation had been replaced by a homogeneous breed of people. Of those wretched avatars, issued from folksy patriotism and fatal nationalism, which had produced Walpurgis

Night—like excesses here too, hardly more than allegorical traces remained visible. On the façades of the former Deutsches Haus, Dom Polski, Romanian Casa Poporului and Ukrainian Narodni Dim could still be discerned, though faded by the strongly contrasting local weather, the frescoes of imposing female figures with bared bosoms and all kinds of symbolic appurtenances—sword, book, lyre, wheat sheaves, eagles, throttled snakes—meant to epitomize in Art Nouveau style the spirit of every nationality, each but a single component among the many of the *spiritus loci* of Czernowitz.

But the primary base element of Czernowitz had always been a cynically healthy derision for all types of lofty conviction. Any true Czernowitzer watched an exhibition of overflowing nationalistic sentiment with no greater personal involvement than that which he reserved for the Purim masquerades put on by street urchins.

Still, it was anything but shoulder-shrugging imperturbability that was responsible for letting these strongholds of conceited, chauvinistically overheated pettiness remain standing just as they had been built and decorated a century ago in the heyday of patriotic romanticism. Among all the spooky, soullessly preserved testimonies to a turbulent past, these were the only ones that appeared dilapidated. I had the impression that behind their now shabby façades these buildings were nothing but empty shells, like houses after a ruthlessly extinguished conflagration, when the firemen have done more damage than the flames—as if, at one time, the aggression they harbored had flared too violently and the people who then exterminated the spreading infection had proceeded so drastically that they also annihilated all the productive antagonisms, all the color and vivid tension that had characterized the city's contiguous admixture of a dozen nationalities.

In this connection I tried to reconstruct a scene from the past in my legendary Czernopol: a youth from the Junimea, the Romanian Youth Movement, steps from the Casa Poporului wearing the well-known costume of short, sleeveless and colorfully embroidered sheepskin jacket, and coarse linen shirt over linen trousers tightly belted in blue-yellow-and-red; there's a suggestion of a whiff of pine needles from the Carpathian forests in his hair and his eyes shine with the pride of the Dacians (whom Trajan's cohorts could never subdue, though they managed to overcome them in battle). As chance will have it, a German student passes by, a member of the folk-German fraternity Arminia, in its usual uniform: stiff collar, kepi worn at a snappy angle, fraternity colors displayed across the chest on a broad ribbon. At the sight of the Romanian he snorts contemptuously through the adhesive plaster covering a recent saber cut—an unambiguous signal that he considers the Romanian a lumpish yokel and potential adversary, even though both sit in the same lecture halls at the university. Such an encounter might all too easily lead to blows. But this time both are distracted by the appearance of a Hasidic rabbi in black caftan, with the pale skin of a bookworm and long corkscrew side-locks under a fox-pelt hat, an apparition that forthwith unites the former opponents in the happy recognition that the newcomer is the natural target of their aggression. For the time being, they content themselves with jeers and taunts, obscene gestures and curses. For the time being—I was writing of the year 1930. The great signal had not yet been given that would produce all its evil consequences.

In the Chernovtsy of 1989 such a scene is unimaginable. It haunts my mind but not those neatly kept streets. What now moved through the streets before my confused and astonished eyes was utterly uniform and obviously homogeneous, nothing provoking any particularizing pride. People strolled about at all hours of the day like a mass of workers streaming from factories at the end of their shift. Despite the occasional colorful getup, the ready-to-wear mass clothing seemed mostly to be a uniform gray. The faces were—as the saying goes—all of the same stamp: of Slavic broadness and angularity with coarse skin and light-colored hair. These were Ukrainians. In the old days we called them Ruthenians, one of the many minorities in a place where there was no majority. In all the Bukovina they did not make up more than a third of the population, in the Czernowitz of old Austria even less, and a smaller proportion still in the Romanian

Cernăuţi. Now they were the only ones left, those people's comrades of the Soviet Republic of the Ukraine, which, as the former
"Little Russia" enlarged by the annexation of Galicia and the
northern Bukovina, now accounts for more than half the European territory of the Soviet Union. Nor were these people different from other Russians. The women were almost without
exception plump, the men stocky and puffy, a people of cabbage
eaters, not in dire want, not dissatisfied but inclined to submit
resignedly to God's will, serious and well behaved. Very well
behaved, it seemed. Femininity found its expression solely and
ostentatiously in a petit-bourgeois motherliness—and perhaps
also in a fatal predilection for dyed fire-red hair. Only very young
girls wore slacks; and only a few teenagers made weak attempts
to imitate Elvis Presley hairdos. But this was mere modishness
and not an expression of a sociopolitical essence.

All in all, this certainly was not a world of ease and plenty, and
it was entirely free of the mad waste and squandering that is the
hallmark of late Occidental consumer paradises. There was no
sales talk, no urging to buy this or that, nor did anything irritate
by junky superabundance. The moderation was pleasing,
whether or not it was voluntary. I felt no obligation to purchase or
become the user of anything, and this circumstance may have
given me the deceptive impression that the people here were
possessed of the dignity of those who voluntarily do without and
content themselves with little. I could not help thinking that they
would have been to Hitler's liking.

Nor was Chernovtsy entirely without color, as I had thought at
first: the sounds of a military band were heard from what was
once called Austria Square. In the past, this had been the great
downtown market square, whither the rattling peasant carts all
converged on Mondays for the week's market, where—under a
fragrant cloud of garlic, freshly tanned sheepskins, sharp cheeses,
the smoke of *machorska* tobacco and cheap rotgut, cooking oil
and cow dung—everything under the sun was sold and bought,
from cowhides and calico kerchiefs to rusty padlocks, coachmen's whips, embroidered linen shirts, mouth organs, chickens

bundled together by their feet, butter on coltsfoot leaves, baskets of eggs, sandals (the heavy *opanka*s of the region) made of cut-up rubber tires, pocket knives, lambskin caps and innumerable other things of the greatest variety. Under the blue of the open sky, this motley, multifaceted scene resembled nothing so much as one of those drip paintings by Jackson Pollock and, at the same time, the wildly confused swarming of an anthill. There Jews haggled for used clothing, Armenians bought corn, linen rolls and skeins of wool by the carload, while Lipovanians hawked their beautiful fruit and shoemakers vaunted their while-you-wait services. Huzule women would get into a violent squabble with a gaggle of Swabians from Bistriţa; drunks beat up on each other; the blind, lame and leprous went begging; gypsies fiddled, while crafty monte players, shuffling two black aces and one red ace with hypnotizing speed from one side to the other and back again, extracted hard-earned pennies from gaping rustic simpletons as easily as did the ubiquitous pickpockets hustling in the thick of the crowd, always anxiously on the lookout for the police who, at any moment, could arrest them or extract horrendous bribes from them. It had been a place of the most intense life, teeming and full of pungent ferment, the navel of that *cosmopolis* which Czernowitz was in a much more literal sense than many a world capital.

At present this civic rectangle is a concrete-covered parade ground, wide, empty and painstakingly scrubbed. Yet not entirely gray on gray: one of its narrow sides, where the square slopes down toward the suburb of Klokuczka, has been taken over completely by a gigantic, glaring red billboard. Jumping out from the crimson background in richly golden yellow is a huge, severely stylized portrait of Lenin, dwarfing the four- and five-storied houses on the long sides of the square. A few dozen marching paces in front of it, a handful of notables were sitting at a long table, half of them in uniform, their epaulets glittering with stars, the women among them with blond hair permed in aspiring-Hollywood-starlet fashion. Another two dozen marching paces in front of the rostrum, three military bands had taken up position, each under the command of a bulbous drum major, and one after the other competing in the performance of jaunty marches and musical favorites both cheerful and solemn.

I was told that I was witnessing a competition among garrison bands. Any number of regiments and various branches of the armed services were represented in their parade uniforms. It was a colorful scene, and each band, in addition to playing its regular program, sought to distinguish itself by some optional virtuoso piece, from the Radetzky March by way of the Andreas Hofer tune all the way to the overture of *Der Freischütz*—in a word, Russian popular music. This had already lasted all morning, a Sunday morning to boot, and I would have surmised that such a performance was bound to attract a fair crowd of onlookers. Yet only a few passersby stopped briefly to look and listen—even when, toward the end, some battalions paraded by in historical uniforms, soldiers of the imperial army that had triumphed over Napoleon, and—less colorful but eerily scary in aardvarklike camouflage—of the forces that had subdued the armies of Hitler. The performance concluded with groups of dancers in regional costume, but these so obviously came from the property department of the local theater that in this place where only a few decades ago such brightly variegated garb could be seen every day and everywhere, they aroused no interest at all.

I too, the foreigner, clearly recognizable as such by clothing and comportment, aroused no interest. No curious glances were cast my way and no sign gave me to understand that I might in any way be conspicuous. It was as if I were transparent or simply did not exist. The feeling of on the one hand being very much and undeniably at home in this place, and on the other being half a century and a whole world removed from it now intensified into the irreal density of dreamed reality. I was there and yet I was not. I dreamed while fully awake—I dreamed not only this tangibly real town but also myself in it. Thus removed from my usual placement in either space or time, I started out to search for the house of my childhood. Let me anticipate right away the outcome: of all the houses in Czernowitz, of which not a stone seemed out of place, my house was the only one missing.

The house of a childhood lying half a century in the past in any case is a mostly airy structure. It consists more of views in and out of it than of solid walls: of partial views of corners, nooks and crannies, certain pieces of furniture, foregrounds and backgrounds—in short, something fragmentary, like the disparate sets in a film studio for a movie shot from the perspective of a knee-high nipper. Nevertheless I well knew—and still know—that our house had been just beyond what had then been the outermost periphery of the city, set in a large garden and giving out on three sides to open countryside. I knew—and still know—that like innumerable other neoclassical villas of its kind, its façade was supported by columns with a narrow terrace crowned by a tympanumlike gable, and that a glassed-in porch at the back looked toward the depth of the garden. It had been reached by a long street bordered by many gardens, Garden Street, in the so-called villa district of the town. I found the street without difficulty. It too was unchanged—at least for most of the way. Of dreamlike surreality, just as I had left it fifty-three years earlier, it ran between two rows of prosperous one-family houses of the kind that had incited Karl Emil Franzos to compare them to cottages in the Black Forest. Some of them greeted me as fond memories; some others, lining the street where in my own time there had been vacant lots, upset me: I knew they had not been there before, but I could not deny their factual presence. They showed no stylistic characteristic, no particular newness or lesser degree of wear and tear to differentiate them from their neighbors. No historical feature distinguished them—neither a nationally emphasized particularity denoting Romanian sovereignty in architectural terms, nor any signs of fifty years of Communist housing precepts. Back of the lilac bushes and mulleins in their front gardens, these houses, in all the idyllic romanticism extolled by Franzos, ivy-clad up to the gables, oriels and bartizans, challenged my presumption that they could not have been built in the same global period of irreality as the rest of Chernovtsy. I began to lose the unerring determination with which I had been seeking my objective. This Garden Street had become longer by a third, just as in a dream a familiar path lengthens into endlessness. And when I finally did reach the end, there, before my very eyes, rose row after row of twelve-, fourteen- and sixteen-story high-rises blocking the view of what had been open country.

I should have expected this. It was logically consistent: when considering the steep slope down to the Prut River valley which encircles much of the city, this was the reasonable and indeed sole direction in which it could have expanded—and that it would have expanded in fifty-three years I had anticipated. In any case the city had grown with an astounding mindfulness of what had been there in the past—in a spirit of such careful preservation that the results transposed me to a no-man's-land in time and into a state somewhere between dreaming and the most acute wakefulness. Not only did everything from my own time remain untouched, but the additions made to it were heavily reminiscent of that period. All the harder was it, therefore, to accept that only the house of my childhood was omitted from this reverential preservation of the past. I clearly remembered that from our southeastern windows one had a view of the poplars lining Transylvania Avenue, leading straight through the open country all the way to the airy blue horizon: the path of my childhood's deepest longings. And the road still existed, although its length could no longer be encompassed at a glance. No longer was it lined by poplars, their branches swarming with birds, but instead by residential blocks and shopping centers (in which only paltry goods were for sale). Between these and the squadron of high-rises, untidy tracts of land remained partly vacant and partly built up, haphazardly—here a student colony, there an orphanage (looking typically Romanian), here a home for the blind among some remains of tree groves, there some one-family houses of a size more appropriate for weekend cottages. In between, in front or behind, our house had once stood. But it was no longer. It had disappeared without a trace. It did not help to inquire after it. Everyone was as helpful as could be imagined, but no one knew it: they were too young or had come here too late or simply could not remember that far back. The more intense my search, the more hopelessly did I lose my way in the thickets of the unknown.

After two days of unavailing inquiry and search, the house of my childhood had become a specter that haunted only my own mind.

To test whether I was not simply the victim of schizophrenic hallucination, I once more took up my search—but this time a search for my own self, and in the center of town. I looked for the town house where my mother had lived after separating from my father, with its big garden, unique relic of Czernowitz's small-town and even rural past. And this house was still there. It stood, with gaps to its left and right, across from a quite substantial apartment house; but what once had been its garden now unfortunately lay under an expanse of concrete. What was more—and this seemed to defy logic—it somehow appeared to have shifted closer to the street. Its roof was covered with rusty sheets instead of shingles, and its walls, once hidden behind jasmine bushes, were naked and painted a horrid coffee-brown shade. The porch had disappeared. Here too, new buildings had materialized that had not been there during my time: all kinds of cozy little small-town cottages, as well as an already dilapidated factory built of yellow clinker bricks and a whole enfilade of cavelike dwellings reaching to the depth of the erstwhile garden. Again, there was not the slightest indication that all of this had not always been there, for the architectural styles were the same; everything seemed to have originated in the small-town past of Czernowitz and showed the same degree of shabby wear and tear.

I thought I was losing whatever remained of my mind: if anything had been built here since my own time, surely it had to be something more substantial than this proletarian colony! Even in the 1920s this piece of ground had been the object of lustful greed on the part of many real estate speculators and builders, all of whom my mother had heroically resisted. Since my mother's "expatriation" in 1940, the ground had been ownerless. An impressive block of apartment houses could have been built in its place, something exemplary of Communist progress; there even would have been space for some greenery around. Whatever had prevented this? It couldn't have been a historically preservative piety that saved the space for these dumps, which merely marred the neat image of the city. I could have sworn that they had not yet been there in 1936, but all appearances contradicted this sworn assertion. I could do nothing but affirm something completely implausible.

I was saved by an angel in the person of one of the local dwellers. No, no, I was quite right, these additional houses had not been there, only the ancient one in the middle, and all the rest had been added in the 1950s, a time of dire poverty in which more substantial constructions were out of the question. And yes, the horrible industrial installation had also been built then, and in great haste. And yes, indeed, the house had once had a glassed-in porch, and over there, where now there are those pre-fab row houses, that's where the stables had been, and the floors there were still always moist. Yes, over there, there indeed had been also some large cherry trees. And wouldn't I want to come into the house and see for myself that the premises still were the same, even though now they were occupied by three families?

The stone that fell from my heart sank heavily into my soul. What I had remembered from my boyhood had not been *all* phantasmagorical illusion or pure imagination. It was a great relief to be reassured on this account. But I had to pay a price. No longer could I ever think of that house of my mother's without its being superseded by the present ugly reality. The real house of my childhood had been spared this fate but instead had turned into irreality, haunted by a mythic quality that made me fear that I could never again believe in my own reality. So be it! It was indeed in the realm of the unbelievable and fabulous that my own Czernopol, the imagined counterpart of the factual Czernowitz, was located. The reality I had found in Chernovtsy threatened to destroy even this. I had to leave as quickly as possible. You must never undertake the search for time lost in the spirit of nostalgic tourism.

A Note About the Author

Gregor von Rezzori was born in the Bukovina in 1914. He studied at the University of Vienna and for a time lived in Bucharest. In West Germany after World War II, he became active as a writer and in radio broadcasting and filmmaking.

Mr. Rezzori's first books included *Maghrebinische Geschichten* (1953) and *Oedipus siegt bei Stalingrad* (1954). Another novel, *Ein Hermelin in Tschernopol,* which appeared in the United States under the title *The Hussar* in 1960, won the author the Theodor Fontane Prize in 1959. American readers first discovered Mr. Rezzori as a writer in English in 1969 with the appearance in *The New Yorker* of a story entitled "Memoirs of an Anti-Semite," which subsequently appeared as a section of the novel of the same name, published in 1981. His most recent novel, *The Death of My Brother Abel,* was published in 1985.

Mr. Rezzori lives with his wife, Beatrice Monti della Corte, in Tuscany.

A Note on the Type

The text of this book was set in Sabon, a type face designed by Jan Tschichold (1902–1974), the well-known German typographer. Because it was designed in Frankfurt, Sabon was named for the famous Frankfurt type founder Jacques Sabon, who died in 1580 while manager of the Egenolff foundry.

Based loosely on the original designs of Claude Garamond (c. 1480–1561), Sabon is unique in that it was explicitly designed for hot-metal composition on both the Monotype and Linotype machines as well as for film composition.